Register Now for Online Access
to Your

SPRINGER PUBLISHING COMPANY
CONNECT™

Your print purchase of *The Psychology of Eating Disorders,* **includes online access to the contents of your book**—increasing accessibility, portability, and searchability!

Access today at:

http://connect.springerpub.com/content/book/978-0-8261-5502-3 or scan the QR code at the right with your smartphone and enter the access code below.

WS0WNU6G

Scan here for quick access.

If you are experiencing problems accessing the digital component of this product, please contact our customer service department at cs@springerpub.com

The online access with your print purchase is available at the publisher's discretion and may be removed at any time without notice.

Publisher's Note: New and used products purchased from third-party sellers are not guaranteed for quality, authenticity, or access to any included digital components.

SPC

SPRINGER ꭍ PUBLISHING COMPANY
View all our products at springerpub.com

Christine L. B. Selby, PhD, CEDS, is an associate professor of psychology at Husson University in Bangor, Maine, and a licensed psychologist in part-time private practice. She is a Certified Eating Disorder Specialist with the International Association of Eating Disorders Professionals (IAEDP).

She is currently a member of the Academy for Eating Disorders (AED), the IAEDP, the Association for Applied Sport Psychology (AASP), and the American Psychological Association (APA). Christine was co-founder of the AASP Eating Disorders Special Interest Group in 2008 and served as co-chair of this group until 2014. She has also been active with the Society for Sport, Exercise, and Performance Psychology—a division of the APA—serving as president-elect, president, and past-president from 2012 to 2015.

Dr. Selby has published primarily in the area of eating disorders in athletes for nonacademic audiences. She has presented locally and nationally on eating disorders and related topics at professional conferences, to allied professionals who work directly with those dealing with eating disorders and related concerns, and on issues related to anti-fat bias and countertransference. Christine has been interviewed for sport-focused podcasts and articles for online and print trade magazines including *Runner's World* and *The Costco Connection*.

Dr. Selby is the author of *Chilling Out: The Psychology of Relaxation*, and *The Body Size and Health Debate*.

THE PSYCHOLOGY OF EATING DISORDERS

Christine L. B. Selby, PhD, CEDS

SPRINGER PUBLISHING COMPANY

Springer Publishing Company, LLC
11 West 42nd Street
New York, NY 10036
www.springerpub.com

Acquisitions Editor: Rhonda Dearborn
Compositor: diacriTech, Chennai

ISBN: 978-0-8261-5501-6
ebook ISBN: 978-0-8261-5502-3
DOI: 10.1891/9780826155023

The author and the publisher of this Work have made every effort to use sources believed to be reliable to provide information that is accurate and compatible with the standards generally accepted at the time of publication. The author and publisher shall not be liable for any special, consequential, or exemplary damages resulting, in whole or in part, from the readers' use of, or reliance on, the information contained in this book. The publisher has no responsibility for the persistence or accuracy of URLs for external or third-party Internet websites referred to in this publication and does not guarantee that any content on such websites is, or will remain, accurate or appropriate.

Library of Congress Cataloging-in-Publication Data
Names: Selby, Christine L. B., author.
Title: The psychology of eating disorders / Christine L. B. Selby.
Description: New York, NY : Springer Publishing Company, LLC, [2018] |
    Includes bibliographical references and index.
Identifiers: LCCN 2018039711| ISBN 9780826155016 | ISBN 9780826155023 (e-book)
Subjects: | MESH: Feeding and Eating Disorders | Feeding and Eating
    Disorders–psychology
Classification: LCC RC552.E18 | NLM WM 175 | DDC 616.85/260651–dc23 LC record available at
https://lccn.loc.gov/2018039711

Contact us to receive discount rates on bulk purchases.
We can also customize our books to meet your needs.
For more information please contact: sales@springerpub.com

ORCID: https://orcid.org/0000-0002-7981-9419

Publisher's Note: New and used products purchased from third-party sellers are not guaranteed for quality, authenticity, or access to any included digital components.

Printed in the United States of America.

This book is dedicated to those who are currently struggling with an eating disorder and to those who died from their eating disorder despite tirelessly fighting to overcome the devastation their eating disorder caused.

CONTENTS

PREFACE

This book will primarily benefit those who do not know a lot about eating disorders or who have not had any formal education with respect to the complexities of these disorders. It was written for undergraduate and graduate students formally learning about eating disorders for the first time and for practitioners who need an introduction to what eating disorders are, what puts someone at risk for developing an eating disorder, and basics regarding prevention, treatment, and dealing with complex emotional reactions to individuals with eating disorders. This book is in no way intended to provide the breadth or depth of information required to be proficient at diagnosing or treating someone who may have an eating disorder. That requires extensive training and supervision at the graduate level and ongoing education to keep up to date with what is newly learned about these disorders.

I chose to write this book because I believe that students interested in learning about eating disorders would benefit from content that is more extensive than a chapter's worth of information in a textbook on abnormal psychology but less detailed than resources intended for those who need to understand the challenges associated with the diagnosis and treatment of these disorders. It is also important to note that I chose to focus this book exclusively on what have traditionally been considered eating disorders. The newest edition of the *Diagnostic and Statistical Manual of Mental Disorders* (5th ed.; *DSM-5*: American Psychiatric Association, 2013), which describes and classifies psychiatric illnesses, recategorized eating disorders along with feeding disorders under the category *Feeding and Eating Disorders*. Thus, the focus of this book is on eating disorders previously categorized independently of other disorders: anorexia nervosa, bulimia nervosa, and binge eating disorder.

This book is organized into several parts designed to address different aspects of eating disorders. Part I describes what eating disorders are and who develops them, including a brief history as well as signs and symptoms of the disorders, and who is likely or less likely to develop an eating disorder. Part II of the book describes factors that can be considered risk factors, co-occurring factors, or consequences of having an eating disorder. These factors are discussed in terms of whether they are biological or medical, psychological, interpersonal, or sociocultural in nature. Part III guides the reader through how to identify those who might be at risk for developing an eating disorder and how to effectively refer someone for an evaluation. This section includes a discussion of what types of professionals should be part of treating someone with an eating disorder and important sources of support who should be involved in the treatment process or kept informed about how treatment is progressing. Part IV describes prevention and treatment efforts commonly used and a brief overview of their effectiveness. It also includes a chapter on identifying and managing one's own emotional reactions to someone with an eating disorder. Finally, the book concludes with several scenarios designed to illustrate for the reader what an eating disorder might "look like" in the real world and what initial treatment efforts might entail.

There are a few elements of this book that may help readers to more fully understand how complex and varied eating disorders and those who have them can be. This book provides a discussion of syndromes and disorders that are related to eating disorders but are not diagnosed or classified as such. These include exercise dependence, orthorexia, bigorexia, and compulsive overeating. Also included is a discussion of *unique populations* that are often overlooked (e.g., older adults), about which we know little in terms of how common eating disorder diagnoses are and how they affect someone who is a part of one of these groups (e.g., individuals with physical or intellectual difficulties), or that require an approach that may be different than that taken with the typical individual with an eating disorder (e.g., athlete, individual diagnosed with autism spectrum disorder). The scenarios provided at the end of the book illustrate some of these unique populations. Another unique feature of this book is the chapter entitled "Identifying and Managing Reactions to Individuals With Eating Disorders". This chapter introduces the reader to what is known about the range of reactions someone can have to an individual diagnosed with an eating disorder. These reactions, particularly when they occur in a treatment provider, are referred to as *countertransference* reactions and can range from love and affection to frustration and rage. This section also discusses the fact that such reactions must be acknowledged, identified, and managed if treatment is to be successful.

Finally, a note about word choice and usage. I have elected to never provide an acronym for anorexia nervosa, bulimia nervosa, and binge eating disorder. In my experience, those new to a content area often find themselves frustrated by having to remind themselves what a particular acronym stands for. I have, however, provided acronyms for names such as the *Diagnostic and Statistical Manual of Mental Disorders* (DSM), the American Psychiatric Association (APA), and others, in part because they are long identifiers and are not as critical for the reader in comparison to the names of the eating disorders. Additionally, I never refer to anorexia nervosa as "anorexia" or bulimia nervosa as "bulimia" because without the term *nervosa* anorexia and bulimia refer to medical conditions that do not necessarily have a psychological component. When referring to someone diagnosed with an eating disorder I do not refer to him or her as a "bulimic" or "anorexic," primarily because using a term in this way reduces an individual to the disorder only, and those with eating disorders are far more complex in terms of who they are as individuals. Finally, when discussing someone diagnosed with an eating disorder, particularly in the context of treatment, I will use the term *patient* instead of *client*. This is because the term *patient* more accurately describes both the nature and purpose of care required for recovery and also that the individual requires formal treatment rather than the use of services per se.

I hope you learn more than you knew about eating disorders prior to reading this book. I also hope you develop an appreciation for how debilitating these disorders are, how many factors are involved in the development and maintenance of these disorders, and how recovery from an eating disorder can be exceptionally challenging and is not a reflection of how hard someone is trying to recover. In my experience, individuals diagnosed with an eating disorder work remarkably hard to recover and fight against a multitude of internal and external forces designed to thwart their efforts.

ACKNOWLEDGMENTS

First and foremost, I would like to thank my husband for his unyielding support of me in general and of this project in particular. I have no doubt that this book would not have been completed without him. I also extend my thanks to my students, Lincoln Bois, Olivia Duron, Krista Jordan, and Jaclyn MacDonald, who provided helpful resources getting this project started and who were actively engaged in my undergraduate course on eating disorders that helped to shape the content of this book.

In addition, I thank Nancy Hale who originally approved this project with Springer Publishing Company and Debra Riegert for seeing this project through after taking over for Nancy. I have appreciated Debra, Mindy Chen, and Kate Dimock checking in with me throughout the process and offering words of encouragement as the deadline for this book approached.

I also thank my two boys, Braeden and Brody—who are actually wonderful young men—simply for being who they are. Their personalities, conversations with me, and activities in which I have been able to take part help to remind me what and who is truly important in my life. Finally, I must thank Susan Berd for her ability to make me smile and for providing daily entertainment that helped me in the final days and weeks of finishing this book.

I

EATING DISORDERS: WHAT ARE THEY AND WHO HAS THEM?

THE PRIMARY EATING DISORDER DIAGNOSES: GENERAL DESCRIPTION, HISTORY, AND MYTHS

Introduction

According to the gold standard for diagnosis of mental health disorders, the ***Diagnostic and Statistical Manual of Mental Disorders*** (5th ed.; *DSM-5*; American Psychiatric Association [APA], 2013), eating disorders can be described generally as a group of disorders that involves problems with eating and eating-related behaviors. Ultimately these issues with eating result in the individual consuming amounts of food that may be significantly less than or more than someone without an eating disorder would consume. Additionally, eating disorders, by virtue of the fact that they are considered illnesses, significantly and negatively affect other aspects of one's life such as interpersonal relationships, physical health, and overall psychological well-being.

In this chapter, an overview of each eating disorder will be provided along with a brief look at related syndromes and disorders. Eating disorders are now classified in the *DSM-5* (APA, 2013) along with feeding disorders usually diagnosed first in childhood (i.e., **Pica, Rumination Disorder,** and **Avoidant/Restrictive Food Intake Disorder**), whereas previously, in the *DSM-IV* (APA, 1994), eating disorders comprised a category of their own. The focus of this and all remaining chapters will be on the disorders that made up the eating disorders category in earlier editions of the *DSM* (i.e., **Anorexia Nervosa, Bulimia Nervosa, Binge Eating Disorder**). Finally, this chapter will end with an exploration of common myths associated with eating disorders.

Anorexia Nervosa

General Description

According to the *DSM-5* (APA, 2013) there are three primary features that someone diagnosed with anorexia nervosa will experience (see Chapter 2). The first feature is that he or she will consistently consume less food than his or her body needs. This is usually referred to as *energy restriction* and means that the individual is consuming far fewer calories than he or she needs given the individual's age, sex, height, and level of physical activity. The second feature is that the individual is terrified of gaining weight or may be engaged in behaviors that prevent him or her from gaining weight. Finally, the individual inaccurately perceives what his or her body looks like or how much his or her body weighs. This means that when the individual looks at himself or herself in a mirror or when he or she focuses on how his or her body feels, the body will seem to be and will feel larger than it actually is.

Descriptions of this disorder have varied throughout history and there is disagreement with respect to whether ancient cases of females intentionally fasting without a medical reason truly reflect anorexia nervosa as it is understood currently. However, the first modern instance of anorexia nervosa discussed among medical professionals paints a picture of the disorder that closely resembles how this disorder is characterized by the *DSM-5* (APA, 2013).

History

The term **anorexia** refers to the absence of an appetite for food. When a diagnosis of anorexia is rendered by a medical professional it means that there is a medical basis for the lack of appetite. Anorexia nervosa is a diagnosis made when someone refuses to eat out of fear of being or becoming fat. Anorexia nervosa was not first officially identified until the late 1800s. Prior to that time, however, there were accounts of individuals, often women, who displayed symptoms of what would now be diagnosed as anorexia nervosa.

The history of anorexia nervosa may date back over eight centuries. Brumberg (1989) published a detailed account of the history of anorexia nervosa in which she described what seemed to be a relatively common practice in medieval Europe: refusing food or fasting for spiritual reasons. During this era stories were recounted about female saints, without any mention of male saints, engaging in this practice. The most well-known of these saints was Saint Catherine of Siena. She lived from 1347 to 1380 and reportedly ate only herbs. When she was forced to eat any more than that she would make herself vomit. The practice of women refusing to eat for spiritual reasons—including the notion that they could subsist on things other than food such as prayer or only ingesting the Eucharist (wafer and wine representing the body and blood of Christ)—was considered to be miraculous. This practice had become so common that by the 1600s and 1700s physicians labeled the practice *anorexia mirabilis*, which, when translated, means "miraculously inspired loss of appetite."

Brumberg (1989) noted that not all who write about the history of anorexia nervosa agree on whether or not these ancient expressions of self-control through food reflect anorexia nervosa as we understand it today. She contends that it is appropriate to consider the fasting practices of women for the purpose of expressing the depth of their faith, and the fasting behaviors diagnosable today as distinct and disparate experiences with the common denominator being the use of food and starvation as a way to communicate. Interestingly, Brumberg points out that by the 1600s and 1700s, around the time medical practitioners of the day started paying closer attention to what these fasting women were doing, fasting behaviors began to decline. There was a shift from seeing fasting from food and feasting on the substance of one's faith as an expression of a highest form of holiness to viewing these behaviors as being the result of evilness. As such, fasting became regarded as evidence of being possessed by the devil and thus something to be strongly discouraged. Despite this radical shift in perspective on the meaning of fasting, many women continued to eat nothing or very little, believing they did not need food to nourish their bodies. Some claimed they kept their bodies alive through smell or that they were fed by angels. Brumberg details numerous stories of people (predominantly female) who refused to eat for a variety of reasons; however, it was not until the late 1800s that anorexia nervosa, as it is understood today, was first described.

In the late 1800s two physicians, working independently, identified a version of anorexia that did not have a medical cause. Sir William Withey Gull published a paper entitled "Anorexia Nervosa (Apepsia Hyesterica, Anorexia Hysterica)" (1873/1997). During that same year, but a few months earlier, Dr. Charles Lasègue published his work entitled "On Hysterical Anorexia" (1873/1997). There are some interesting differences in terms of how each physician described the disorder as he saw it and what his experiences were with respect to outcome.

Gull (1873/1997) presented a medically clinical description of the disorder. He listed physical symptoms involving vital signs such as pulse, heart-sounds, respiration, and weight. He also described treatment in terms of what was offered to his patients with respect to medicines and food. Although Gull initially used the term *hysterica* he believed that *nervosa* was a more appropriate term since he had seen this affliction in males as well as females (hysteria was, at the time, only associated with females). He also noted that *anorexia* was the more accurate term to use, and was the term used by Lasègue (1873/1997) rather than *apepsia* (digestive failure), since any food that was consumed was, in fact, digested. Gull made note of this in his paper and acknowledged that his French colleague published the term anorexia in this context before he did—though he noted that prior to Lasègue's publication a few months before his own he had already come to the conclusion that anorexia was the better term to describe this disorder. Gull contends, however, that he was truly the first person to describe this condition since he presented his observations of this disorder in a talk presented at Oxford in 1868. The fact that Lasègue did not refer to Gull's talk in his own paper signaled to Gull that Lasègue was unaware of it and thus they were both independently documenting the same disorder.

Lasègue (1873/1997) reported only seeing anorexia in females, which may explain why he named the disorder "hysterical anorexia." His description of the disorder was markedly different than Gull's. While his description did include physical symptoms, it also included observations about how his patients acted and what they thought with respect to food, their weight, and their overall health. He noted that his patients stated that they did not need more food and that they were healthy despite not eating much and losing weight to the point of emaciation. Since these patients remained highly active prior to severe emaciation, this was reportedly further evidence to the patients that they were well.

Lasègue (1873/1997) also documented his observations with respect to the friends and families of those diagnosed with this disorder. He reported that families relied heavily on making urgent requests of the patient to eat or resorting to threats if he or she did not eat. He also offered advice to physicians on how to treat someone with this disorder including the notion that it is a mistake to think a patient with this disorder can be treated in a conventional way using medicines along with the imposition of their authority as a doctor. Rather, he suggested taking a much more subdued approach, warning that any other approach is likely to be perceived by the patient as a form of hostility. He noted that a hostile approach is likely to result in a lack of trust that may be insurmountable and stated: "a first medical fault is never reparable" (Lasègue, 1873/1997, p. 493).

Though Gull (1873/1997) may have been the first to formally describe what is now known as anorexia nervosa, both Gull's and Lasègue's (1873/1997) work provided insight into the medical symptomology associated with the disorder. Additionally, they shed light on the psychology of these patients and how they may affect their families and the physicians attempting to treat them. Together Gull and Lasègue addressed the physical impact of starvation in the context of this disorder and the psychological presentation of someone who is often unaware of or unwilling to acknowledge the gravity of his or her illness. More than 80 years after Gull presented his opinion at Oxford, anorexia nervosa was formally identified as a mental disorder requiring treatment.

Anorexia nervosa appeared in the first *DSM* published by the APA in 1952; however, it was one among many examples of the diagnosis *psychophysiologic gastrointestinal reaction*, which was the category for gastrointestinal problems "in which emotional factors play a causative role" (APA, 1952, p. 30). In the *DSM-II* (APA, 1968), anorexia nervosa was reclassified as an example of the diagnosis *feeding disturbance*. In 1980 (APA), the third edition of the *DSM* was published and included the category called *eating disorders*, which specifically identified symptoms of anorexia nervosa that are similar to those used in the current edition. The *DSM-IV* (APA, 1994) provided a great deal more in terms of the description of the disorder including information about etiology, prevalence, and associated physical and psychological symptoms. Finally, the *DSM-5* (APA, 2013), the most current version of the manual, provides additional, updated information on how and in whom this disorder develops as well as providing some changes as to how the disorder is diagnosed (see Chapter 2).

Historical documentation of how some people (primarily females) interacted with food shows that anorexia nervosa may have existed as early as the 1300s. Several hundred years later our understanding of the disorder is still being refined by those who regularly diagnose and treat individuals with the symptoms of anorexia nervosa. Similarly, our understanding of bulimia nervosa, a diagnostic cousin to anorexia nervosa, is that it is a disorder in its own right rather than as a variant of anorexia nervosa. The professional community's understanding of this disorder continues to be refined as well.

Bulimia Nervosa

General Description

The elements of bulimia nervosa, as described in the following section, have changed very little since it was first formally identified in the late 1970s (Russell, 1979). Currently, this disorder involves three primary components according to the *DSM-5* (APA, 2013; see Chapter 2). Colloquially, this disorder is referred to as the binge-purge disorder, reflecting the first two components of the disorder. The first element involves episodes of binge eating and the second involves what are called **compensatory behaviors** or, loosely, the purge part of the disorder. Compensatory behaviors can involve a multitude of behaviors including self-induced vomiting or fasting in between binges. The third component of bulimia nervosa involves the fact that someone with this disorder will believe that his or her worth as a human being is dependent on how much he or she weighs and/or what his or her body looks like.

Bulimia nervosa is relatively new in terms of its inclusion in the *DSM* as a formal diagnosis. Indeed, some, including the psychiatrist who first named and described this disorder, believe that it is relatively new because very few instances of anything resembling bulimia nervosa appear in general historical accounts of the human experience, or in historical records of psychiatric clinics.

History

Dr. Gerald Russell (1979) was the first to formally identify bulimia nervosa and initially identified this disorder as a variant of anorexia nervosa. Russell stated that prior to his publication on bulimia nervosa others had proposed the possibility that presentations of anorexia nervosa might indicate two distinct types of the disorder. He noted this because others had observed, with relative frequency, the presence of self-induced vomiting and other means of getting rid of calories in patients diagnosed with anorexia nervosa. Russell himself concluded that the condition he described should not be considered as distinct from anorexia nervosa but that it may be an outcome or consequence of having been anorectic prior to developing the symptoms of bulimia nervosa.

Russell's (1979) description of bulimia nervosa is similar to the current description and understanding of the disorder (see Chapter 2). He reported that the 30 patients he observed, who were predominantly female, experienced periods in which they had urges to overeat that were characterized as "powerful and intractable" (Russell, 1979, p. 445). He also noted that immediately following periods of overeating his patients would engage in some behavior designed to prevent weight gain. The most common behavior he observed was self-induced vomiting. He also stated that some patients used laxatives, fasted for a period of time, engaged in excessive exercise, or used diuretics all for the purpose of preventing weight gain. Finally, Russell stated his patients showed an intense fear of gaining weight or becoming fat and noted that this final observation was the only one shared with patients to whom he referred as having "true anorexia nervosa." He noted that some patients with anorexia nervosa did engage in self-induced vomiting or other behaviors designed to prevent weight gain but that this behavior did not follow an episode of overeating. Rather, it occurred following the ingestion of any amount of food no matter how small.

In their descriptions of overeating episodes, Russell (1979) reported that his patients stated they felt a type of hunger that was not connected to the need for food but rather to satisfy an emotional feeling or a sense of emptiness. They described eating several cartons or packages of various foods with one patient estimating that she consumed at least 15,000 calories during her evening time episodes. Although not identified as such, Russell seemed to indicate that this was evidence of the loss of control that is part of the current clinical understanding of how a **binge** episode is experienced. To that end, he noted that his patients would report trying just a small amount of a favorite or high calorie food, which immediately led to a binge as patients stated that once they started to eat they could not stop.

Following Russell's description of bulimia nervosa in 1979, the third edition of the *DSM* (*DSM-III*; APA, 1980) was published and included the diagnosis of *bulimia* as an eating disorder with diagnostic symptoms distinct from anorexia nervosa. Although the first edition of the *DSM* (APA, 1952) included the term **bulimia** it was only included in an appendix entitled "Supplementary Terms" and was not listed as something diagnosable as a mental disorder. In his review of what had been published in the 1960s and 1970s regarding bulimic type behaviors, Vandereycken (1994) reported that similar behavior patterns identified by Russell were found by other researchers and clinicians who used a variety of terms for the behavior. Some of the terms used included hyperorexia nervosa, hyperphagia with vomiting, bulimarexia, binging/vomiting syndrome, dietary chaos syndrome, and compulsive bulimia. Vandereycken noted that the prominence of Russell's article, in comparison to others who attempted to describe similar behavior patterns before Russell, is likely due to the fact that he provided a lucid and clinically useful description of what his 30 patients experienced. He was able to distill their symptoms into commonalities as well as identify what made them unique from those who were diagnosed with the "pure" version of anorexia nervosa.

Despite Russell's (1979) paper being considered the first description of a "new" disorder, others (Casper, 1983; Stein & Laakso, 1988) have suggested the history of bulimia as a syndrome extends much further back in time. Casper (1983) observed that instances of bulimia (overeating) were identified as early as 1892 but that bulimia as a mental disorder with accompanying purging surfaced in the late 1930s or early 1940s; approximately 40 years prior to Russell's description of bulimia nervosa. Casper suggested that the absence of a formal description of bulimia as a mental illness prior to the 1940s was likely due to the fact that it was not until then that people, especially females, were focused on body shape with a desire for thinness.

Stein and Laakso (1988) provide a discussion of the history of bulimia, which they indicate existed prior to the 1800s, providing evidence that there may have been writings about bulimia as early as 200 AD. Although some of the descriptions of bulimia seem to point to the purely medical definition—overeating—other descriptions indicated that for some people overeating was followed by vomiting. Stein and Laakso noted that some of these early descriptions involving overeating (and subsequent vomiting in some cases) may have been indicative of disease or infection, or of a learned behavior via receiving attention when overeating. However, they further noted historical descriptions of bulimia that include depressive-like symptoms, which suggest it is possible bulimia nervosa, as it is known today, may have existed hundreds of years ago.

In 2004, Palmer published an article examining what we have learned about bulimia nervosa since it was described by Russell 25 years earlier. He stated that Russell's initial description was compelling and seemed to capture constellations of symptoms that have since been acknowledged as distinct from anorexia nervosa. The current criteria used to diagnose bulimia nervosa (see Chapter 2) has amended and expanded Russell's proposed criteria, thereby refining clinical professionals' ability to accurately diagnose this disorder. Palmer notes, however, that despite these changes much more is needed by way of refining the diagnoses of both bulimia nervosa and anorexia nervosa. He came to this conclusion in part because the most commonly used diagnosis with eating disorders, prior to the publication of the *DSM-5* (APA, 2013), was *eating disorder not otherwise specified* (EDNOS). This led Palmer to conclude that prior to the 2013 publication of the *DSM-5,* the "classification of the eating disorders cannot be considered to be definitive, or even satisfactory" (p. 448).

Twenty-five years after his 1979 publication describing a new variant of anorexia nervosa, Russell (2004) noted that his original description of bulimia nervosa has stood the test of time, adding that his initial characterization of bulimia nervosa as an "ominous" variant of anorexia nervosa was born from his idea that the emergence of these new symptoms was a result of a failure of recovery from anorexia nervosa. Indeed, he points to others (e.g., Eddy et al., 2002; Fairburn, 2000; Soundy, Lucas, Suman, & Melton, 1995) who have documented the transition that can take place within a patient from his or her initial experience of anorexia nervosa, then bulimia nervosa, or vice versa. Russell stated that he may be one of the few people genuinely interested in trying to figure out if bulimia nervosa simply appeared in the late 20th century, or if it had always existed but we did not have the language to describe it or the means by which to diagnose it. He acknowledged that its formal description in the 1970s likely meant that more clinicians and researchers would recognize and subsequently identify patients with this disorder as opposed to seeing the symptoms of bulimia nervosa as a variant of anorexia nervosa. He also postulated that the attention the disorder received by clinicians and the media may very well have influenced vulnerable individuals into taking on these symptoms. Ultimately, however, Russell (2004) concluded that bulimia nervosa is, compared to anorexia nervosa, a new disorder. He points to the fact that there is a dearth of descriptions in the literature of anything similar to bulimia nervosa prior to the 1950s, noting that archives of a well-known clinic do not have records of many cases of patients experiencing bulimia nervosa-like symptomology, and that three cohort studies published within 15 years of Russell's (1979) original description found that bulimia nervosa seemed to have materialized in the 1960s/1970s.

Our understanding of bulimia nervosa has taken a circuitous route to our current understanding of it today. Historically, ancient accounts of binge eating behaviors did not always include accompanying purging behaviors, and more contemporary descriptions of the disorder suggested that bulimia nervosa was likely a variant of anorexia nervosa, meaning it was not a distinct disorder. However, further examination of some individuals' experiences with the symptoms of bulimia nervosa have led researchers and clinicians to conclude that it is a disorder distinguishable from anorexia nervosa. It is possible that some of the historical accounts of binge eating behavior reflected not bulimia nervosa but another disorder altogether; one that took longer to be identified as a third type of eating disorder. Binge eating disorder shares some symptoms of bulimia nervosa but diverges from this disorder in important ways.

Binge Eating Disorder

General Description

Although the concept of binge eating has been around for quite some time, it was not until the most recent version of the *DSM* (*DSM-5*; APA, 2013) was published that Binge Eating Disorder was included as a diagnosis distinct from the other eating disorders. Binge eating disorder involves instances when someone is engaged in binge eating behavior (see Chapter 2), which is characterized by eating a high volume of food (often of high caloric value) that is more than most people would eat given the amount of time it took as well as the context in which the person consumed the food. In addition to binge eating episodes, someone with binge eating disorder is markedly distressed by his or her behavior. That is, these individuals do not want to keep doing what they are doing but they also feel like they cannot or do not know how to stop.

The time following a binge eating episode is often characterized by things such as feeling so full that people are in discomfort or pain, feeling disgusted with themselves, and feeling embarrassed by what they have done. Binge eating disorder is distinguished from bulimia nervosa due to the fact that someone with this disorder does not engage in the compensatory behaviors explicitly designed to compensate for or get rid of what he or she has consumed (e.g., excessive exercise, self-induced vomiting).

History

Much of the history of binge eating disorder is connected to descriptions of binge eating, which are often included in the context of bulimia nervosa. This is likely due to the fact that bulimia nervosa was formally described in the late 1970s and diagnosable in 1980 when the *DSM-III* (APA, 1980) was published. Binge eating disorder by contrast did not achieve diagnosable status until the *DSM-5* (APA, 2013) was published.

In 1959, Albert Stunkard published a paper entitled "Eating Patterns and Obesity": He was interested in understanding obesity and in determining whether or not different causes of obesity yielded different eating patterns. His initial conclusions were based on studies with mice; however, he noted that while studies conducted with mice may yield more precise results with respect to amount of food consumed and patterns of eating behaviors, studies with human beings afforded researchers and clinicians the opportunity to hear about the experience of binge eating directly from the individual himself or herself. As a result of his inquiry with obese patients Stunkard identified three patterns of eating: night eating, binge eating, and eating without satiation. He further noted that based on direct reports from his patients he was able to determine the degree to which factors such as self-condemnation, personal meaning, and amount of stress were present in the various eating patterns.

Night eating syndrome according to Stunkard (1959) involves a lack of appetite for food in the morning followed by excessive hunger and eating large amounts of food in the evening. He identified the primary factor contributing to this eating pattern was life-stress; thus, when the stress abated the abnormal eating pattern usually did as well. Binge eating was described by Stunkard as involving "enormous amounts of food. . . consumed in relatively short periods" (1959, p. 289) accompanied by what he referred to as an "orgiastic quality." This eating pattern, too, not only appears during periods of life-stress but also carries with it a personal or unconscious meaning. The binge episodes are also followed by what he called self-condemnation, which likely represents something like feeling disgusted with one's self and thinking badly about one's self. Finally, the eating without satiation pattern involves the experience of being unable to stop eating once the individual has started. He stated that after commencing there is no increase in hunger or desire to eat, which might otherwise explain periods of continuous eating. This pattern is further differentiated from the other two in that none of the three factors (self-condemnation, personal meaning, and life stress) were found to be present.

The binge eating pattern that Stunkard (1959) described is of particular interest to the history of binge eating disorder. Stunkard did not suggest that this pattern, along with the other two patterns of eating, were disorders to be diagnosed, but rather that they were behavioral patterns that helped to explain why someone might be obese.

Interestingly, each of the three behavior patterns he identified, in one way or another, are part of our current eating disorder diagnoses. Binge eating as Stunkard described it is not dissimilar from how a binge is currently described. Additionally, his characterization of eating without satiation—inability to stop eating once started—is explicitly part of the binge eating disorder diagnosis. The night eating pattern is currently identified as night eating syndrome in the *DSM-5* (APA, 2013) and is one among many possibilities for the diagnosis Other Specified Feeding or Eating Disorder (see Chapter 2).

There is considerable evidence that binge eating disorder was believed to be a disorder distinguishable from other eating disorders prior to its inclusion in the *DSM-IV* (APA, 1994) as a diagnosis requiring further study, and prior to its formal inclusion in the *DSM-5* (APA, 2013). A great deal of research was conducted on binge eating disorder symptomology prior to its official inclusion in either the *DSM-IV* or the *DSM-5*. The disorder is mentioned by name in studies on prevalence (Hudson, Hiripi, Pope, & Kessler, 2007; Stunkard et al., 1996), diagnosis (Brewerton, 1999; Spitzer et al., 1992; Spitzer et al., 1993), effectiveness of various types of treatment (Brewerton, 1999; Brownley, Berkman, Sedway, Lohr, & Bulik, 2007; Wiser & Telch, 1999), associated symptoms or disorders (Colles, Dixon, & O'Brien, 2008; De Zwaan et al., 1994), and risk factors (Fairburn et al., 1998; Striegel-Moore, Dohm, Pike, Wilfley, & Fairburn, 2002; Striegel-Moore, Fairburn, Wilfley, Pike, & Dohm, 2005). Additionally, in 2008, prior to the publication of the *DSM-5*, the *Binge Eating Disorder Association* (BEDA) was formed (BEDA, n.d.). Finally, 2 years following the publication of the *DSM-5,* the U.S. Food and Drug Administration (FDA) approved the use of lisdexamfetamine dimesylate (trade name: Vyvanse; U.S. FDA, 2015), suggesting that research on medications for binge eating had been in progress prior to publication of the *DSM-5*.

Binge eating disorder has a seemingly shorter history than the other two primary eating disorder diagnoses. If taking into account the historical reports of binge eating that are associated with the history of bulimia nervosa, binge eating disorder may have a history as long-standing as bulimia nervosa. Despite this seemingly shared history, binge eating disorder was not recognized as a diagnosable eating disorder until 2013 (APA) when the *DSM-5* was published.

Common Myths of Eating Disorders

There are a multitude of myths surrounding eating disorders, including who does and who does not get eating disorders, who or what is to blame for the development of eating disorders, and how long someone will have an eating disorder. The reality is that eating disorders are complex and serious disorders that involve one's biology (e.g., genetics), one's environment (e.g., the media, and interpersonal and cultural influences), and one's psychological functioning (e.g., unique thoughts, feelings, and perceptions about themselves and the world around them). Some of the more common and persistent myths are drawn from a talk by Dr. Cynthia Bulik (2014) to attendees of the National Institute of Mental Health Alliance for Research Progress. In her talk, entitled "9 Eating Disorder Myths Busted," Bulik outlined nine common myths related to eating disorders and offered evidence debunking those myths. The content of her talk led the Academy for Eating Disorders (AED; with contributions from other prominent eating disorder organizations) to create and adopt the "Nine Truths About Eating Disorders" (AED,

2015). Although other well regarded organizations have addressed persistent myths related to eating disorders (e.g., National Eating Disorders Association, 2016), this section will focus on Dr. Bulik's nine myths as they seem to comprehensively capture the erroneous ideas many people have about eating disorders.

Myth 1: You Can Tell by Looking at Someone That He or She Has an Eating Disorder

It is common for people to picture an emaciated young woman when they think about eating disorders. Although emaciation is possible for some people with anorexia nervosa, the reality is that someone of any weight classification, based on any body mass index (BMI) chart (e.g., Centers for Disease Control and Prevention, 2017), can have an eating disorder. What matters are the specific behaviors in which someone is engaged as well as the individual's perception of and reaction to his or her body size, eating behaviors, and weight loss or weight gain (see Chapters 3 to 7).

Myth 2: Families Are to Blame

Historically, the blame for eating disorders fell squarely on the shoulders of someone's family, particularly the parents. The thinking was that any concerns a child, adolescent, or adult had with eating and **body image** were the result of either modeling on the parent's part (e.g., a parent's dieting behavior, negative comments about his or her own body size, negative comments about certain types of food), or comments parents made about their child's body shape and size or his or her eating habits. While parent behaviors such as these can be harmful in a variety of ways, they do not cause an eating disorder to develop. Although this myth is a difficult one to combat, even among treatment providers, families are now considered to be an integral part of treatment and its success, especially for those who live full-time with their parents (see Chapter 12).

Myth 3: Mothers Are to Blame

This myth is an extension of Myth 2. Mothers in particular have been blamed for numerous mental health disorders ultimately diagnosed in their children and eating disorders are no different. Mothers have been particularly targeted when it comes to anorexia nervosa. Eating disorders are far too complex to place the blame on any one person. Although not an eating disorder, obesity in children is not immune to mother blame. Since food selection and preparation often are, or are presumed to be, the domain of the mother, it is not a stretch to presume that the body shape and size of her children is her responsibility as well. The reality is that eating disorders (and other issues) are far too complex to place the blame on any one person (see Chapters 5 to 7).

Myth 4: Eating Disorders Are a Choice

This myth is perpetuated in part due to mainstream culture's obsession with thinness in females and leanness in males which can be confused with anorexia nervosa, particularly in women. Additionally, the number one risk factor for developing an eating disorder is going on a diet (i.e., a pattern of eating that involves some sort of restriction—calories, types of foods, and/or amount of food). Since most people consciously decide to go on (and off) a diet, it is assumed by many that the eating disorder itself is a choice. Researchers and clinicians in the field now know that something like dieting may be akin to lighting a fuse. That is, the predisposition for an eating disorder already existed in the person and some experience they may have (whether by choice or not) activates the eating disorder (see Chapters 3 to 7).

Myth 5: Eating Disorders Are the Province of White Upper-Middle Class Teenage Girls

When thinking of someone with an eating disorder, most people probably do picture a White, thin, teenaged female who is in a financially successful family. The reality is, however, that eating disorders are not selective. Eating disorders do not target one race or socioeconomic status over another anymore than it seeks out females and ignores males. Increasing numbers of children (as young as 7 or 8), middle aged or older adults, and males seek help for an eating disorder. Unfortunately, this particular myth is often held not only by members of the public but by treatment providers as well. If a provider believes this myth, then when patients express concern that they or their child might have an eating disorder, their concerns may be dismissed if they do not fit this myth's profile. The danger of that, of course, is that they do not get the treatment they need as quickly as they need it (see Chapters 3 to 7).

Myth 6: Eating Disorders Are Benign

Eating disorders are serious illnesses that not only involve one's mental well-being but also his or her physical well-being. Eating disorders as a group, but anorexia nervosa in particular, have the highest mortality rate of any psychiatric illness despite the fact that they are statistically uncommon (Harris & Barraclough, 1998; Neumärker, 2000; Smink, van Hoeken, & Hoek, 2012). In addition to the possibility of reproductive damage, osteoporosis, heart damage, and gastrointestinal problems—some of which may not be reversible—someone with an eating disorder may die by suicide or due to cardiac arrest, which are the two most common causes of death (see Chapters 5 to 7).

Myth 7: Society Alone Is to Blame

There are studies that have identified a connection between the hundreds or thousands of media messages we are exposed to throughout a day (see Chapter 7); however, current research is painting a clearer picture in terms of the role genetics play in the presence and development of eating disorders (see Chapter 5). It is known, for example, that eating disorders can be inherited and thus run in families. It is also likely that there is an interaction between the environment and one's genetics, but what that means is if you do not have the "right" genetics then a society with a strong focus on a particular standard of attractiveness alone cannot bring about an eating disorder.

Myth 8: Genes Are Destiny

Despite the fact that the genetic picture is becoming clearer as it relates to eating disorders, the fact of the matter is that someone's genetics does not paint the entire picture. That is, if genetics were the sole factor in the development of eating disorders, then any genetic findings associated with this category of disease would reveal that genes are 100% responsible. Depending on the study, genetics (see Chapter 5) have been shown to account for somewhere in the neighborhood of 50% of the reason an eating disorder develops. The remainder comes from sources such as environmental factors or an individual's psychology (i.e., how he or she processes and interprets experiences, interpersonal interactions, etc.; see Chapters 5 to 7).

Myth 9: Eating Disorders Are for Life

Many patients, families, and treatment providers believe that eating disorders cannot be cured, or at best they are very difficult to cure and only a handful at that will no longer have an eating disorder. The question of "cure" is, in many ways, as complicated as the disorders themselves. Defining what it means to be cured from any eating disorder can vary from one person to the next. Some may say it is the absence of eating disorder behaviors (i.e., no more restricting, no more binging, no more purging). Others may say a cure does not exist until the behaviors are gone and the accompanying thoughts and feelings related to the desire to have a particular body shape, weight, or size are as well. Despite this confusion, it is possible for someone with an eating disorder to learn how to refrain from eating disorder behaviors, and how to change his or her thought processes and relationships with others so that both are more healthy and supportive (see Chapter 12).

Conclusion

Eating disorders as a group have a history that dates back several hundred years and may date back to as early as 200 AD. Despite our growing understanding of these disorders and refinement of how they are diagnosed, there remain many myths about eating disorders that still persist, including myths about how you can tell if someone has an eating disorder, what causes them, who gets them, how serious they are, and whether or not they can be cured. In the chapters that follow, many of these myths will be addressed via eating disorders' specific signs and symptoms, demographics of those who are diagnosed with eating disorders, what factors are involved in the development and maintenance of eating disorders, and how to prevent and treat eating disorders.

References

Academy for Eating Disorders. (2015). *Nine truths about eating disorders*. Retrieved from https://www.aedweb.org/learn/publications/nine-truths

American Psychiatric Association. (1952). *Diagnostic and statistical manual of mental disorders*. Washington, DC: Author.

American Psychiatric Association. (1968). *Diagnostic and statistical manual of mental disorders* (2nd ed.). Washington, DC: Author.

American Psychiatric Association. (1980). *Diagnostic and statistical manual of mental disorders* (3rd ed.). Washington, DC: Author.

American Psychiatric Association. (1994). *Diagnostic and statistical manual of mental disorders* (4th ed.). Washington, DC: Author.

American Psychiatric Association. (2013). *Diagnostic and statistical manual of mental disorders* (5th ed.). Arlington, VA: American Psychiatric Publishing.

Binge Eating Disorder Association. (n.d.). *Founder's history: About Chevese Turner*. Retrieved from https://bedaonline.com/beda-founder-history

Brewerton, T. D. (1999). Binge eating disorder: Diagnosis and treatment options. *CNS Drugs, 11*, 351–361. doi:10.2165/00023210-199911050-00003

Brownley, K. A., Berkman, N. D., Sedway, J. A., Lohr, K. N., & Bulik, C. M. (2007). Binge eating disorder treatment: A systematic review of randomized controlled trials. *International Journal of Eating Disorders, 40*, 337–348. doi:10.1002/eat.20370

Brumberg, J. J. (1989). *Fasting girls: The history of anorexia nervosa*. New York, NY: Vintage Books.

Bulik, C. (2014). *9 eating disorder myths busted. Proceedings of the National Institutes of Mental Health Alliance for Research Progress Winter Meeting*. Retrieved from https://www.nimh.nih.gov/news/science-news/2014/9-eating-disorders-myths-busted.shtml

Casper, R. C. (1983). On the emergence of bulimia nervosa as a syndrome: A historical view. *International Journal of Eating Disorders, 2*(3), 3–16. doi:10.1002/1098-108X(198321)2:3<3::AID-EAT2260020302>3.0.CO;2-D

Centers for Disease Control and Prevention. (2017, August 29). *About adult BMI*. Retrieved from https://www.cdc.gov/healthyweight/assessing/bmi/adult_bmi/index.html

Colles, S. L., Dixon, J. B., & O'Brien, P. E. (2008). Loss of control is central to psychological disturbance associated with binge eating disorder. *Obesity, 16*, 608–614. doi:10.1038/oby.2007.99

de Zwaan, M., Mitchell, J. E. Seim, H. C., Specker, S. M., Pyle, R. L., Raymond, N. C. & Crosby, R. B. (1994). Eating related and general psychopathology in obese females with binge eating disorder. *International Journal of Eating Disorders, 15*, 43–52. doi:10.1002/1098-108X(199401)15:1<43::AID-EAT2260150106>3.0.CO;2-6

Eddy, K. T., Keal, P. K., Dorer, D. J., Alinshy, S. F., Franko, D. L., & Herzog, D. B. (2002). Longitudinal comparison of anorexia nervosa sub-types. *International Journal of Eating Disorders, 31*, 191–201. doi:10.1002/eat.10016

Fairburn, C. G. (2000). Bulimia nervosa. In M. G. Gelder, J. J. López-Ibor, & N. C. Andreason (Eds.), *New Oxford textbook of psychiatry* (pp. 856–867). Oxford, UK: Oxford University Press.

Fairburn, C. G., Doll, H. A., Welch, S. L., Hay, P. J., Davies, B. A., & O'Connor, M. E. (1998). Risk factors for binge eating disorder: A community-based, case-control study. *Archives of General Psychiatry, 55*, 425–432. doi:10.1001/archpsyc.55.5.425

Gull, W. W. (1997). Anorexia nervosa (apepsia hysterica, anorexia hysterica). *Obesity Research, 5*, 498–502. (Originally published in 1873). doi:10.1002/j.1550-8528.1997.tb00677.x

Harris, E. C., & Barraclough, B. (1998). Excess mortality of mental disorder. *British Journal of Psychiatry, 173*, 11–53. doi:10.1192/bjp.173.1.11

Hudson, J. I., Hiripi, E., Pope, H. G., & Kessler, R. C. (2007). The prevalence and correlates of eating disorders in the national comorbidity survey replication. *Biological Psychiatry, 61*, 348–358. doi:10.1016/j.biopsych.2006.03.040

Lasègue, C. (1997). On hysterical anorexia. *Obesity Research, 5*, 492–497. (Originally published in 1873). doi:10.1002/j.1550-8528.1997.tb00676.x

National Eating Disorders Association. (2016). *Eating disorder myths*. Retrieved from https://www.nationaleatingdisorders.org/toolkit/parent-toolkit/eating-disorder-myths

Neumärker, K.-J. (2000). Mortality rates and causes of death. *European Eating Disorders Review, 8*, 181–187. doi:10.1002/(SICI)1099-0968(200003)8:2<181::AID-ERV336>3.0.CO;2-#

Palmer, R., (2004). Bulimia nervosa: 25 years on. *British Journal of Psychiatry, 185*, 447–448. doi:10.1192/bjp.185.6.447

Russell, G. F. M. (1979). Bulimia nervosa: An ominous variant of anorexia nervosa. *Psychological Medicine, 9*, 429–448. doi:10.1017/S0033291700031974

Russell, G. F. M. (2004). Thoughts on the 25th anniversary of bulimia nervosa. *European Eating Disorders Review, 12*, 139–152. doi:10.1002/erv.575

Smink, F. R. E., van Hoeken, D. & Hoek, H. W. (2012). Epidemiology of eating disorders: Incidence, prevalence and mortality rates. *Current Psychiatry Reports, 14,* 406–414. doi:10.1007/s11920-012-0282-y

Soundy, T. J., Lucas, A. R., Suman, V. J., & Melton, L. J. (1995). Bulimia nervosa in Rochester, Minnesota from 1980-1990. *Psychological Medicine, 25,* 1065–1071. doi:10.1017/S0033291700037557

Spitzer, R. L., Devlin, M., Walsh, B. T., Hasin, D., Wing, R., Marcus, M., . . . Nonas, C. (1992). Binge eating disorder: A multisite field trial of the diagnostic criteria. *International Journal of Eating Disorders, 11,* 191–203. doi:10.1002/1098-108X(199204)11:3<191::AID-EAT2260110302>3.0.CO;2-S

Spitzer, R. L., Yanovski, S., Wadden, T., Wing, R., Marcus, M. D., Stunkard, A., . . . Horne, R. L. (1993). Binge eating disorder: Its further validation in a multisite study. *International Journal of Eating Disorders, 13,* 137–153. doi:10.1002/1098-108x(199303)13:2<137::aid-eat2260130202>3.0.co;2-#

Stein, D. M., & Laakso, W. (1988). Bulimia: A historical perspective. *International Journal of Eating Disorders, 7,* 201–210. doi:10.1002/1098-108X(198803)7:2<201::AID-EAT2260070207>3.0.CO;2-I

Striegel-Moore, R. H., Dohm, F., Pike, K. M., Wilfley, D. E., & Fairburn, C. G. (2002). Abuse, bullying, and discrimination as risk factors for binge eating disorder. *American Journal of Psychiatry, 159,* 1902–1907. doi:10.1176/appi.ajp.159.11.1902

Striegel-Moore, R. H., Fairburn, C. G., Wilfley, D. E., Pike, K. M., & Dohm, F. (2005). Toward an understanding of risk factors for binge eating disorder in black and while women: A community-based case-control study. *Education Faculty Publications, 35,* 907–917. doi:10.1017/S0033291704003435

Stunkard, A. J., Berkowitz, R., Wadden, T., Tanrikut, C., Reiss, E., & Young, L. (1996). Binge eating disorder and the night-eating syndrome. *International Journal of Obesity, 20,* 1–6.

Stunkard, A. J. (1959). Eating patterns and obesity. *Psychiatric Quarterly, 33,* 284–295. doi:10.1007/BF01575455

U.S. Food & Drug Administration. (2015, January 15). *FDA expands uses of Vyvanse to treat binge-eating disorder.* Retrieved from https://ohsonline.com/Articles/2015/02/03/FDA-Expands-Uses-of-Vyvanse-to-Treat-Binge.aspx

Vandereycken, W. (1994). Emergence of bulimia nervosa as a separate diagnostic entity: Review of the literature from 1960-1979. *International Journal of Eating Disorders, 16,* 105–116. doi:10.1002/1098-108X(199409)16:2<105::AID-EAT2260160202>3.0.CO;2-E

Wiser, S., & Telch, C. F. (1999). Dialectical behavior therapy for binge-eating disorder. *Journal of Clinical Psychology, 55,* 755–768. doi:10.1002/(SICI)1097-4679(199906)55:6<755::AID/break-JCLP8>3.0.CO;2-R

SIGNS AND SYMPTOMS

Introduction

The various editions of the *Diagnostic and Statistical Manual of Mental Disorders (DSM)* are focused on accurately identifying *symptoms* that reflect the diagnosis of a particular disorder, whereas *signs* of any psychiatric disorder may or may not reflect a specific symptom of a disorder. Signs are evidence of a disease or disorder that can be observed by someone else, whereas a symptom is evidence of a disease or disorder that is experienced internally by the individual themselves. A sign of an eating disorder, for example, would be someone refusing to eat, whereas a symptom would be someone's fear of becoming fat. Signs of a disorder are intended to alert the individual, family or friends, or evaluating healthcare professional that there *may* be a problem that can be diagnosed and treated (see Chapter 8). The more signs of a particular disorder someone displays, the more likely it is that a specific diagnosis may be appropriate; however, as with any disorder, the diagnosis itself must be left to a licensed professional trained to evaluate and render mental disorder diagnoses. This chapter presents general signs that an eating disorder may be present. Each specific eating disorder is presented in terms of the signs that may signal that particular disorder followed by a description of diagnostic symptoms that are indicative of that disorder.

General Signs of Eating Disorders

There are a multitude of signs that someone may have an eating disorder. This section takes a look at what may be an indicator that an eating disorder of some kind may be developing or has already developed. As with any disorder, the presence of any one sign (or symptom for that matter) is not a guarantee that the disorder has developed or that it will in the future; however, when an individual shows multiple signs of an eating disorder there is a greater chance that an eating disorder is developing or has already developed.

In 2015, the National Eating Disorder Association (NEDA) published its third edition of the *Parent Toolkit*. This guide was designed to assist parents in identifying an eating disorder in their child as well as to assist with the challenges of having a family member with an eating disorder, such as finding the right treatment and how to deal with insurance companies. This toolkit also provides a list of signs for eating disorders in general and for each eating disorder in particular. NEDA grouped the general signs of an eating disorder in two categories: emotional and behavioral signs, and physical signs, and noted that anyone showing any of the signs should be taken seriously and the individual should be strongly encouraged to seek help. The National Institute of Mental Health (2018) also published materials designed to inform people about eating disorders that included a list of signs and symptoms. What follows is a brief description of many of the signs noted in these two publications.

Emotional and Behavioral Signs

Emotional signs of an eating disorder can involve specific changes in emotions, the expression of particular emotions, or the experience of things that can negatively impact someone's emotions (see Chapter 6).

Emotional Signs

Fear is a common sign of an eating disorder and can be experienced in a variety of contexts involving an individual's body shape and size. This emotional sign can include the fear of gaining weight or the fear of eating where others can see them (i.e., eating in public). Related to this are feelings of self-worth and self-esteem which are inextricably linked to body shape, weight, and size. This means that depending on how much their body weighs, how their body looks, how they feel in their body, or how their clothes feel on their body, their sense of who they are will be dictated by whether or not the experiences are positive (e.g., weight is lost) or negative (e.g., clothes feel tight). Thus, self-esteem and self-worth are dependent on the state of or perception of one' body.

Someone who may show signs of an eating disorder may express his or her emotions in an unusual way. For some, this may mean not showing much emotion at all, which is typically referred to as "flat affect." This means that things that would usually evoke some type of emotion, whether a positive (e.g., happiness) or a negative (e.g., anger or sadness) emotion, result in the individual not displaying any or a very subtle emotional reaction. By contrast, it is possible that the unusual emotional experiences may be expressed in terms of irritability. Someone showing this sign is likely easily stressed by seemingly insignificant things and he or she is unable to cope with or tolerate such inconveniences. As a result, the individual gets frustrated and acts irritable at a variety of situations and other people. Others may be restless or hyperactive and thus have a difficult time sitting still or physically staying in one spot. Finally, someone showing signs of an eating disorder may have dramatic mood swings. Such a person may seem to be okay or even having a good time and then quickly and suddenly become very sad, angry, or irritable. The person may not know why his or her mood shifted so rapidly and dramatically

Behavioral Signs

Behavioral signs of an eating disorder can range from body checking to elaborate food rituals that may be noticeable to others. Unusual food rituals literally involve the manner in which someone eats his or her food. The individual may cut his or her food into very small pieces, eating one piece at a time, or take very small bites of food. The person may count the number of times he or she chews the food before swallowing it and eating very slowly overall. Other unusual eating behaviors can involve the person developing complex rituals around food that involve how the food is prepared (e.g., time of day, specific pots/pans/utensils used), how the food is arranged on the plate, and so on. Failure to follow such rituals or being prevented from following such rituals may precipitate some of the emotional signs noted previously.

In an effort to ensure that they are losing weight and/or only putting "healthy" foods in their body, some people showing signs of an eating disorder may be likely to participate in fad diets that are usually restrictive in nature. The diet may require a follower to cut out entire food groups and/or to limit the amount of certain types of foods or the overall amount of food consumed in a day. By contrast, it may be possible that someone showing signs of an eating disorder will hoard or hide foods. This may be due to fear of having foods taken away by others, or because they have a stash of "junk food" they are saving for a later binge.

Food rituals have the potential of turning into rules that must be followed such as only eating certain types of food that are identified as being "safe" foods or "healthy" foods. Over time, the number of safe and/or healthy foods will likely shrink, leaving the person unable to eat very many types of food without breaking a rule, which can result in self-punishment and self-loathing.

Preoccupation with food can manifest in a variety of ways. It can certainly include thinking about food consistently and throughout the day on most days. As a result, the person may talk about food more than seems typical of most people. These people may routinely ask about what others have had to eat or what their favorite foods are, they may be drawn to the smell of cooking food, and they may subscribe to food related magazines. Similarly, someone showing preoccupation with food may display his or her preoccupation with food by watching as many cooking shows as possible.

Body checking is another behavioral sign of eating disorders. Body checking may occur by looking in the mirror and scrutinizing one's appearance. When someone does this, he or she is likely looking for flaws in the body, particularly as it relates to weight and shape. Body checking may stem, in part, from another sign of eating disorders, which is having a negative or distorted **body image**. Someone showing signs of an eating disorder will not be satisfied with how his or her body looks, no matter how much weight and/or body fat the person may lose. Someone who has an extremely distorted view of his or her body may believe he or she is fat or obese when the individual is, in fact, emaciated.

Given the rampant dissatisfaction with one's body, it is common for people showing signs of an eating disorder to try to hide their body by wearing bulky and often loose fitting clothes. This can make it more difficult, for example, for others to determine how much weight someone struggling with **anorexia nervosa** may have lost. Regardless of one's body shape and size, loose fitting clothes that hide or disguise one's body may be a sign of an eating disorder.

Another behavioral sign of an eating disorder can include excessive exercise. This can be difficult to define; however, generally speaking, if the individual is not a competitive athlete but is exercising as if he or she is one, it is possible that the individual is using exercise as a part of his or her eating disorder. Moreover, regardless of one's athletic status, if someone is continuing to exercise despite being sick or injured, it is possible that he or she is using exercise in a way that is unhealthy and that may be part of an eating disorder.

Physical Signs

In addition to emotional and behavioral signs, there are many physical signs indicative of an eating disorder that can affect potentially every system in one's body (see Chapter 5).

One physical sign of an eating disorder that, depending on the disorder itself may ultimately be a symptom, involves fluctuations in weight. These fluctuations will be noticeable and can involve either weight loss or weight gain. Other physical signs include general gastrointestinal problems (e.g., constipation, acid reflux), irregular menstrual functioning in females (e.g., infrequent menstrual cycles or cessation of menstruation), difficulty concentrating, dizziness or fainting, sleep difficulties, and frequent complaints of being cold. Those showing physical signs of an eating disorder may also evidence problems with their teeth, skin, nails, and hair. The enamel on their teeth may show signs of erosion or cavities. Their skin, hair, and nails may become dry and brittle, and they may have frequent sleep difficulties and impaired immune system functioning.

Some of the signs discussed previously may seem contradictory (e.g., restricting food or hoarding food) and may make it difficult to tell if someone has an eating disorder or not. The reality is some individuals may show many of these signs, even ones that seem to be at odds with one another, or only a few of these signs. Additionally, showing any of these signs does not mean that the person definitively has or will have an eating disorder. Regardless, since these emotional, behavioral, and physical signs have been associated with eating disorders, they should be taken seriously and considered as possible indicators of one of the eating disorders.

Signs and Symptoms of Specific Eating Disorders

In their discussion of how difficult eating disorders, in particular anorexia nervosa, are to treat, Abbate-Daga, Amianto, Delsedime, De-Bacco, and Fassino (2013) described the symptoms of eating disorders as "highly valuable" (p. 13). This may seem strange given the fact that these disorders have one of, if not the highest, mortality rate of any psychiatric illness (Harris & Barraclough, 1998; Neumärker, 2000; Smink, van Hoeken, & Hoek, 2012).

Both the National Eating Disorders Association (2015) and the National Institute of Mental Health (2018) have identified signs that tend to indicate a particular eating disorder may be developing or has already developed. Some of these signs will be briefly summarized prior to describing the diagnostic symptoms of each eating disorder.

Anorexia Nervosa

Signs

Some of the signs associated specifically with anorexia nervosa include a preoccupation with one's weight, and with food in general, which may include calorie counting and the number of grams of fat consumed. Despite one's weight (including emaciation), someone showing signs of anorexia nervosa may often say that he or she "feels fat," which may be accompanied by an intense fear of gaining weight or of being fat. As such, these people are likely to refuse to maintain a healthy weight and may restrict the types and quantities of food they eat, and engage in rigid food rituals when they do eat. Someone showing signs of anorexia nervosa may also seem to require a need for being in control, which can be accompanied by inflexible thinking. Their need for control may also be displayed through a restricted range of emotional expression as well as the inflexible food rituals noted in the previous paragraph.

Overall, someone who may show signs of anorexia nervosa will be preoccupied with food (e.g., frequently cooks for others, watches cooking shows, talks about food) despite not eating very much or making excuses about why he or she is not eating with others at meal times. Excessive weight loss as a result of not eating enough will likely result in the individual having gastrointestinal issues and frequently feeling cold. The individual's malnourishment is also predictive of signs such as dry and brittle skin, hair and nails, anemia, muscle weakness, and low blood pressure.

Symptoms

As discussed in Chapter 1, anorexia nervosa has a long history that more or less reflects the primary symptom of anorexia nervosa: not eating enough. To consider anorexia nervosa purely as a disorder in which someone does not eat enough is an oversimplification for sure. In this section further detail will be provided describing the symptoms used to diagnose someone with anorexia nervosa.

In the *DMS-5* (American Psychiatric Association [APA], 2013) there are three criteria and several specifiers used to diagnose Anorexia Nervosa. Each of the three criteria must be met in order for someone to be diagnosed with this disorder. The first criterion begins with the phrase "(r)estriction of energy intake relative to requirements" (APA, 2013, p. 338), which in the simplest of terms means that the individual is not eating enough. As a result, he or she will lose weight to the point of "significantly low body weight" (p. 338), which is determined based on the individual's age, sex, what his or her weight history has been, and what the individual requires in order to be physically healthy. The phrase *significantly low body weight* is not something that can be specified in diagnostic criteria for all who may be diagnosed with anorexia nervosa; however, it refers to a weight that is below the lowest healthy weight for that person. For children and adolescents who are still physically growing, a significantly low weight is a weight that is below the healthiest weight expected based on the individual's age, sex, and height.

In addition to weight loss resulting in a lower than healthy body weight, the individual will also be scared to the point of feeling terrified about gaining weight or of becoming fat. This is the second diagnostic criterion. Accompanying this intense fear, the individual may also consistently engage in behaviors that interfere with his or her ability to gain weight despite being at a very low weight. The third criterion involves the perception the person has of his or her own body and how it may affect the individual's sense of self. People with anorexia nervosa have difficulty seeing and experiencing their body the way it actually is. They may fail to recognize how dangerous their body weight is, they may believe themselves to be "good" or "bad" based on how their body looks, and they may grossly misperceive the actual size of their body. Many individuals with anorexia nervosa will see a fat person when looking in the mirror despite having an emaciated body.

These three criteria must be met in order for someone to be diagnosed with anorexia nervosa. It is, however, important for those rendering this diagnosis to consider whether a **subtype** or **specifier** is appropriate. Anorexia nervosa has two subtypes: restricting type and binge-eating/purging type. Someone with the restricting type of anorexia nervosa loses weight predominantly through limiting how much food he or she eats, not eating at all for a period of time, and/or engaging in exercise that is considered to be excessive. Individuals with this subtype of anorexia nervosa do not regularly engage in binging or purging episodes. Someone who does regularly engage in binge eating or purging behaviors would be categorized by the second type of anorexia nervosa: binge-eating/purging type. For this subtype of anorexia nervosa, weight loss is primarily achieved via **purging** behaviors such as self-induced vomiting or the misuse of laxatives, diuretics, or enemas. The purpose of the purging behaviors is to, in one way or another, get rid of the food that has been consumed even if the amount of food consumed is quite small. With the restricting type, the food is not gotten rid of per se but the individual will rigidly limit what and how much he or she can eat, and whatever is eaten is compensated for by fasting or burning it off via overexercising.

There are two sets of specifiers for the diagnosis of anorexia nervosa. The first set of specifiers refers to whether or not the individual is in any type of remission. Someone who is in **partial remission** will have previously met all criteria for anorexia nervosa, but when this specifier is appropriate he or she will no longer meet the first criterion (i.e., the individual is no longer significantly underweight); however, the individual will continue to meet the remaining two criteria. Someone who is in **full-remission** will have previously met all criteria for the disorder, but when this specifier is appropriate he or she will no longer meet any of the criteria for an ongoing period of time. The second set of specifiers indicates how severe someone's symptoms are based on what his or her current **body mass index (BMI)** is if the person is an adult, or his or her BMI percentile if the person is a child or adolescent. The severity specifiers are mild (BMI more than or equal to 17), moderate (BMI ranging from 16 to 16.99), severe (BMI ranging from 15 to 15.99), and extreme (BMI less than 15).

Bulimia Nervosa

Signs

There is some overlap between anorexia nervosa and **bulimia nervosa** with respect to signs of the disorders, including signs such as engaging in food rituals, being uncomfortable eating around others, and skipping meals altogether. Signs that are more likely to be found among those who may be dealing with bulimia nervosa include behaviors such as going to the bathroom immediately following meals. This can be suggestive of purging behaviors as the individual may eat what appears to be a "normal" meal but feels the need to get rid of the food as quickly as possible. Additionally, a sign of bulimia nervosa may also include large quantities of food going missing from the household in a relatively short period of time. There may also be food stashed away in unusual places and possibly evidence of large quantities of food that had been previously eaten such as a lot of empty food wrappers.

Signs of self-induced vomiting can include "puffy cheeks" or swelling of the cheeks and jaw area. The person who self-induces vomiting may also have calluses on the back of his or her hand (i.e., Russell's sign) and discolored teeth. Binge eating and purging episodes are likely to be done in secret and thus, the individual may rearrange his or her schedule to ensure he or she has time to engage in these behaviors without being caught.

Symptoms

The diagnosis of Bulimia Nervosa according to the *DSM-5* (APA, 2013) involves five criteria and several specifiers. The first criterion involves regular binge eating episodes that must meet two subcriteria. The first subcriterion is that whatever the individual eats is consumed during a distinct period of time and that the amount of food eaten is much more than what a typical person would eat under the same circumstances and length of time. The second subcriterion of a binge eating episode is that the individual feels like he or she does not have control over his or her eating. This means that the person is aware of not being able to stop once he or she has started or cannot decide to eat less than what he or she is eating.

The second criterion for bulimia nervosa is that in addition to binge eating the individual regularly engages in **compensatory behaviors** designed to prevent weight gain. These behaviors, however, are deemed to be inappropriate and include self-induced vomiting, fasting, excessive exercising, or misusing laxatives, diuretics, enemas, or any other medication that results in weight loss. The third criterion for bulimia nervosa involves the number of times and how often the binge eating and inappropriate compensatory behaviors occur. In this case, someone with the diagnosis of bulimia nervosa must average at least one binge-purge episode per week for at least 3 months. The fourth criterion involves the individual's self-concept and sense of self-worth, both of which are overly affected by what his or her body looks like and how much his or her body weighs. The final criterion is that the first four criteria do not occur only when someone has anorexia nervosa. In short, this means that if someone meets the criteria for anorexia nervosa and he or she engages in binge-purge behaviors as defined here, the individual would be diagnosed with anorexia nervosa.

There are no subtypes of bulimia nervosa; however, there are two sets of specifiers. The first set involves where the individual may be in terms of remission. Someone is in partial remission when he or she has previously met all of the criteria for the disorder and at the time this specifier is appropriate the individual has met some of the criteria for bulimia nervosa for an ongoing length of time. By contrast, someone who is in full remission has previously met all criteria for the disorder but at the time this specifier is appropriate he or she no longer meets any of the criteria for an ongoing length of time. The second set of specifiers involves how severe the individual's symptoms are and is based on how frequently the individual engages in inappropriate compensatory behaviors. Someone who can be identified as having mild bulimia nervosa will average one to three episodes of inappropriate compensatory behaviors per week. A moderate level of severity involves four to seven episodes, while a severe level of bulimia nervosa will involve eight to 13 episodes per week. The extreme specifier is appropriate when someone engages in 14 or more inappropriate compensatory behaviors each week.

Binge Eating Disorder

Signs

Common signs of **binge eating disorder** overlap with those of bulimia nervosa, including things such as large quantities of food going missing, food hoarding, large number of empty food wrappers, and altering their schedule to make time for binge eating episodes. Someone who may be dealing with binge eating disorder may also have food rituals, and may also skip meals altogether or will only eat small amounts of food when eating with others at regular meal times. It is also possible that a sign of binge eating disorder includes fasting or repeated dieting.

Symptoms

The formal diagnosis of Binge Eating Disorder has only been possible since the *DSM-5* (APA, 2013) was published. Criteria had been proposed for binge eating disorder in the *DSM-IV* (American Psychiatric Association, 1994), and were largely identical to those that would come to define the disorder in the *DSM-5* (although the *DSM-5* criteria include the addition of specifiers).

The first criterion of binge eating disorder is the same as the first criterion for bulimia nervosa. This criterion reflects the presence and nature of binge eating episodes. The two subcriteria required for a binge eating episode are also the same: consuming a large amount of food that is more than most people would eat under similar circumstances, which is consumed over a distinct period of time, and there is a sense of not being in control of how much is eaten or when to stop. The second criterion for the diagnosis of binge eating disorder involves experiencing three or more items from a list of behaviors and experiences that may occur during a binge eating episode. The five items according to the *DSM-5* are:

1. Eating much more rapidly than normal
2. Eating until feeling uncomfortably full
3. Eating large amounts of food when not feeling physically hungry
4. Eating alone because of feeling embarrassed by how much one is eating
5. Feeling disgusted with oneself, depressed, or very guilty afterward. (APA, 2013, p. 350)

The third and fourth criteria, respectively, for binge eating disorder are that the individual feels significant distress about the binge eating, and that the individual has binge eating episodes that occur at least once per week for 3 months. The final criterion states that the binge eating episodes are not accompanied by regularly engaging in the inappropriate compensatory behaviors as defined in criterion two for bulimia nervosa, and that the binge eating episodes do not occur only when the individual can also meet the criteria for bulimia nervosa or anorexia nervosa.

There are no subtypes of binge eating disorder but there are two sets of specifiers. The first set of specifiers refers to the type of remission in which someone may be. Being in partial remission means that the individual previously met all criteria for binge eating disorder but at the time this specifier is appropriate their binge eating episodes occur less than once per week for an extended period of time. Being in full remission means that after meeting all criteria for binge eating disorder the individual no longer meets any of the criteria for an extended period of time. The second set of specifiers involves the degree of severity of the disorder and refers specifically to the frequency of binge eating episodes. A mild form of binge eating disorder is characterized by one to three binge eating episodes per week, and a moderate degree of severity is identified by the individual having four to seven binge eating episodes per week. Having binge eating disorder that can be identified as severe means that the individual has eight to 13 binge eating episodes per week, and someone with an extreme form of binge eating disorder egages in 14 or more episodes each week.

Other Specified Feeding and Eating Disorder

A diagnosis of Other Specified Feeding and Eating Disorder (OSFED) is used when an individual shows symptoms of a feeding disorder (e.g., **Pica**) or eating disorder that do not meet any of the specific feeding or eating disorder diagnoses. The symptoms will be highly distressful and/or cause significant impairment in at least one area of normal functioning (e.g., school, work, relationships). This diagnosis is used when the clinician rendering the diagnosis wishes to specifically describe why the symptoms do not fit one of the other feeding or eating disorders. Five specific symptom presentations are identified by the *DSM-5* (APA, 2013) for the OSFED diagnosis.

The first specific presentation is identified as *atypical anorexia nervosa* characterized by significant weight loss that has not resulted in a significantly low weight. The second presentation is *bulimia nervosa (of low-frequency and/or limited duration)*, which reflects symptoms that otherwise meet the criteria for bulimia nervosa except the individual's binge–purge episodes occur less than once per week and/or the episodes have occurred for less than 3 months. *binge eating disorder (of low-frequency and/or limited duration)* is the third specified presentation that is effectively the same as bulimia nervosa (of low-frequency and/or limited duration) except that the frequency and duration of the episodes in question are binge episodes rather than binge–purge episodes. The fourth presentation is *purging disorder*, which involves purging behaviors for the purpose of manipulating one's weight or shape; however, the person does not engage in binge eating episodes. The final presentation listed as part of the OSFED diagnosis is *night eating syndrome*. This presentation of symptoms involves eating at nighttime, either after waking from sleep or eating a large amount of food after dinner. Night eating syndrome is not diagnosed when this pattern of eating may result from changes to the individual's typical sleep–wake cycle, or when this pattern of eating is part of the culture in which one lives. Additionally, the symptoms of night eating syndrome cause a great deal of distress in the individual and likely interfere with normal functioning. Finally, night eating syndrome is not diagnosed if the symptoms can be explained by a medical diagnosis or another mental disorder such as substance use disorder or binge eating disorder.

Unspecified Feeding or Eating Disorder

The Unspecified Feeding or Eating Disorder (UFED) diagnosis is used when an individual experiences feeding or eating disorder-related symptoms that do not meet the full criteria of any of the specific disorders. Additionally, the individual's symptoms interfere with his or her ability to function normally and cause a great deal of distress. The UFED diagnosis is used by the rendering clinician when he or she does not want to specify why the symptoms do not meet the specific criteria of another feeding or eating disorder.

The UFED diagnosis is also appropriate when there is not enough information provided to more specifically indicate a particular diagnosis. The *DSM-5* (APA, 2013) notes that an example of this diagnosis might be when a patient is evaluated in an emergency room/department setting at a hospital. Those rendering a diagnosis may not have enough time to collect sufficient information and/or the individual may not be able to provide specific information.

Related Syndromes and Disorders

Most of the terms discussed in the following subsections are not diagnosable mental disorders in and of themselves. These syndromes are discussed because they frequently appear in popular media and at times in academic papers and are included here because they are thought to be directly or tangentially related to eating disorders in one way or another.

Exercise Dependence

Exercise is known to be beneficial in a multitude of ways and can improve one's quality of life and overall health (Penedo & Dhan, 2005). Regular exercise has been linked to improved self-esteem (Fox, 2000), lower levels of anxiety (DeBoer, Powers, Utschig, Otto, & Smits, 2012), and improved quality of life for those who are seriously mentally ill (Alexandratos, Barnett, & Thomas, 2012). Despite these known benefits, it is possible to utilize exercise in such a way that harms one's overall mental and physical well-being (e.g., overuse injuries; Grave, 2008). Not all who engage in exercise in a harmful way are necessarily mentally ill (Taranis, Touyz, & Meyer, 2011) and some may consider exercise dependence or "addiction to exercise" as a "badge of honor" (Sachs, 2018, p. 335); however, a misuse of exercise has been linked to eating disorders (Beaumont, Arthur, Russell, & Touyz, 1994; Hechler, Beumont, Marks, & Touyz, 2005; Penas-Lledo, Vaz Leal, & Waller, 2002) and is, in fact, part of the description of anorexia nervosa and bulimia nervosa in the *DSM-5* (APA, 2013). One way that both clinical and nonclinical populations may experience a problem with exercise is known as *exercise dependence*.

In addition to the term **exercise dependence**, there are a multitude of other terms used to describe a misuse of exercise. These include exercise addiction (Aidman & Wollard, 2003; Sachs & Pargman, 1979), drive exercise (Stiles-Shields, Goldschmidt, Boepple, Glunz, & Le Grange, 2011), exercise abuse (Davis, 2000), and exercise anorexia (Touyz, Beumont, & Heok, 1987). It is possible that the last term is reflective of anorexia nervosa itself, during which someone uses exercise as a means of weight loss above and beyond what is lost via insufficient caloric intake.

Exercise dependence can be most simply characterized as the misuse of exercise, resulting in a withdrawal experience when exercise is discontinued for any period of time and for any reason. A formal definition provided by Downs and Hausenblas (2014) states that exercise dependence involves "a craving for leisure time physical activity that results in uncontrollable excessive exercise behavior and that manifests in physiological symptoms (e.g., tolerance, withdrawal) and/or psychology symptoms (e.g., anxiety, depression)" (p. 390).

As few as 3% and as many as 13% of adults who exercise may show symptoms of exercise dependence (Allegre, Souville, Therme, & Griffiths, 2006; Hausenblas & Downs, 2002; Terry, Szabo, & Griffiths, 2004), and it has been linked to eating disorders, though it is also hypothesized to exist independent of eating disorders (Lichtenstein, Christiansen, Elklit, Bilenbert, & Støving, 2014).

Although not diagnosable as a mental disorder, it is important for those working with individuals who may be at risk for overexercising and eating disorders to be aware of what exercise dependence is and understand its possible negative effects. Smith, Hale and Selby (2017) specifically noted that those who work directly with athletes and exercisers should not only know how to identify problematic exercise but should also have a strategy in place to facilitate help for those who are at risk for damaging themselves physically and psychologically. In a related vein, Selby (2017) stated that those who work with individuals with eating disorders should fully understand how someone's use of exercise may inhibit his or her treatment and recovery process.

Orthorexia

The term *orthorexia* can be found in popular media fairly regularly, especially in discussions of various diets that promote "clean eating." The physician Steven Bratman, who is credited with coining the term orthorexia in 1996 and who formally wrote about it a year later (Bratman, 1997), has a website devoted to the syndrome (Bratman, n.d.). Some have suggested that there is considerable overlap of symptoms between orthorexia, anorexia nervosa, and obsessive-compulsive disorder (OCD; Koven & Abry, 2015). Although it is not currently listed as a possible eating disorder, nor is it listed in the *DSM-5* (APA, 2013) as a condition of future study, orthorexia is often referred to as a disorder, and criteria for identifying the disorder have been proposed.

Orthorexia is characterized by eating healthy foods but to such a degree that the types of foods individuals will allow themselves to eat becomes increasingly narrow. Dunn and Bratman (2016) noted that instead of focusing on weight as someone with anorexia nervosa is apt to do, someone dealing with orthorexia is focused on "purity." These individuals seek to avoid eating foods that may make them feel impure or unclean. Orthorexia has received some scientific attention in Europe and to a much lesser degree in the United States (Dunn & Bratman, 2016), including the development of an assessment tool called the ORTO-15. This tool was developed for the purpose of identifying those who have a "'maniacal obsession for health food'" (Donini, Marsili, Graziani, Imbriale, & Cannella, 2005, p. e28).

Formal criteria for the identification and possible diagnosis of orthorexia were proposed by Dunn and Bratman (2016). They identified two primary criteria. The first is characterized by a focus on eating that can be considered obsessive in nature and that involves a rigid set of beliefs about eating that may result in significant distress when the person is faced with unhealthy food options. This criterion also notes that weight loss is possible but that weight loss itself is not the focus of the individual, whereas achieving a healthy ideal is the primary focus. When someone with orthorexia consumes food that violates his or her self-identified rules, the individual is afraid that he or she has been contaminated or will develop a disease. This is frequently accompanied by a sense of shame and anxiety. The second criterion is that the individual's focus on eating in a pure way impairs his or her ability to maintain nutritional health and/or a healthy weight, as well as the individual's ability to maintain relationships or meet academic or work-related expectations. The focus on what these individuals put in their body overwhelms them to the point that all other things in their life become secondary. The second criterion also involves the notion that how they feel about themselves, who they are, and what their body looks like is contingent on whether or not they have complied with their rules around eating healthy.

Despite the individual's focus on only eating healthy and pure foods, someone dealing with orthorexia will ultimately compromise his or her mental and physical well-being to the point that the individual may lose relationships, experience an increase in anxiety, no longer be able to eat in an intuitive fashion (i.e., eat when hungry and stop when full), and in some cases may become severely malnourished and die as a result of his or her inability to adequately provide nourishment for the body.

Bigorexia/Muscle Dysmorphia

Bigorexia is also known as *muscle dysmorphia*—a subtype of body dysmorphic disorder. Body dysmorphic disorder involves an obsession or preoccupation with a flaw in one's physical appearance that is either slightly or not at all noticeable to others (APA, 2013). Accompanying this concern is some combination of behaviors such as repeatedly checking one's appearance in the mirror, excessive grooming, repeatedly picking at one's skin, seeking reassurance from others that they look okay, and/or consistently comparing one's appearance to others'. This experience is different from eating disorders in that the focus on physical appearance is not on body weight or body fat. When diagnosing body dysmorphic disorder it can be specified whether or not the person is dealing with muscle dysmorphia, which refers to a concern about whether or not one's muscles are believed to be too small or insufficient.

Muscle dysmorphia was first discussed in 1993 by Pope, Katz, and Hudson; however, they referred to the symptoms as *reverse anorexia*. They interviewed over 100 body builders and found that nearly 3% of those they talked to had symptoms consistent with anorexia nervosa and just over 8% of the body builders stated that they thought their bodies were small despite the fact that others observed them to have large and muscular bodies. In 1997, Pope, Gruber, Choi, Olivardia, and Phillips identified muscle dysmorphia by name and suggested that it should be considered a type of body dysmorphic disorder. They offered potential criteria to be used for formal diagnosis of the condition. The culmination of their work on understanding muscle dysmorphia was the publication of *The Adonis Complex: The Secret Crisis of Male Body Obsession* (Pope, Phillips, & Olivardia, 2000). Muscle dysmorphia was included as a variant of Body Dysmorphic Disorder for the first time in the *DSM-5* (APA, 2013). The criteria included therein are similar to but different from those proposed by Pope and his colleagues.

Since it was first identified, a great deal of research has been conducted on muscle dysmorphia to better understand what it is, how it develops, who develops it, and the best ways to treat it; however, much of that research was conducted with small sample sizes and the use of case studies (Tod, Edwards, & Cranswick, 2016). Muscle dysmorphia is believed to be found predominantly among male body builders (Mosley, 2009) and as already noted is a variant of body dysmorphic disorder, which is classified under the Obsessive-Compulsive and Related Disorders category in the *DSM-5*. Murray, Maguire, Russell, and Touyz (2012), however, have suggested that it may be better categorized as an eating disorder. Although based on a single case, they concluded that assessment of muscle dysmorphia should also include assessment of specific eating disorder symptomology such as compulsive exercising, binging and purging, and inflexible eating patterns that are often restrictive in nature. Kinnaird (2017), in part, supports this reclassification. She noted that both eating disorder and muscle dysmorphia criteria are important but that neither sufficiently captures the experiences of males dealing with body image concerns. She suggested the use of a "male eating disorder framework" (Kinnaird, 2017, p. 9) reflecting the idea that males have a set of experiences distinct from females. Those who have written about body dysmorphia generally concede that more research needs to be conducted in order to more fully and adequately understand this constellation of symptoms.

Compulsive (Over)Eating

Neither the term *compulsive eating* nor *compulsive overeating* appear anywhere in the *DSM-5* (APA, 2013); when used, however, these terms, particularly compulsive overeating, likely refer to behavior seen in those diagnosed with binge eating disorder (Izydorczyk, 2012). Compulsive overeating appears in the *DSM-IV* (APA, 1994) in the context of the sleep disorder *primary hypersomnia* (excessive sleepiness with episodes of prolonged sleep or daytime sleeping nearly daily) as an indicator of behavioral disinhibition. As noted earlier in this chapter and in Chapter 1, binge eating disorder is characterized by recurrent binge eating episodes that are accompanied by a sense of being out of control when eating; that is, someone with binge eating disorder cannot stop eating once he or she has started. The use of the word *compulsion* can be clinically problematic, which is likely the reason compulsive eating does not appear anywhere in the *DSM*. According to the *DSM-5*, a compulsion in the context of OCD involves a repetitive behavior or thought done for the purpose of reducing one's anxiety resulting from his or her particular obsession (intrusive and unwanted thoughts or urges). The repetitive behavior (e.g., handwashing, checking) or thought (e.g., counting, repetition of a specific word) is done based on a set of rigid rules such as engaging in the behavior or thought a certain number of times in a specific way. If not done according to these rules, the compulsion has to be repeated. This is not what compulsive eating is like, although as noted those who engage in binge eating episodes often feel like they cannot stop and may very well say that they eat compulsively.

Another possible similarity between clinical compulsions and compulsive eating can be found among studies with animals. Just as those with OCD may engage in compulsive behaviors to reduce the obsession-related anxiety, someone who is eating compulsively may also do so in order to make himself or herself feel better (Di Segni, Patrono, Patella, Puglisi-Allegra, & Ventura, 2014). Di Segni and his colleagues suggested that compulsive overeating may be comparable to addiction to other substances. They suggest, in particular, that those who engage in binge eating behaviors, which they indicated is equitable to compulsive eating, tend to eat highly refined foods and will continue to eat and overeat these types of foods despite any negative consequences. This, they say, is the hallmark of addiction and therefore compulsive eating or binge eating should be considered in this context. Indeed, researchers out of Yale University (Gearhardt, Corbin, & Brownell, 2009) developed what they call the *Yale Food Addiction Scale*, designed to measure food addiction despite its absence from the *DSM*.

Conclusion

There are a multitude of signs that someone may be dealing with an eating disorder. Some of these signs may be more indicative of one eating disorder than another, whereas other signs are general enough that they may indicate the possibility of any eating disorder. The symptoms of each disorder are specific; however, there is some overlap between the disorders (e.g., binge eating) that can make for a less clear diagnostic picture. What can further complicate what an eating disorder is and is not involves several-related syndromes that are often associated with eating disorders but that are not eating disorders in and of themselves. Such complexity points to the importance of sufficient education and training to properly recognize what is an eating disorder and what is not.

References

Abbate-Daga, G., Amianto, F., Delsedime, N., De-Bacco, C., & Fassino, S. (2013). Resistance to treatment and change in anorexia nervosa: A clinical overview. *BMC Psychiatry, 13*, 1–18. doi:10.1186/1471-244X-13-294

Aidman, E. V., & Wollard, S. (2003). The influence of self-reported exercise addiction on acute emotional and physiological responses to brief exercise deprivation. *Psychology of Sport and Exercise, 4*, 225–236. doi:10.1016/S1469-0292(02)00003-1

Alexandratos, K., Barnett, F., & Thomas, Y. (2012). The impact of exercise on the mental health and quality of life of people with severe mental illness. *The British Journal of Occupational Therapy, 75*, 48–60. doi:10.4276/030802212X13286281650956

Allegre, B., Souville, M., Therme, P., & Griffiths, M. (2006). Definitions and measures of exercise dependence. *Addiction Research and Theory, 14*, 631–646. doi:10.1080/16066350600903302

American Psychiatric Association. (1994). *Diagnostic and statistical manual of mental disorders* (4th ed.). Washington, DC: Author.

American Psychiatric Association. (2013). *Diagnostic and statistical manual of mental disorders* (5th ed.). Arlington, VA: American Psychiatric Publishing.

Beaumont, P. J. V., Arthur, B., Russell, J. D., & Touyz, S. W. (1994). Excessive physical activity in dieting disorder patients: Proposals for a supervised exercise program. *International Journal of Eating Disorders, 15*, 21–36. doi:10.1002/1098-108X(199401)15:1<21::AID-EAT2260150104>3.0.CO;2-K

Bratman, S. (n.d.). *Orthorexia*. Retrieved from http://www.orthorexia.com

Bratman, S. (1997, September/October). Health food junkie. *Yoga Journal*, pp. 42–50.

Davis, C. (2000). Exercise abuse. *International Journal of Sport Psychology, 31*, 278–289.

DeBoer, L. B., Powers, M. B., Utschig, A. C., Otto, M. W., & Smits, J. A. (2012). Exploring exercise as an avenue for the treatment of anxiety disorders. *Expert Review of Neurotherapeutics, 12*, 1011–1022. doi:10.1586/ern.12.73

Di Segni, M., Patrono, E., Patella, L., Puglisi-Allegra, S., & Ventura, R. (2014). Animal models of compulsive eating behavior. *Nutrients, 6*, 4591–4609. doi:10.3390/nu6104591

Donini, L., Marsili, D., Graziani, M., Imbriale, M., & Cannella, C. (2005). Orthorexia nervosa: Validation of a diagnosis questionnaire. *Eating and Weight Disorders, 10*, e28–32. doi:10.1007/BF03327537

Downs, D. S., & Hausenblas, H. (2014). Exercise dependence. In R. C. Eklund & G. Tenenbaum (Eds.), *Encyclopedia of sport and exercise psychology* (Vol. 1, pp. 266–269). Thousand Oaks, CA: Sage.

Dunn, T. M., & Bratman, S. (2016). On orthorexia nervosa: A review of the literature and proposed diagnostic criteria. *Eating Behaviors, 21*, 11–17. doi:10.1016/j.eatbeh.2015.12.006

Fox, K. R. (2000). Self-esteem, self-perceptions and exercise. *International Journal of Sport Psychology, 31*, 228–240.

Gearhardt, A. N., Corbin, W. R., & Brownell, K. D. (2009). Preliminary validation of the Yale Food Addiction Scale. *Appetite, 52*, 430–436. doi:10.1016/j.appet.2008.12.003

Grave, R. D. (2008). Excessive and compulsive exercises in eating disorders: Prevalence, associated features, and management. *Directions in Psychiatry, 28*, 273–282.

Harris, E. C. & Barraclough, B. (1998). Excess mortality of mental disorder. *British Journal of Psychiatry, 173*, 11–53. doi:10.1192/bjp.173.1.11

Hausenblas, H., & Downs, D. S. (2002). Relationship among sex, imagery, and exercise dependence symptoms. *Psychology of Addictive Behaviors, 16*, 169–172. doi:10.1037/0893-164X.16.2.169

Hechler, T., Beumont, P., Marks, P., & Touyz, S. (2005). How do clinical specialists understand the role of physical activity in eating disorders? *European Eating Disorders Review, 13*, 125–132. doi:10.1002/erv.630

Izydorczyk, B. (2012). Neuroticism and compulsive overeating: A comparative analysis of the level of neuroticism and anxiety in a group of females suffering from psychogenic binge eating, and in individuals exhibiting no mental or eating disorders. *Archives of Psychiatry and Psychotherapy, 3*, 5–13.

Kinnaird, E. (2017). From anorexia to bigorexia: A discussion of current research and future directions in male eating disorders. *PsyPAG Quarterly, 2017* (102), 6–10.

Koven, N. S., & Abry, A. W. (2015). The clinical basis of orthorexia nervosa: Emerging perspectives. *Neuropsychiatric Disease and Treatment, 11*, 358–394. doi:10.2147/NDT.S61665

Lichtenstein, M. B., Christiansen, E., Elklit, A., Bilenbert, N., & Støving, R. K. (2014). Exercise addiction: A study of eating disorder symptoms, quality of life, personality traits and attachment styles. *Psychiatry Research, 215*, 410–416. doi:10.1016/j.psychres.2013.11.010

Mosley, P. E. (2009). Bigorexia: Body building and muscle dysmorphia. *European Eating Disorders Review, 17*, 191–198. doi:10.1002/erv.897

Murray, S. B., Maguire, S., Russell, J., & Touyz, S. W. (2012). The emotional regulatory features of bulimic episodes and compulsive exercise in muscle dysmorphia: A case report. *European Eating Disorders Review, 20*, 68–73. doi:10.1002/erv.1088

National Eating Disorders Association. (2015). *Parent toolkit* (3rd ed.). New York, NY: Author.

National Institute of Mental Health. (2018). *Eating disorders: About more than food* (NIH Publication No. TR 17-4901). Washington, DC: U.S. Government Printing Office.

Neumärker, K. J. (2000). Mortality rates and causes of death. *European Eating Disorders Review, 8*, 181–187. doi:10.1002/(SICI)1099-0968(200003)8:2<181::AID-ERV336>3.0.CO;2-#

Penas-Lledo, E., Vaz Leal, F. J., & Waller, G. (2002). Excessive exercise in anorexia nervosa and bulimia nervosa: Relation to eating characteristics and general psychopathology. *International Journal of Eating Disorders, 31*, 370–375. doi:10.1002/eat.10042

Penedo, F. J., & Dahn, J. R. (2005). Exercise and well-being: A review of mental and physical health benefits associated with physical activity. *Current Opinion in Psychiatry, 18*, 189–193. doi:10.1097/00001504-200503000-00013

Pope, H. G., Gruber, A. J., Choi, P., Olivardia, R., & Phillips, K. A. (1997). Muscle dysmorphia: An unrecognized form of body dysmorphic disorder. *Psychosomatics, 38*, 548–557. doi:10.1016/S0033-3182(97)71400-2

Pope, H. G., Katz, D. L., & Hudson, J. I. (1993). Anorexia nervosa and "reverse anorexia" among 108 male bodybuilders. *Comprehensive Psychiatry, 34*, 406–409. doi:10.1016/0010-440X(93)90066-D

Pope, H. G., Phillips, K. A., & Olivardia, R. (2000). *The Adonis complex: The secret crisis of male body obsession.* New York, NY: The Free Press.

Sachs, M. L. (2018). Exercise addiction. In S. Razon & M. L. Sachs. (Eds.), *Applied exercise psychology: The challenging journey from motivation to adherence* (pp. 330–337). New York, NY: Routledge.

Sachs, M. L., & Pargman, D. (1979). Running addiction: A depth interview examination. *Journal of Sport Behavior, 2*, 143–155.

Selby, C. L. B. (2017). Eating disorders and exercise. In S. Razon & M. Sachs (Eds.), *Applied exercise psychology: The challenging journey from motivation to adherence* (pp. 377–398). New York, NY: Routledge.

Smink, F. R. E., van Hoeken, D., & Hoek. H. W. (2012). Epidemiology of eating disorders: Incidence, prevalence and mortality rates. *Current Psychiatry Reports, 14*, 406–414. doi:10.1007/s11920-012-0282-y

Smith, D., Hale, B. D., & Selby, C. (2017). Exercise dependence. In S. Cotterill, N. Weston, & G. Breslin (Eds.), *Applied sport and exercise psychology: Practitioner case studies* (pp. 437–456). Chichester, West Sussex, UK: Wiley.

Stiles-Shields, E. C., Goldschmidt, A. B., Boepple, L., Glunz, C., & Le Grange, D. (2011). Driven exercise among treatment-seeking youth with eating disorders. *Eating Behaviors, 12*, 328–331. doi:10.1016/j.eatbeh.2011.09.002

Taranis, L., Touyz, S., & Meyer, C. (2011). Disordered eating and exercise: Development and preliminary validation of the Compulsive Exercise Test. *European Eating Disorders Review, 19*, 256–268. doi:10.1002/erv.1108

Terry, A., Szabo, A., & Griffiths, M. (2004). The exercise addiction inventory: A new brief screening tool. *Addiction Research and Theory, 12*, 489–499. doi:10.1080/16066350310001637363

Tod, D., Edwards, C., & Cranswick, I. (2016). Muscle dysmorphia: Current insights. *Psychology Research and Behavior Management, 9*, 179–188. doi:10.2147/PRBM.S97404

Touyz, S. W., Beumont, P. J. V., & Heok, S. (1987). Exercise anorexia: A new dimension in anorexia nervosa? In P. J. V. Beumont, G. D. Burrows, & R. C. Caspar (Eds.), *Handbook of eating disorders, Part 1: Anorexia and bulimia nervosa* (pp. 143–157). Amsterdam, Netherlands: Elsevier.

AGE, SEX, RACE, AND SOCIOECONOMIC STATUS

Introduction

The stereotype of someone with an eating disorder is a young, White female who is likely from a household that could be classified as having middle to upper socioeconomic status (SES). To date, this particular description does represent a significant proportion of those diagnosed with an eating disorder; however, only seeing this type of person when considering who has an eating disorder means that many others may be missed. For example, friends and family may not believe someone if he or she says "I have an eating disorder," or may dismiss their own fears if they suspect their loved one may have an eating disorder if that person falls outside of the stereotypical picture. Moreover, healthcare providers who hold this particular bias may misdiagnose non-White, non-young, non-female, nonaffluent individuals who present with symptoms that otherwise would be associated with an eating disorder. Practically speaking, what having a restricted view of eating disorders can mean is that many people who may be at risk for developing an eating disorder or who already have diagnosable symptoms may be overlooked and go untreated. Increasing rates of eating disorders are found among males, individuals of all ages, and from an increasing diversity in terms of culture and ethnicity (Lachenmeyer & Muni-Brander, 1988; Weiselberg, Gonzalez, & Fisher, 2011). It is, therefore, important to understand the prevalence rates of eating disorders in general and among various demographic characteristics to paint a more clear picture of who can develop an eating disorder and when.

Age

The prevalence rate for any eating disorder over one's lifetime is relatively low. Although higher numbers are found among those diagnosed with **binge eating disorder**, that number is still lower than 3%. The lifetime prevalence for *anorexia nervosa* is estimated to be 0.6% to 0.69%, 1.0% to 1.69% for **bulimia nervosa,** and 1.43% to 2.8% for binge eating disorder (Duncan, Ziobrowski, & Nicol, 2017; Hudson, Hiripi, Pope, & Kessler, 2007; there are differences between males and females that will be discussed in the Section "Sex").

Among adolescents aged 13 to 18 years, lifetime prevalence rates are similar but slightly different than the overall rates. Swanson, Crow, Le Grange, Swendsen, and Merikangas (2011) reported that 0.3% of adolescents will be diagnosed with anorexia nervosa, 0.9% will be diagnosed with bulimia nervosa, and 1.6% will be diagnosed with binge eating disorder. If an eating disorder develops in adolescence, it is likely to develop by about age 12; more specifically, the median age of onset is 12.3 years old for anorexia nervosa, 12.4 years old for bulimia nervosa, and 12.6 years old for binge eating disorder (Swanson et al., 2011). Campbell and Peebles (2014) reported that it is common for adolescents to not be diagnosed with an eating disorder in a primary care setting and as a result they may not get the treatment they need quickly enough. They also noted that rates of eating disorders among those younger than adolescence are increasing. It is, therefore, possible that the current statistics on how common eating disorders are among children and adolescents are underrepresentative of how many could be diagnosed with an eating disorder.

Although eating disorders are often associated with adolescence, the average age of onset for eating disorders is late teens to mid-twenties. Hudson et al. (2007) reported that anorexia nervosa is likely to start at 18.9 years old, bulimia nervosa at 19.7 years old, and binge eating disorder at 25.4 years old. Although the average age of onset for any eating disorder is within young adulthood, it is clear by the data reported for adolescents that it can often develop much younger than that. Additionally, there is evidence that eating disorders do occur during the middle to older adulthood years for both males and females (Reas & Stedal, 2015; Scholtz, Hill, & Lacey, 2010). What is not clear, however, is whether these are individuals who have had a lifelong struggle with an eating disorder or whether these individuals developed an eating disorder for the first time in older adulthood (see Chapter 4). A recent study examining differences between young adults (ages 18–39) and middle-aged adults (40 years old and above) found some differences between age groups on the various eating disorder diagnoses (Elran-Barak et al., 2015). Their results indicated that the rate of **anorexia nervosa** did not change from one period of adulthood to the next; however, fewer individuals in midlife had a diagnosis of Bulimia Nervosa, and more individuals in midlife had a diagnosis of Binge Eating Disorder or Otherwise Specified Feeding and Eating Disorder (see Chapter 2).

The average age of onset of any eating disorder tends to be adolescence to young adulthood; however, there is evidence that individuals in much younger and much older age groups can also develop these disorders. In the next section, eating disorders are discussed in terms of prevalence rates among males and females.

Sex

It is believed that among all of those who are diagnosed with either anorexia nervosa or bulimia nervosa, males make up approximately 10% of those diagnosed; among those diagnosed with binge eating disorder, the proportion increases to 25% (Weltzin et al., 2005). Males have been found to seek treatment in increasing numbers (Braun, Sunday,

Huang, & Halmi, 1999) though they are still less likely than females to seek treatment in general (Oliver, Pearson, Coe, & Gunnell, 2005; Weltzin et al., 2005), and more likely to delay seeking treatment when they do (Galdas, Cheater, & Marshall, 2005). Treatment seeking behaviors may therefore affect the reported prevalence rates of eating disorder diagnoses among males.

Historically, not much is known about males and eating disorders. This is due in large part to the fact that most studies only looked at behaviors and associated characteristics among females (Ulfvebrand, Birgegård, Norring, Högdahl, & von Hausswolff-Juhlin, 2015) as such eating disorders are typically associated with females (Mitchison & Mond, 2015). There may, however, be differences between males and females with respect to a focus on muscularity, which is more likely to be found among males and is associated with behaviors such as using drugs, engaging in binge drinking, and using supplements marketed for muscle growth (Field et al., 2013). Thus, healthcare professionals may fail to identify these behaviors as rising to the level of a weight-related disorder due to a presentation of symptoms that is atypical compared to that which is presented by females. This may mean that our current assessment and diagnosis of eating disorders may need to be modified to reflect this possible sex difference (Mitchison & Mond, 2015).

Additional factors that may account for which males develop an eating disorder and which do not include competing in athletics—particularly in sports with an expectation for leanness putting males at greater risk for developing exercise dependence (Hausenblas & Downs, 2002)—and being homosexual (Dakanalis et al., 2012; Russell & Keel, 2002). When eating disorder diagnoses do not highlight a focus and desire for thinness, such as with binge eating disorder or **avoidant/restrictive food-intake disorder**, the prevalence rates between males and females are more equivalent (Murray et al., 2017).

As noted in the section on age, adolescents have a lifetime prevalence rate of 0.3% for anorexia nervosa, 0.9% for bulimia nervosa, and 1.6% for binge eating disorder; however, there are differences with respect to lifetime prevalence between males and females (Swanson et al., 2011). Both male and female adolescents have 0.3% lifetime prevalence for anorexia nervosa; however, males have a lower lifetime prevalence for bulimia nervosa (0.5% males and 1.3% females) and binge eating disorder (0.8% males and 2.3% females). Overall, lifetime prevalence rates are higher for adults with marked differences between the sexes. Adult females have a lifetime prevalence rate of 0.69% for anorexia nervosa whereas adult males have a 0.19% lifetime prevalence rate. The lifetime prevalence rates for bulimia nervosa for females and males are 1.68% and 0.55%, respectively, and for binge eating disorder the lifetime prevalence rates are 2.97% for women and 1.59% for men.

The differences between prevalence rates between males and females may reflect a true difference; however, it is possible that other factors are at play that may result in the underreporting of eating disorders in males. One issue is that in the ***Diagnostic and Statistical Manual of Mental Disorders*** (*DSM-IV*; American Psychiatric Association [APA], 1994) the diagnosis of *eating disorder not otherwise specified* (EDNOS) historically constituted the majority of eating disorder diagnoses rather than anorexia nervosa or bulimia nervosa (Fairburn & Bohn, 2005; Fairburn & Cooper, 2007). When compared to the previous criteria used in the *DSM-IV*, using the new *DSM-5* criteria resulted in an increase in diagnoses of both anorexia nervosa and bulimia nervosa and a decrease in the use of the EDNOS diagnosis (Serrano-Troncoso, et al., 2017). The improvement of the diagnostic criteria for eating disorders in the *DSM-5* is important not only for the proper identification and treatment of eating disorders but also with respect to how males are identified in the context of eating disorders (Gualandi, Simoni, Manzato, & Scanelli, 2016). Results from a study examining how prevalent the EDNOS diagnosis was in the United States showed that the majority of both adolescents and adults diagnosed with an eating disorder fell under this category and that more than 83% of males compared to more than 71% of females were diagnosed with EDNOS (Le Grange, Swanson, Crow, & Merikangas, 2012). Thus, even when males were identified with an eating disorder, they were more likely to be diagnosed with the category designed to include those who do not meet full criteria for either anorexia nervosa or bulimia nervosa and therefore may have been overlooked as having a disorder requiring clinical attention. The diagnosis of EDNOS has been referred to as "subclinical" and as being less serious than the primary eating disorder diagnoses (Fairburn & Bohn, 2005).

When eating and body-related disturbances are considered among males, they are often done in the context of disorders that are more likely to be associated with males such as muscle dysmorphia, which is a subtype of body dysmorphic disorder, and overexercising that is focused on muscle development (Mitchison & Mond, 2015). In a recent examination of the literature on eating disorders in males, Murray et al. (2017) concluded that among clinical professionals and males themselves, eating disorders among males are still considered to be an unusual occurrence. This has meant that much has been missed with regard to understanding the ways in which males may or may not differ from females in their presentation and experience of eating disorder symptoms.

Eating disorder diagnoses are significantly and quickly on the rise and this may be truer among males than females (Murray et al., 2017). Acknowledging and developing an understanding of the difference between males and females in how they experience an eating disorder can mean that more males are properly diagnosed and get the help they need as expediently as possible.

Race/Ethnicity

Historically, non-Caucasian racial/ethnic groups were not studied in the context of eating disorders and were in fact deemed to be unlikely to develop this category of disorders (Pike, Hoek, & Dunne, 2014). This belief was perpetuated in large part due to the stereotype that only young, White females from upper SES levels developed eating disorders, a stereotype that may have continued due to the biased clinical sample that treating professionals saw in their inpatient and outpatient practices (Gard & Freeman, 1996). Andersen, Morse, and Santmyer (1985) hypothesized, however, that as minority groups raised their level of SES there would be an accompanying increase in eating disorder diagnoses. Given the persistence of the young, White, upper SES, female as the stereotypical patient with an eating disorder, many researchers have worked to determine if, in fact, there is a difference in prevalence rates between different racial and ethnic groups.

In their review of the literature examining where on the globe eating disorders seem to exist, Pike et al. (2014) found that although specifics about prevalence are not known, eating disorders have been diagnosed on each of the world's major continents and that the narrow concept of eating disorders with respect to race and ethnicity is inaccurate. Others have confirmed that rates of eating disorder diagnoses are on the rise among non-Western cultures (Soh & Walter, 2013). Pike and Dunne (2015) noted that Western cultural influences, however, are insufficient to explain any increases in eating disorders among other cultures and pointed to changes observed globally with respect to urbanization and industrialization that explain these changes.

There are some differences among various ethnic and racial groups. For example, among those identifying as Asian, prevalence rates for eating disorders have been found to be lower than those found among non-Asian individuals (Sue, Cheng, Saad, & Chus, 2012), whereas bulimia nervosa may be more prevalent among Latino or African American individuals in comparison to non-Latino Whites (Marques et al., 2011; Smink, van Hoeken, & Hoek, 2012). By contrast, anorexia nervosa is either equivalent or more likely to be found among Whites or mixed-race individuals compared to those identifying as Black or African American (Keel & Forney, 2013; Marques et al., 2011). African American individuals may have risk and protective factors for eating disorders that are different from those seen among White girls (Bodell et al., 2018; Dye, 2016; Hoek et al., 2005; Talleyrand, 2010; Taylor et al., 2013), whereas risk factors may be the same between Latina and European American women (Cachelin, Gil-Rivas, & Vela, 2014). With regard to binge eating disorder, some research has found that when compared to White individuals Black and Hispanic/Latino individuals have a similar prevalence rate but Black individuals reported binging more frequently and had a higher BMI (Lydecker & Grilo, 2016). Among, Asian Americans prevalence rates for BED seem to be higher than those found among White individuals though they were less likely to report feeling a loss of control or associated distress from binge eating (Lee-Winn, Mendelson, & Majtabai, 2014).

Boisvert and Harrell (2014) examined the literature on eating disorders among the majority and minority racial and ethnic cultures in North America. They looked at the intersection between race/ethnicity and SES when it comes to diagnosis and treatment of eating disorders. They concluded that those who are not Caucasian were less likely to be diagnosed with an eating disorder and were also less likely to seek treatment when there was an eating disorder diagnosis or concern. This was also identified as an issue of concern by Franko (2007), who noted that the heterogeneous presentation of eating disorder symptomology may contribute to eating disorders being overlooked by treatment professionals in those who are of a nonmajority race or ethnicity. These ideas were echoed by Boisvert and Harrell (2014). who noted that possible explanations for the disparity in identifying eating disorder cases included a lack of understanding of cultural differences between Whites and non-Whites among treatment providers, which can mean that eating disorder symptomology may be presented differently and therefore missed. Boisvert and Harrell (2014) noted that individuals who have an Asian, Hispanic/Latino, or Black/African American racial/ethnic heritage may feel ashamed of their problems and fear that they will be stigmatized. They may, therefore, minimize the seriousness of their symptoms, and if they do decide treatment is a good idea they may not have adequate access to healthcare services due to proximity, financial, or language constraints.

Boisvert and Harrell (2014) identified an aspect of coming from a non-White background that may protect someone from developing an eating disorder who is in the process of adjusting to living in a North American country. They found that women who are from an ethnic minority were less likely to develop an eating disorder if they remained strongly connected to their culture of origin. It is possible that encouraging women to remain faithful to the traditions associated with their culture may help them resist the North American and Western cultural pressure to be thin. The strongest finding revealed in this study was that non-White women with a high SES were less likely to report eating disorder behaviors compared to non-White women with a lower SES.

Soh and Walter (2013) reviewed the literature involving cross-cultural examinations of eating disorders. They found that while an increase in empirical attention has been devoted to understanding eating disorders among various cultures, they noted that there is still not enough known to fully understand how members of different cultural groups may differ from others. For example, they noted that among minority ethnic and cultural groups that have been studied, African and African American groups have received the most attention, adding that having a well-developed understanding of one cultural group does not generalize to understanding another. They concluded by noting that rates of treatment among non-Western groups is substantially lower than among Western groups. This can perpetuate a lack of understanding of how culture may influence the development and maintenance of an eating disorder, which in turn can become an obstacle to providing effective treatment.

Socioeconomic Status

Part of the stereotype of the typical person with an eating disorder is that he or she is of high SES. In their review of studies published in the 1970s through the early 1990s, Gard and Freeman (1996) found that studies prior to the mid-1980s that included SES as a variable of interest identified a relationship between SES and anorexia nervosa such that those with a higher SES were more likely to be diagnosed with anorexia nervosa. These studies did not include bulimia nervosa as this disorder was not formally identified and diagnosed until the mid-1980s; however, when bulimia nervosa was included a similar relationship between the disorder and SES was found. It was not until the mid-1980s and onward that researchers published more studies including SES as a demographic variable. Collectively, the findings revealed that there was either no relationship between a high SES and eating disorders, or that the reverse was more likely, particularly among those diagnosed with bulimia nervosa (Pope, Champoux, & Hudson, 1987), including higher rates among homeless people than in the general population (Gard & Freeman, 1996). Gard and Freeman (1996) noted that one reason the stereotype that females with high SES backgrounds were the most likely to develop an eating disorder was due in part to the biased nature of who sought treatment. Clinicians were recording and reporting who sought treatment, which included demographics such as age, sex, and SES. Since those with money were more likely to be able to afford treatment, treating professionals were more likely to think only those with higher SESs were developing eating disorders. Similarly, the belief in a highly specific demographic diagnosed with eating disorders extended to being female, Caucasian, young adult, and from an industrialized or westernized culture (Walcott, Pratt, & Patel, 2003). This is due in large part to convenience samples of research participants found among those who attend university or who were being treated for an eating disorder and extends back to the late 1800s. Walcott et al. (2003) further cited research showing that eating disorders are being detected in increasing numbers among males and females of various racial/ethnic heritages, among girls aged younger than puberty, and in countries around the world not considered to be westernized.

While the bulk of this section will be spent on whether or not there is an equal or skewed distribution of eating disorders among various levels of SES, one study examined eating disorders from the perspective of how much people at various levels of SES know about a variety of mental illnesses including eating disorders.

A group of German and Austrian researchers (von dem Knesebeck et al., 2013) surveyed over 2,000 people regarding how much they knew about schizophrenia, depression, and eating disorders, including their ability to recognize the disorders, how much they knew about the treatment of these disorders, and how common these disorders are. Each participant in the survey also provided information about his or her education level, what his or her occupation was, and what his or her income was. The intent of the researchers was to see if knowledge and beliefs about these disorders differed based on one's SES. Overall, they discovered that the lower someone's SES the less he or she knew about the disorders including eating disorders, and the more likely he or she was to believe that the cause of any of these disorders might be due, in part, to one's "weak will." With respect to eating disorders, those with higher levels of SES were found to believe that psychotherapy as a form of treatment can be effective compared to their lower SES counterparts. Overall, these researchers concluded that there is a lack of knowledge about these disorders, including eating disorders, among those with lower SESs, suggesting that any public campaigns designed to educate people about these disorders should focus on those with lower levels of education, lower income levels, and those who have an occupation status considered to be low (e.g., unemployed).

Although it is difficult to predict with a significant degree of certainty how successful an adolescent may be in his or her adult years when considering things like occupational status and income, some studies have found that when an adolescent is diagnosed with an eating disorder he or she is more likely to experience negative consequences that extend into his or her adulthood years. Interestingly, these consequences do not affect males and females equally. Tabler and Utz (2015) accessed a database of information including information that allowed them to examine data collected on males and females during various points along their developmental trajectory. These researchers specifically examined the data collected when the study participants were between 11 and 18 years old, again when these same participants were between approximately 17 and 25 years old, and finally when they were about 24 to 32 years old. This provided useful data during adolescence, young adulthood, and adulthood. Their results showed that females were more negatively impacted by eating disorder-related behaviors than males on things such as how much education they achieved, how much income they earned in adulthood, and whether or not they owned a home. They noted, however, that they were unable to examine the ways in which race/ethnicity may play a role due to the relatively small amount of people who participated in the study, resulting in even fewer people identifying as being a member of a racial/ethnic minority group.

A related but separate concept from SES is known as social rank. This refers to one's perceived social status among peers. Social status is freely given to others based on the value they have to their peers. Gilbert (1997) examined social rank and how it helps to keep social interactions in balance. He found that those who have higher social status tend to be able to effectively compete with others and generally succeed, as well as being attractive to those whom they may want to date. Higher social status is also bestowed on those who easily command the attention of others not through force or aggression, but by how attractive they are socially. Various studies on how social rank might interact with eating disorder behaviors have found that one's social rank does seem to affect eating disorder symptoms (Troop, Allan, Treasure, & Katzman, 2003; Troop, Andrews, Hiskey, & Treasure, 2014; Troop & Baker, 2008). Specifically, the more severe the eating disorder psychopathology, the more likely it is for those individuals to perceive themselves as having a low social status (Troop et al., 2003) and additionally to engage in socially submissive behaviors (Troop & Baker, 2008). A recent study, however, found that over a period of 6 months one's perceived social rank had a significantly negative effect on symptoms related to anorexia nervosa in comparison to symptoms reflective of bulimia nervosa (Troop et al., 2014), that is, the lower one's perceived social rank, the more severe one's symptoms of anorexia nervosa.

Contrary to the conclusion that in some instances eating disorders are more likely to be found among those with lower SESs (Gard & Freeman, 1996), a more contemporary study seems to have confirmed at least part of the eating disorder stereotype: those with eating disorders are more likely to come from a higher socioeconomic background compared to those who do not have an eating disorder (Nevonen & Norring, 2004). These researchers acknowledged that previous examinations of the relationship between SES and eating disorders have been mixed. Their findings provide support for the idea that those with eating disorders come from high status areas, but more aligned with the findings of Troop et al. (e.g., Troop et al., 2003, 2014) that those with eating disorders were more likely to have a lower social status than those without an eating disorder diagnosis.

Linking race and ethnicity with SES, Andersen et al. (1985) suggested that a higher SES was a factor in the development of eating disorders, indicating that as individuals from various minority groups raise their SES more minority individuals will be diagnosed with eating disorders.

In their review of various demographic variables and their relationship to eating disorders, Nagel and Jones (1992) concluded their review by stating that treating professionals are already aware of the pressure adolescents feel to adhere to societal norms (e.g., standards for appearance) and that this pressure is felt among males and females, minority and majority cultures, and all levels of SES.

Conclusion

There are identifiable differences between those of a different age, sex, race/ethnicity, and SES when it comes to eating disorder diagnoses and issues related to eating disorders such as body image dissatisfaction. Understanding these differences can help us understand why some people struggle with eating disorders and related issues and others do not, though it remains important to be wary of stereotyping for any group as making an assumption about the presence or absence of an eating disorder based on what is currently known can mean someone with an eating disorder will be overlooked and not get the treatment he or she needs.

References

American Psychiatric Association. (1994). *Diagnostic and statistical manual of mental disorders* (4th ed.). Washington, DC: Author.

American Psychiatric Association. (2013). *Diagnostic and statistical manual of mental disorders* (5th ed.). Washington, DC: Author.

Andersen, A. E., Morse, C., & Santmyer, K. (1985). Inpatient treatment for anorexia nervosa. In D. M. Garner & P. E. Garfinkel (Eds.), *Handbook of psychotherapy for anorexia nervosa and bulimia*. New York, NY: Guilford Press.

Bodell, L. P., Wildes, J. E., Cheng, Y., Goldschmidt, A. B., Keenan, K., Hipwell, A. E., . . . Stepp, S. D. (2018). Associations between race and eating disorder symptom trajectories in Black and White girls. *Journal of Abnormal Child Psychology, 46*, 625–638. doi:10.1007/s10802-017-0322-5

Boisvert, J. A., & Harrell, W. A. (2014). Ethnicity, socioeconomic status, and eating disorder symptomatology in Canada: Implications for mental health care. *Ethnicity and Inequalities in Health and Social Care, 7*, 158–177. doi:10.1108/EIHSC-10-2013-0038

Braun, D. L., Sunday, S. R., Huang, A., & Halmi, K. A. (1999). More males seek treatment for eating disorders. *International Journal of Eating Disorders, 25*, 415–424. doi:10.1002/(SICI)1098-108X(199905)25:4<415::AID-EAT6>3.0.CO;2-B

Cachelin, F. M., Gil-Rivas, V., & Vela, A. (2014). Understanding eating disorders among Latinas. *Advances in Eating Disorders, 2*, 204–208. doi:10.1080/21662630.2013.869391

Campbell, K., & Peebles, R. (2014). Eating disorders in children and adolescents: State of the art review. *Pediatrics, 134*, 582–592. doi:10.1542/peds.2014-0194

Dakanalis, A., Di Mattei, V. E., Bagliacca, E. P., Prunas, A., Sarno, L., Riva, G., . . . Zanetti, A. (2012). Disordered eating behaviors among Italian men: Objectifying media and sexual orientation differences. *Eating Disorders, 20*, 356–367. doi:10.1080/10640266.2012.715514

Duncan, A. E., Ziobrowski, H. N., & Nicol, G. (2017). The prevalence of past 12-month and lifetime *DSM-IV* eating disorders by BMI category in US men and women. *European Eating Disorders Review, 25*, 165–171. doi:10.1002/erv.2503

Dye, H. (2016). Are there differences in gender, race, and age regarding body dissatisfaction? *Journal of Human Behavior in the Social Environment, 26*, 499–508. doi:10.1080/10911359.2015.1091240

Elran-Barak, R., Fitzsimmons-Craft, E. E., Benyamini, Y., Crow, S. J., Peterson, C. B., Hill, L. L., . . . Le Grange, D. (2015). Anorexia nervosa, bulimia nervosa, and binge eating disorder in midlife and beyond. *The Journal of Nervous and Mental Disease, 203*, 583–590. doi:10.1097/NMD.0000000000000333

Fairburn, C. G., & Bohn, K. (2005). Eating disorder NOS (EDNOS): An example of the troublesome "not otherwise specified" (NOS) category in *DSM-IV*. *Behaviour Research and Therapy, 43*, 691–701. doi:10.1016/j.brat.2004.06.011

Fairburn, C. G., & Cooper, Z. (2007). Thinking afresh about the classification of eating disorders. *International Journal of Eating Disorders, 40*, S107–S110. doi:10.1002/eat.20460

Field, A. E., Sonneville, K. R., Crosby, R. D., Swanson, S. A., Eddy, K. T., Camargo, C. A., . . . Micali, N. (2013). Prospective associations of concerns about physique and the development of obesity, binge drinking, and drug use among adolescent boys and young adult men. *Journal of the American Medical Association, 168*, 34–39. doi:10.1001/jamapediatrics.2013.2915

Franko, D. L. (2007). Race, ethnicity, and eating disorders: Considerations for *DSM-V*. *International Journal of Eating Disorders, 40*, S31–S34. doi:10.1002/eat.20455

Galdas, P. M., Cheater, G., & Marshall, P. (2005). Men and health-seeking behavior: Literature review. *Journal of Advanced Nursing, 49*, 616–623. doi:10.1111/j.1365-2648.2004.03331.x

Gard, M. C. E., & Freeman, C. P. (1996). The dismantling of a myth: A review of eating disorders and socioeconomic status. *International Journal of Eating Disorders, 20*, 1–12. doi:10.1002/(SICI)1098-108X(199607)20:1<1::AID-EAT1>3.0.CO;2-M

Gilbert, P. (1997). The evolution of social attractiveness and its role in shame, humiliation, guilt and therapy. *The British Journal of Medical Psychology, 70,* 113–147. doi:10.1111/j.2044-8341.1997.tb01893.x

Gualandi, M., Simoni, M., Manzato, E., & Scanelli, G. (2016). Reassessment of patients with eating disorders after moving from *DSM-IV* towards *DSM-5:* A retrospective study in a clinical sample. *Eating and Weight Disorders, 21,* 617–624. doi:10.1007/s40519-016-0314-4

Hausenblas, H., & Downs, D. S. (2002). Relationship among sex, imagery, and exercise dependence symptoms. *Psychology of Addictive Behaviors, 16,* 169–172. doi:10.1037/0893-164X.16.2.169

Hoek, H. W., van Harten, P. N., Hermans, K. M., Katzman, M. A., Matroos, G. E., & Susser, E. S. (2005). The incidence of anorexia nervosa on Curacao. *American Journal of Psychiatry, 162,* 748–752. doi:10.1176/appi.ajp.162.4.748

Hudson, J. I., Hiripi, E., Pope, H. G., & Kessler, R. C. (2007). The prevalence and correlates of eating disorders in the national comorbidity survey replication. *Biological Psychiatry, 61,* 348–358. doi:10.1016/j.biopsych.2006.03.040

Keel, P. K., & Forney, K. J. (2013). Psychosocial risk factors for eating disorders. *International Journal of Eating Disorders, 46,* 433–439. doi:10.1002/eat.22094

Lachenmeyer, J. R., & Muni-Brander, P. (1988). Eating disorders in a nonclinical adolescent population: Implications for treatment. *Adolescence, 90,* 303–312.

Le Grange, D., Swanson, S. A., Crow, S. J., & Merikangas, K. R. (2012). Eating disorder not otherwise specified presentation in the US population. *International Journal of Eating Disorders, 45,* 711–718. doi:10.1002/eat.22006

Lee-Winn, A., Mendelson, T., & Mojtabai, R. (2014). Racial/ethnic disparities in binge eating: Disorder prevalence, symptoms presentation, and help-seeking among Asian Americans and non-Latino Whites. *American Journal of Public Health, 104,* 1263–1265. doi:10.2105/AJPH.2014.301932

Lydecker, J. A., & Grilo, C. M. (2016). Different yet similar: Examining race and ethnicity in treatment-seeking adults with binge eating disorder. *Journal of Consulting and Clinical Psychology, 84,* 88–94. doi:10.1037/ccp0000048

Marques, L., Alegria, M., Becker, A. E., Chen, C. N., Fang, A., Chosak, A., . . . Diniz, J. B. (2011). Comparative prevalence, correlates of impairment, and service utilization for eating disorders across US ethnic groups: Implications for reducing ethnic disparities in health-care access for eating disorders. *International Journal of Eating Disorders, 44,* 412–420. doi:10.1002/eat.20787

Mitchison, D., & Mond, J. (2015). Epidemiology of eating disorders, eating disordered behaviour, and body image disturbance in males: A narrative review. *Journal of Eating Disorders, 3,* 1–9. doi:10.1186/s40337-015-0058-y. Retrieved from https://jeatdisord.biomedcentral.com/track/pdf/10.1186/s40337-015-0058-y?site=jeatdisord.biomedcentral.com

Murray, S. B., Nagata, J. M., Griffiths, S., Calzo, J. P., Brown, T. A., Mitchison, D., . . . Mond, J. M. (2017). The enigma of male eating disorders: A critical review and synthesis. *Clinical Psychology Review, 57,* 1–11. doi:10.1016/j.cpr.2017.08.001

Nagel, K. L. & Jones, K. H. (1992). Sociological factors in the development of eating disorders. *Adolescence, 27,* 107–113.

Nevonen, L., & Norring, C. (2004). Socio-economic variables and eating disorders: A comparison between patients and normal controls. *Eating and Weight Disorders, 9,* 279–284. doi:10.1007/BF03325082

Oliver, M. I., Pearson, N., Coe, N., & Gunnell, D. (2005). Help-seeking behaviour in men and women with common mental health problems: Cross-sectional study. *British Journal of Psychiatry, 186,* 297–301. doi:10.1192/bjp.186.4.297

Pike, K. M., & Dunne, P. E. (2015). The rise of eating disorders in Asia: A review. *Journal of Eating Disorders, 3,* 1–14. doi:10.1186/s40337-015-0070-2

Pike, K. M., Hoek, H. W., & Dunne, P. E. (2014). Cultural trends and eating disorders. *Current Opinion in Psychiatry, 27*, 436–442. doi:10.1097/YCO.0000000000000100

Pope, H. G., Champoux, R. F., & Hudson, J. I. (1987). Eating disorder and socioeconomic class: Anorexia nervosa and bulimia in nine communities. *The Journal of Nervous and Mental Disease, 175*, 620–623. doi:10.1097/00005053-198710000-00007

Reas, D. L., & Stedal, K. (2015). Eating disorders in men aged midlife and beyond. *Maturitas, 81*, 248–255. doi:10.1016/j.maturitas.2015.03.004

Russell, C. J., & Keel, P. K. (2002). Homosexuality as a specific risk factor for eating disorders in men. *International Journal of Eating Disorders, 31*, 300–306. doi:10.1002/eat.10036

Scholtz, S., Hill, L. S., & Lacey, H. (2010). Eating disorders in older women: Does late onset anorexia nervosa exist? *International Journal of Eating Disorders, 43*, 393–397. doi:10.1002/eat.20704

Serrano-Troncoso, E., Cañas, L., Carbonell, X., Carulla, M., Palma, C., Matali, J., . . . Dolz, M. (2017). Diagnostic distribution of eating disorders: Comparison between *DSM-IV-TR* and *DSM-5. Actas Españolas de Psiquiatría, 45*, 32–38.

Smink, F. R. E., van Hoeken, D., & Hoek, H. W. (2012). Epidemiology of eating disorders: Incidence, prevalence and mortality rates. *Current Psychiatry Reports, 14*, 406–414. doi:10.1007/s11920-012-0282-y

Soh, N. L. W., & Walter, G. (2013). Publications on cross-cultural aspects of eating disorders. *Journal of Eating Disorders, 1*, 1–4. doi:10.1186/2050-2974-1-4

Sue, S., Cheng, J. K. Y., Saad, C. S., & Chus, J. P. (2012). Asian American mental health: A call to action. *American Psychologist, 67*, 532–544. doi:10.1037/a0028900

Swanson, S. A., Crow, S. J., Le Grange, D., Swendsen, J., & Merikangas, K. R. (2011). Prevalence and correlates of eating disorders in adolescents: Results from the national comorbidity survey replication adolescent supplement. *Archives of General Psychiatry, 68*, 714–723. doi:10.1001/archgenpsychiatry.2011.22

Tabler, J., & Utz, R. L. (2015). The influence of adolescent eating disorders or disordered eating behaviors on socioeconomic achievement in early adulthood. *International Journal of Eating Disorders, 48*, 622–632. doi:10.1002/eat.22395

Talleyrand, R. M. (2010). Eating disorders in African American girls: Implications for counselors. *Journal of Counseling & Development, 88*, 319–324. doi:10.1002/j.1556-6678.2010.tb00028.x

Taylor, J. Y., Caldwell, C. H., Baser, R. E., Matusko, N., Faison, N., & Jackson, J. S. (2013). Classification and correlates of eating disorders among Blacks: Findings from the national survey of American life. *Journal of Health Care for the Poor and Underserved, 24*, 289–310. doi:10.1353/hpu.2013.0027

Troop, N. A., Allan, S., Treasure, J. L., & Katzman, M. (2003). Social comparison and submissive behaviour in eating disorder patients. *Psychology and Psychotherapy: Theory, Research and Practice, 76*, 237–249. doi:10.1348/147608303322362479

Troop, N. A., Andrews, L., Hiskey, S., & Treasure, J. L. (2014). Social rank and symptom change in eating disorders: A 6-month longitudinal study. *Clinical Psychology and Psychotherapy, 21*, 115–122. doi:10.1002/cpp.1830

Troop, N. A., & Baker, A. H. (2008). The specificity of social rank in eating disorder versus depressive symptoms. *Eating Disorders, 16*, 331–341. doi:10.1080/10640260802115993

Ulfvebrand, S., Birgegård, A., Norring, C., Högdahl, L., & von Hausswolff-Juhlin, Y. (2015). Psychiatric comorbidity in women and men with eating disorders results from a large clinical database. *Psychiatry Research, 230*, 294–299. doi:10.1016/j.psychres.2015.09.008

von dem Knesebeck, O., Mnich, E., Daubmann, A., Wegscheider, K., Angermeyer, M. C., Lambert, M., . . . Kofahl, C. (2013). Socioeconomic status and beliefs about depression, schizophrenia and eating disorders. *Social Psychiatry, 48*, 775–782. doi:10.1007/s00127-012-0599-1

Walcott, D. D., Pratt, H. D., & Patel, D. R. (2003). Adolescents and eating disorders: Gender, racial, ethnic, sociocultural, and socioeconomic issues. *Journal of Adolescent Research, 18*, 223–243. doi:10.1177/0743558403018003003

Weiselberg, E. C., Gonzalez, M., & Fisher, M. (2011). Eating disorders in the twenty-first century. *Minerva Ginecologica, 63,* 531–545.

Weltzin, T. E., Weisensel, N., Franczyk, D., Brunett, K., Klitz, C., & Bean, P. (2005). Eating disorders in men: Update. *Journal of Men's Health and Gender, 2,* 186–193. doi:10.1016/j.jmhg.2005.04.008

UNIQUE POPULATIONS

Introduction

Identifying the groups in this section as "unique" might erroneously imply that some of the populations discussed in Chapter 3 (e.g., males, racial and ethnic minorities) are not unique. They are; however, the growing recognition that eating disorders can affect anyone at any age, at any socioeconomic status, and of any race or ethnicity has resulted in an increase in scientific studies examining the extent to which eating disorders among those who do not reflect the stereotype are similar to or different from a young, White, middle-class female with an eating disorder. Some of the populations discussed in this chapter, too, have seen an increase in study (e.g., athletes); however, their inclusion here reflects the need to approach the identification and treatment of individuals from these groups differently.

In their book entitled *The Hidden Faces of Eating Disorders and Body Image,* Reel and Beals (2009) explore the often overlooked populations when it comes to understanding **body image** issues and eating disorders themselves. They caution that in practice, regardless of whether someone with an eating disorder fits the stereotypically young, White, affluent, female stereotype or fits within one of the often overlooked categories, it is important to discard what is known to be typical of any group and focus on developing an understanding of who the individual is in the context of his or her unique group status and the eating disorder itself. The unique populations included herein are a reminder that characteristics of and affiliations to various groups (e.g., physical disability and religious affiliation) may mean that special consideration is needed when screening, preventing, and treating individuals affiliated with these groups.

Athletes

Athletes are believed to be at greater risk for eating disorders than the general population (Holm-Denoma, Scaringi, Gordon, Van Orden, & Joiner, 2009; Sundgot-Borgen &

Torstveit, 2004; Torstveit, Rosenvinge, & Sundgot-Borgen, 2008). However, a meta-analysis conducted on studies that examined the prevalence of eating disorders in athletes compared to nonathlete populations found that while eating problems were more prevalent in the athlete population overall, the difference was small (Smolak, Murnen, & Ruble, 2000). Additionally, many more athletes experience what are referred to as *subclinical* eating-related issues (i.e., problematic eating behaviors that may cause distress but that do not meet the criteria for any eating disorder; Petrie & Greenleaf, 2007). Regardless of whether or not an athlete's behaviors are explicitly diagnosable, the literature points to the likelihood that many athletes struggle with eating disorders and related concerns. This is believed to be due to the dual pressures of looking a particular way based on societal expectations and the pressure to maintain a specific weight or to have a specific aesthetic depending on the athlete's sport (Becker, McDaniel, Bull, Powell, & McIntyre, 2012; de Bruin, 2010; Thompson & Sherman, 2010).

Several sport-specific factors have been identified that may contribute to the increased risk for athletes and include an expectation for a lower weight or lower body fat for the purpose of improving performance, a requirement of wearing revealing uniforms, or maintaining a pleasing aesthetic in sports where the athlete himself or herself is judged (Petrie & Greenleaf, 2007; Thompson & Sherman, 2010). Given that these factors have each been linked to eating problems and related issues (e.g., body image dissatisfaction) it is possible that any sport that has more than one of the aforementioned factors places an athlete at even greater risk of engaging in pathogenic behaviors designed to change his or her body weight or shape, thereby putting himself or herself at risk for developing an eating disorder. Interestingly, it may seem as if identifying these athletes may be relatively easy to do; however, Thompson and Sherman (1999) noted that many of the characteristics found among those typically diagnosed with **anorexia nervosa** are also found among high performing and/or highly dedicated athletes.

The similarities found between successful athletes and anorexia nervosa, respectively, are: mental toughness and asceticism, commitment to training and excessive exercise, pursuit of excellence and perfectionism, coachability and overcompliance, unselfishness and selflessness, and performance despite pain and denial of discomfort (Thompson & Sherman, 1999). The strong overlap between the personality characteristics of someone with anorexia nervosa and a competitive athlete can make identifying an athlete who is at risk for or who is already in the midst of an eating disorder tricky at best. What, under other circumstances, may appear to be a highly dedicated athlete may in fact mask a serious mental illness that if not identified quickly will lead to a decline in performance and a potentially serious decline in physical and psychological health with the possibility of death. In an article detailing effective ways to identify and refer athletes who may be at risk for an eating disorder, Selby and Reel (2011) cautioned that relying on stereotypes with respect to eating disorders in general or athletes in particular can mean that an athlete in need of treatment may be overlooked.

An additional area of interest with respect to eating disorders as they might be seen in female athletes is what is called the female athlete triad. The female athlete triad consists of compromised bone density (i.e., osteopenia or osteoporosis; see Chapter 5), irregularities with menstruation (e.g., amenorrhea), and energy deficiency (i.e., not consuming enough food given energy expenditure; Hoch et al., 2009; Nattiv et al., 2007). All three of these elements are interrelated and the idea is that if one element of the triad is present in an athlete then the other two should be assessed as well. The athlete may or may not have an eating disorder since that is a diagnosis with specific criteria to be met; however, the presence of symptoms of the female athlete triad may warrant an eating disorder screening and potentially a full evaluation (see Chapter 8).

Should an eating disorder be identified in an athlete, the care provided for an athlete may involve more people than one would see with a nonathlete. Technically, those providing the actual treatment would not differ from those providing treatment to a nonathlete (see Chapter 12); however, it is possible and may be recommended that a separate support team is kept informed of the athlete's progress and provided with recommendations for how to best support the athlete prior to and when returning to practice and competition (Thompson & Sherman, 2010). The support team may consist of the athlete's parents or significant other, the coach, athletic trainer or team physician, and other important sport-related staff.

Autism Spectrum Disorder

The newest version of the *Diagnostic and Statistical Manual of Mental Disorders* (5th ed.; *DSM-5*; American Psychiatric Association [APA], 2013) combined several diagnoses from previous editions of the manual under the **Autism Spectrum Disorder (ASD)** diagnosis. ASD "encompasses disorders previously referred to as early infantile autism, childhood autism, Kanner's autism, high-functioning autism, atypical autism, pervasive developmental disorder not otherwise specified, childhood disintegrative disorder, and Asperger's disorder" (APA, 2013, p. 53). ASD is typically first diagnosed in childhood and is characterized by problems with social communication and social interactions, repetitive behaviors, and a narrow range of interests or activities. The diagnosis can also be accompanied by impairments in intellect or language, genetic or medical factors, and other psychiatric disorders. The severity of ASD can range from mild to profound, meaning that an individual diagnosed with ASD may require minimal support for daily living orrequire substantial support depending on the severity of the diagnosis. Thus, the ASD diagnosis, as implied by the term *spectrum,* includes a range of behaviors and overall level of functioning.

With regard to the association between ASD and eating disorders, much of the research in this area predates the *DSM-5*; therefore, studies included participants based in their specific diagnosis (e.g., *Asperger's disorder*). Since these specific disorders are now subsumed under the ASD diagnosis, for ease of reading the following summary of findings will refer to study participants in terms of a diagnosis of ASD.

Given the potential for a severe or profound level of ASD, it is perhaps not surprising that researchers have investigated the degree to which those with ASD may experience other behavioral and psychiatric problems (Bradley, Summers, Wood, & Bryson, 2004; Gillberg & Billstedt, 2000). Those diagnosed with ASD and an intellectual disability, for example, may be three times more likely to have other behavioral (e.g., self-injury and impulse control issues) or psychiatric disturbances (e.g., depression, anxiety, eating disorders, and sleep disorders) compared to those who only have an intellectual disability but do not have ASD (Bradley et al., 2004). When examining the rates of ASD among those with or without an eating disorder, an ASD diagnosis was found to be more common among those with an eating disorder compared to those without an eating disorder (Huke, Turk, Saeidi, Kent, & Morgan, 2013). Among those with anorexia nervosa specifically, a higher rate of ASD-related characteristics were found compared to those without any psychiatric diagnosis (Hambrook, Tchanturia, Schmidt, Russell, & Treasure, 2008).

A study conducted by Bölte, Ozkara, and Poustka (2001) noted that any relationship between those with ASD and a low-body weight (such as that which might be seen in patients with anorexia nervosa) can be explained, in part, by hyperactivity; therefore, any link between ASD and anorexia nervosa specifically is likely due to chance. Studies conducted several years later, however, reveal a different picture regarding the connection between ASD and anorexia nervosa (Oldershaw, Treasure, Hambrook, Tchanturia, & Schmidt, 2011; Zucker et al., 2007). ASD-related symptoms are particularly prevalent among those who have a chronic course of anorexia nervosa (Zucker et al., 2007). There seem to be similarities with respect to how someone diagnosed with ASD and someone diagnosed with anorexia nervosa processes information and how they are each able to manage social interactions (Nazar et al., 2017; Zucker et al., 2007). Additionally, those diagnosed with ASD and anorexia nervosa have been found to respond as effectively as those diagnosed with anorexia nervosa only to treatment for eating disorder-related symptoms (Nazar et al., 2017). This is particularly important given that anorexia nervosa has, historically, been difficult to treat (Lipsman & Lozano, 2014; Walsh, 2013) and has a greater chance of ending in death than other psychiatric illnesses (Harris & Barraclough, 1998; Neumärker, 2000; Smink, van Hoeken, & Hoek, 2012). However, difficulties related to interpersonal interactions and overall functioning linger beyond eating disorder treatment for those who also have a diagnosis of ASD, which indicates that treatment offering a specific focus on "social identity and functioning" (Nazar et al., 2017, p. 178) would be beneficial.

Oldershaw et al. (2011) studied how patients with ASD or anorexia nervosa processed emotions. While similarities were found including the ability to understand emotions in a variety of contexts, those with ASD struggled more with understanding emotions based on the expressiveness of someone's eyes, whereas those with anorexia nervosa were found to have more difficulty in understanding emotions based on observing interpersonal interactions. Additionally, both groups showed similar difficulties on measures of communication and elevated levels of repetitive behaviors. Understanding these two disorders, then, in terms of shared characteristics rather than as separate and distinct diagnoses may help to inform and guide prognosis and treatment effectiveness (Oldershaw et al., 2011; Zucker et al., 2007).

Intellectual Disabilities

The American Association on Intellectual and Developmental Disabilities (2017) noted that an intellectual disability involves both problems with intellectual functioning and adaptive behavior. Intellectual functioning is usually measured via IQ tests and someone who is limited in the abilities measured by such tests typically scores no higher than 75 (100 is the average IQ). Adaptive behavior refers to a person's ability (or inability) to do what he or she needs to do to effectively live his or her life from day to day. This can include things such as the ability to earn and manage money, to appropriately interact with and get along with others, to follow rules including laws, to take care of themselves, and to access services including healthcare, public transportation, and the like.

Sovner (1986) suggested that given the cognitive and communication limitations of someone with an intellectual disability, garnering accurate and complete information to help in rendering an appropriate psychiatric diagnosis can be challenging. With respect to eating disorders in particular, determining whether or not an eating disorder is present in an individual involves someone's ability to talk about how he or she feels about his or her body and the person's eating behaviors. It is also important for an individual to be able to accurately describe what he or she ate, how much, and in what period of time the food was consumed. Inaccuracies in such reports can lead to a missed diagnosis or the rendering of a diagnosis that is inappropriate.

Gravestock (2000) called for a more well-developed understanding of how eating disorders may be understood and diagnosed among adults with an intellectual disability. He stated that the areas of clinical diagnosis and treatment, skills of service providers, and quantity and quality of research conducted in this area need improvement, adding that better understanding and conceptualization of eating disorders among those with an intellectual disability was needed. Gravestock later developed a model that described what an eating disorder might look like in someone with an intellectual disability (Gravestock, 2003). He noted that it is important to distinguish between abnormal eating behaviors that reflect an eating disorder and similar behaviors that might be better understood in the context of another disorder including developmental disorders in which intellectual functioning is compromised. Emerson (2003), however, concluded that children and adolescents with an intellectual disability are at greater risk for developing some types of mental health issues but found no differences in the rates of eating disorder diagnoses when participants were compared based on the presence or absence of an intellectual disability. Emerson's finding might illustrate Gravestock's perspective that eating disorder diagnoses are often missed among those with intellectual disabilities. Gravestock suggested that a broader definition of eating disorders may be warranted so these disorders are no longer underdiagnosed in this population.

Older Adults

Body image issues are known to affect adult women regardless of age (Bedford & Johnson, 2006; Gagne et al., 2012; Peat, Peyerl, & Muehlenkamp, 2008; Runfola et al., 2013), and body image dissatisfaction in general has been directly linked to eating disorders (Ferreiro, Seoane, & Senra, 2011). The proportion of women 30 years and older who are dissatisfied with their bodies may be as high as 71% (Allaz, Bernstein, Rouget, Archinard, & Morabia, 1998), and as many as 60% of older adult women aged 60 to 70 may be unhappy with how their bodies look (Mangweth-Matzek et al., 2006). Despite the prevalence of body image issues, the risk of having an eating disorder may decline as women age (Preti et al., 2009). This may be due in part to the notion that as women age they may be better able to appropriately divest themselves from cultural pressures to be thin (Peat et al., 2008). Despite this, eating disorders do exist among older adults.

Accurately identifying older adults who may have an eating disorder has its challenges. One issue has to do with determining if their cases are truly late onset eating disorders or if they have had a lifelong struggle with their eating disorder, but it was not until later life that they received the diagnosis (Hall & Driscoll, 1993), if they were misdiagnosed and untreated earlier in life (Mangweth-Matzek et al., 2006), or if they never fully recovered from an eating disorder with an earlier onset (Hsu, Crisp, & Callender, 1992). Despite this potential for confusion, late onset of eating disorders has been found to exist (Hall & Driscoll, 1993; Zerbe, 2002).

Recent research has revealed that adults in midlife were less likely to be diagnosed with anorexia nervosa in comparison to adults younger than midlife (Jenkins & Price, 2018). These results also revealed that those in midlife at the time of the study reported that their eating disorder began later in comparison to the younger adults and that their eating disorder had lasted longer. This is consistent with earlier reports that successful outcomes for eating disorder treatment among those who are older lags in comparison to treatment of younger individuals particularly with respect to overall quality of life and interpersonal functioning (Ackard, Richter, Egan, & Cronemeyer, 2014).

Regardless of when the disorder may have emerged in the individual's life, another challenge related to older adults and eating disorders has to do with where he or she can find information and treatment that addresses the needs of those in their older adulthood years. Additionally, some older adults have run into age bias among healthcare professionals, which may mean their concerns are not taken seriously and they do not get the treatment they need. In one study, several cases of eating disorders, predominantly anorexia nervosa, were identified among women aged 50 or older (Scholtz, Hill, & Lacey, 2010). Among those interviewed, several reported their frustration with the fact that online information was geared toward younger patients and healthcare options for people with eating disorders at their age were highly limited. One patient reported that her medical provider told her that she was "too old to have an eating disorder" (Scholtz et al., 2010, p. 396). This "ignoring" of older adults who have an eating disorder, regardless of when the disorder first emerged, may perpetuate misdiagnosis and ignoring a serious, life-threatening disorder in someone who does not fit the stereotypical profile.

Although most of the literature examining eating disorders among older populations has focused on women, cases of eating disorders among older adult men also exist (Reas & Stedal, 2015; Riemann, McNally, & Meier, 1993) although such cases may be quite rare (Lucas, Beard, O'Fallon, & Kurland, 1991) and may go undiagnosed (Hall & Driscoll, 1993).

Physical Disabilities

Eating disorders understood in the context of physical disabilities reveal not so much an issue with respect to effectively and accurately diagnosing an eating disorder but in regard to the degree that body image issues can be pronounced among those who have a physical disability. Body image issues are a known predictor of behaviors related to eating disorders (Ferreiro, Seoane, & Senra, 2011), so evidence that individuals with a physical disability may struggle with body dissatisfaction may point to a need not only for assessment of body image but also of eating disorders. Diving into the complexities and unique effects one particular physical disability may have on someone's psychological functioning compared to another is beyond the scope of this chapter, though research will be discussed that focuses on specific physical disabilities. Regardless of the type of physical disability someone may have, body image pressures exist and may extend beyond those experienced by their able-bodied counterparts (Taleporos & McCabe, 2002).

Lower limb amputation affects a multitude of facets of an individual's life, including how the person views his or her body (Senra, Oliveira, Leal, & Vieira, 2011). Adults who either had one or both lower limbs amputated had self-esteem levels comparable to those without an amputation; however, amputees were found to have a more negative body image (Holzer et al., 2014). What may complicate the effect of body image on someone with an amputation is the likelihood that the person is dealing with multiple body images including what view he or she had of his or her body before the amputation, and the view after the amputation either with or without a prosthesis (Rybarczyk, Szymanski, & Nicholas, 2000).

Another important element in the realm of body image is the degree to which someone with an amputation is satisfied with his or her prosthesis, which includes how well it functions and whether or not the prosthetic is esthetically pleasing (Horgan & MacLachlan, 2004; Murray & Fox, 2002). There were some differences between males and females on body image disturbance. The biggest difference between the sexes was found with respect to esthetics—females were more affected by the esthetics of the prosthesis than males. Males were more affected by the functionality of their prosthesis than females but the difference between the two sexes was much smaller on this element of prosthesis satisfaction.

Scleroderma is another type of physical disability and is an autoimmune disease that affects connective tissue. This can result in hardening of the skin, which is the most noticeable symptom of the disease (Scleroderma Foundation, 2018). Some studies have found that when individuals are physically disabled, including having the diagnosis of scleroderma, they are more vulnerable to feeling badly about their bodies (Benrud-Larson et al., 2003; Jewett et al., 2012) and that psychological distress, which includes body image disturbance, should be part of any comprehensive intervention (Thombs et al., 2012).

Other studies examining body image have included patients with traumatic brain injury (Fuentes, Pazzaglia, Longo, Scivoletto, & Haggard, 2013; Howes, Edwards, & Benton, 2005), spinal cord injuries (Potgieter & Kahn, 2005), and visual impairment (Baker, Sivyer, & Towell, 1998; Greguol, Gobbi, & Carraro, 2014). These studies reveal greater body image issues among these populations in comparison to those without the disability. Regardless of the physical disability, it is clear that body image issues can be part of the individual's psychological struggles and may require clinical attention. However, there are some protective factors that may help to prevent negative body image from developing or becoming a source of significant impairment. For example, engaging in physical activity has been found to lower feelings of body dissatisfaction (Greguol, Gobbi, & Carraro, 2014; Wetterhahn, Hanson, & Levy, 2002). Additionally, the messages individuals with a physical disability receive from their environment may moderate the severity of body image dissatisfaction (Taleporos & McCabe, 2002). When these messages reflect a disdain for bodies that do not fit society's expectations for attractiveness, one's body image can suffer. If, however, one's partner and important others provide positive feedback the individual with the physical disability can experience a more positive body image.

Religion

Refusing to eat or engaging in fasting for spiritual reasons was a common practice during medieval times (Brumberg, 1989). The most well-known individual who engaged in this practice was Saint Catherine of Siena who lived during the mid to late 1300s. Most who fasted for spiritual reasons were canonized as saints; thus, severe asceticism was viewed as a direct path to sainthood (Davis & Nguyen, 2014). In modern times, there has been some skepticism of claims that fasting behaviors are tied to one's religious faith. It is believed, at least for some, that they may have found an acceptable mask for the symptoms of their eating disorder (Banks, 1992). Others, however, have stated that those who have a strong religious faith and who are engaged in ascetic behaviors such as fasting may be misdiagnosed as having an eating disorder such as anorexia nervosa, indicating that modern-day practitioners of this type of asceticism may not be clear-cut cases of anorexia nervosa (Bynum, 1988).

Having a religious faith can be beneficial (Miller & Thoresen, 2003), including the fact that it has been shown to be connected with lower levels of some psychiatric disorders (Bonelli & Koenig, 2013). Some research has shown that both one's physical and psychological well-being can be positively impacted by one's religious or spiritual belief system (Hill & Pargament, 2003; Kendler et al., 2003; Miller & Thoresen, 2003). However, those with "extremely high religiosity" or low religiosity (Bonelli & Koenig, 2013, p. 669) were found to have more mental health issues, and those who endorse being spiritual outside of the context of a formal religious tradition were more susceptible to mental health issues including maladaptive eating patterns (King et al., 2013). Still others have found that spirituality compared to religion has a more robust connection with eating disorder symptoms such that those who expressed having a high degree of spirituality (rather than religion) also had a lower degree of eating disorder symptoms (Boisvert & Harrell, 2012).

The difference between those who benefit from having a religious faith and those who do not may lie in the difference between religion and spirituality. Lelwica (2010) indicated that religion encompasses an "organized system of symbols, rituals, myths, and beliefs" (p. 41), whereas spirituality is "the process through which may of us create and discover the meaning of our lives" (p. 41). Religion, therefore, can be witnessed by others via one's behavioral practice of his or her religious faith (e.g., going to church/temple/mosque, praying); however, spirituality is an inner experience that only the individual himself or herself can fully experience. Bonelli and Koenig (2013) suggested that a religious faith that is beneficial may require "a certain amount of inner freedom and flexibility" (p. 669), which would seem to reflect the more personal nature of spirituality.

Spangler (2010) provided a multifaceted model illustrating how religion, specifically, can negatively impact someone and thereby put him or her at a greater risk of developing an eating disorder. She noted that many religious traditions influence one's view of one's body, which can directly affect body satisfaction and ultimately lead to the development of an eating disorder. Additionally, religious teachings and practices help to frame our sense of self or identity, which in turn can influence our emotional experiences, including negative ones. Eating disorders, therefore, may be used to soothe negative affect, and this salve in the form of an eating disorder then becomes something that is needed in order for the individual to feel good. Spangler acknowledged that there are certainly other factors at play in the development of eating disorders, which helps to explain why not everyone whose religious or spiritual beliefs puts them at risk for developing an eating disorder ultimately develops one.

Some differences have been identified that may help determine how those with a strong religious background may cope with their eating disorder-related symptoms which, in turn, may have implications for treatment. Coping strategies among those with a strong sense of spirituality or religious faith may be more likely to utilize prayer or to read religious or spiritually based materials to help them with their distress (Jacobs-Pilipski, Winzelbert, Wilfley, Bryson, & Taylor, 2005). These researchers noted that spiritual and religious practices may be underutilized strategies for those trying to cope with eating disorder-related symptoms. Other studies have found that when examining what positively influences eating disorder recovery, one's faith played an important role in the recovery process for many (Hsu, Crisp, & Callender, 1992; Mitchell, Erlander, Pyle, & Fletcher, 1990; Rorty, Yager, & Rossotto, 1993).

It is unclear whether maintaining a strong religious faith places one at a greater risk for developing an eating disorder (Banks, 1992; Bell, 1985) or whether it serves as a buffer and therefore a protective factor against developing an eating disorder (Kim, 2006). Some have found that compared to the general population, having a religious ideology was connected to lower body dissatisfaction in males (Carroll & Spangler, 2001) and females (Sandberg & Spangler, 2007). It is possible that there may be differences in rates of body dissatisfaction and risk for eating disorder pathology among various religious faiths (e.g., Latzer, Tzischinsky, & Azaiza, 2007; Mitrany, Lubin, Chetrit, & Modan, 1995). A recent meta-analysis of research examining the relationship between religion and mental illness, however, did not reveal a connection one way or another between religion and eating disorders specifically; however, the authors cautioned that simply because a relationship was not revealed does not mean one does not exist (Bonelli & Koenig, 2013).

Despite this apparent lack of clarity, some have suggested that encouraging patients to reconnect or stay connected with their particular religious beliefs may be beneficial to their treatment and subsequent recovery (Berrett, Hardman, O'Grady, & Richards, 2007; Jacobs-Pilipski et al., 2005). Another way of stating this is that neither one's psychiatric concerns nor one's religious beliefs should be overlooked and that patients who are also spiritual practitioners may benefit from a harmonious inclusion of religion as part of their treatment (Morgan, Marsden, & Lacey, 1999; Spangler & Queiroz, 2009). Clinician's views of and approach to religion in the context of treatment are also important and can affect outcome, which suggests that the inclusion of a clergyperson as part of the treatment team may be beneficial (Marsden, Karagianni, & Morgan, 2007; Richards, Berrett, Hardman, & Eggett, 2006; Smith, Hardman, Richards, & Fischer, 2003).

Conclusion

The unique populations discussed in this chapter were not intended to be an exhaustive accounting of all groups that may go overlooked or that may require a different approach to treatment. In aggregate, the experiences of these groups illustrate the importance of keeping an open mind to who may or may not have an eating disorder or body image concern. Although these people may not fit the stereotype of who has an eating disorder, they may, in fact, be at greater risk.

References

Ackard, D. M., Richter, S., Egan, A., & Cronemeyer, C. L. (2014). Poor outcome and death among youth, young adults, and midlife adults with eating disorders: An investigation of risk factors by age at assessment. *International Journal of Eating Disorders, 46*, 825–835. doi:10.1002/eat.22346

Allaz, A., Bernstein, M., Rouget, P., Archinard, M., & Morabia, A. (1998). Body weight preoccupation in middle-age and ageing women: A general population survey. *International Journal of Eating Disorders, 23,* 287–294. doi:10.1002/(sici)1098-108x(199804)23:3<287::aid-eat6>3.0.co;2-f

American Association on Intellectual and Developmental Disabilities. (2017). *Definition of intellectual disability.* Retrieved from http://aaidd.org/intellectual-disability/definition

American Psychiatric Association. (2013). *Diagnostic and statistical manual of mental disorders* (5th ed.). Washington, DC: Author.

Baker, D., Sivyer, R., & Towell, T. (1998). Body image dissatisfaction and eating attitudes in visually impaired women. *International Journal of Eating Disorders, 24,* 319–322. doi:10.1002/(sici)1098-108x(199811)24:3<319::aid-eat10>3.3.co;2-c

Banks, C. G. (1992). "Culture" in culture-bound syndromes: The case of anorexia nervosa. *Social Science Medicine, 34,* 867–884. doi:10.1016/0277-9536(92)90256-P

Becker, C. B., McDaniel, L., Bull, S., Powell, M., & McIntyre, K. (2012). Can we reduce eating disorder risk factors in female college athletes? A randomized exploratory investigation of two peer-led interventions. *Body Image, 9,* 31–42. doi:10.1016/j.bodyim.2011.09.005

Bedford, J. L., & Johnson, C. S. (2006). Societal influences on body image dissatisfaction in younger and older women. *Journal of Women and Aging, 18,* 41–55. doi:10.1300/j074v18n01_04

Bell, R. M. (1985). *Holy anorexia.* Chicago, IL: University of Chicago Press.

Benrud-Larson, L. M., Heinberg, L. J., Boling, C., Reed, J., White, B., Wigley, F. M., & Haythornthwaite, J. A. (2003). Body image dissatisfaction among women with scleroderma: Extent and relationship to psychosocial function. *Health Psychology, 22,* 130–139. doi:10.1037/0278-6133.22.2.130

Berrett, M. E., Hardman, R. K., O'Grady, K. A., & Richards, P. S. (2007). The role of spirituality in the treatment of trauma and eating disorders: Recommendations for clinical practice. *Eating Disorders, 15,* 373–389. doi:10.1080/10640260701454394

Boisvert, J. A., & Harrell, W. A. (2012). The impact of spirituality on eating disorder symptomology in ethnically diverse Canadian women. *International Journal of Social Psychiatry, 59,* 729–738. doi:10.1177/0020764012453816

Bölte, S., Ozkara, N., & Poustka, F. (2001). ASDs and low body weight: Is there really a systematic association? *International Journal of Eating Disorders, 31,* 349–351. doi:10.1002/eat.10015

Bradley, E. A., Summers, J. A., Wood, H. L., & Bryson, S. E. (2004). Comparing rates of psychiatric and behavior disorders in adolescents and young adults with severe intellectual disability with and without autism. *Journal of Autism and Developmental Disorders, 34,* 151–161. doi:10.1023/b:jadd.0000022606.97580.19

Brumberg, J. J. (1989). *Fasting girls: The history of anorexia nervosa.* New York, NY: Vintage Books.

Bynum, C. W. (1988). *Holy feast and holy fast.* Oakland: University of California Press.

Carroll, A., & Spangler, D. L. (2001). A comparison of body image satisfaction among Latter-day Saint and non-Latter-day Saint college-age students. *Issues in Religion and Psychotherapy, 26,* Article 2. Retrieved from https://scholarsarchive.byu.edu/cgi/viewcontent.cgi?article=1432&context=irp

Davis, A. A., & Nguyen, M. (2014). A case study of anorexia nervosa driven by religious sacrifice. *Case Reports in Psychiatry, 2014,* 512764. doi:10.1155/2014/512764

de Bruin, A. P. K. (2010). *Thin is going to win? Disordered eating in sport.* Amsterdam, The Netherlands: Author.

Emerson, E. (2003). Prevalence of psychiatric disorders in children and adolescents with and without intellectual disability. *Journal of Intellectual Disability Research, 47,* 51–58. doi:10.1046/j.1365-2788.2003.00464.x

Ferreiro, F., Seoane, G., & Senra, C. (2011). A prospective study of risk factors for the development of depression and disordered eating in adolescents. *Journal of Clinical, Child, Adolescent Psychology, 40,* 500–505. doi:10.1080/15374416.2011.563465

Fuentes, C., Pazzaglia, M., Longo, M. R., Scivoletto, G., & Haggard, P. (2013). Body image distortions following spinal cord injury. *Journal of Neurology, Neurosurgery & Psychiatry, 84*, 201–207. doi:10.1136/jnnp-2012-304001

Gagne, D. A., Von Holle, A., Brownley, K. A., Runfola, C. D., Hofmeier, S., Branch, K. E., & Bulik, C. M. (2012). Eating disorder symptoms and weight and shape concerns in a large web-based convenience sample of women ages 50 and above: Results of the gender and body image (GABI) study. *International Journal of Eating Disorders, 45*, 832–844. doi:10.1002/eat.22030

Gillberg, C., & Billstedt, E. (2000). Autism and Asperger syndrome: Coexistence with other clinical disorders. *Acta Psychiatrica Scandinavica, 102*, 321–330. doi:10.1034/j.1600-0447.2000.102005321.x

Gravestock, S. (2000). Eating disorders in adults with intellectual disability. *Journal of Intellectual Disability Research, 44*, 625–637. doi:10.1046/j.1365-2788.2000.00308.x

Gravestock, S. (2003). Diagnosis and classification of eating disorders in adults with intellectual disability: The diagnostic criteria for psychiatric disorders for use with adults with learning disabilities/mental retardation (DC-LD) approach. *Journal of Intellectual Disabilities Research, 47*, 72–83. doi:10.1046/j.1365-2788.47.s1.41.x

Greguol, M., Gobbi, E., & Carraro, A. (2014). Physical activity practice, body image and visual impairment: A comparison between Brazilian and Italian children and adolescents. *Research in Developmental Disabilities, 35*, 21–26. doi:10.1016/j.ridd.2013.10.020

Hall, P., & Driscoll, R. (1993). Anorexia in the elderly—An annotation. *International Journal of Eating Disorders, 14*, 497–499. doi:10.1002/1098-108x(199312)14:4<497::aid-eat2260140413>3.0.co;2-1

Hambrook, D., Tchanturia, K., Schmidt, U., Russell, T., & Treasure, J. (2008). Empathy, systematizing, and autistic traits in anorexia nervosa: A pilot study. *British Journal of Clinical Psychology, 47*, 335–339. doi:10.1348/014466507x272475

Harris, E. C., & Barraclough, B. (1998). Excess mortality of mental disorder. *British Journal of Psychiatry, 173*, 11–53. doi:10.1192/bjp.173.1.11

Hill, P. C., & Pargament, K. I. (2003). Advances in the conceptualization and measurement of religion and spirituality. *American Psychologist, 58*, 64–74. doi:10.1037/0003-066x.58.1.64

Hoch, A. Z., Pajewski, N. M., Moraski, L., Carrera, G. F., Wilson, C. R., Hoffman, R. G., . . . Gutterman, D. D. (2009). Prevalence of the female athlete triad in high school athletes and sedentary students. *Journal of Clinical Sports Medicine, 19*(5), 421–428. doi:10.1097/jsm.0b013e3181b8c136

Holm-Denoma, J. M., Scaringi, V., Gordon, K. H., Van Orden, K. A., & Joiner, T. E. (2009). Eating disorder symptoms among undergraduate varsity athletes, club athletes, independent exercisers, and nonexercisers. *International Journal of Eating Disorders, 42*, 47–53. doi:10.1002/eat.20560

Holzer, L. A., Sevelda, F., Fraberger, G., Bluder, O., Kickinger, W., & Holzer G. (2014). Body image and self-esteem in lower-limb amputees. *PLOS ONE, 9*, e92943. doi:10.1371/journal.pone.0092943

Horgan, O., & MacLachlan, M. (2004). Psychosocial adjustment to lower-limb amputation: A review. *Disability and Rehabilitation, 26*, 837–850. doi:10.1080/09638280410001708869

Howes, H., Edwards, S., & Benton, D. (2005). Female body image following acquired brain injury. *Brain Injury, 19*, 403–415. doi:10.1080/02699050400025158

Hsu, L. K. G., Crisp, A. H., & Callender, J. S. (1992). Recovery in anorexia nervosa: The patient's perspective. *International Journal of Eating Disorders, 11*, 341–350. doi:10.1002/1098-108x(199205)11:4<341::aid-eat2260110408>3.0.co;2-g

Huke, V., Turk, J., Saeidi, S., Kent, A., & Morgan, J. F. (2013). Autism spectrum disorders in eating disorder populations: A systematic review. *European Eating Disorders Review, 21*, 345–351. doi:10.1002/erv.2244

Jacobs-Pilipski, M. J., Winzelbert, A., Wilfley, D. E., Bryson, S. W., & Taylor, C. B. (2005). Spirituality among young women at risk for eating disorders. *Eating Behaviors, 6*, 293–300. doi:10.1016/j.eatbeh.2005.03.003

Jenkins, P. E., & Price, T. (2018). Eating pathology in midlife women: Similar or different to younger counterparts? *International Journal of Eating Disorders, 51*, 3–9. doi:10.1002/eat.22810

Jewett, L. R., Hudson, M., Malcarne, V. L., Baron, M., Thombs, B. D., & Canadian Scleroderma Research Group. (2012). Sociodemographic and disease correlates of body image distress among patients with systemic sclerosis. *PLOS ONE, 7*, e33281. doi:10.1371/journal.pone.0033281

Kendler, K. S., Liu, X., Gardner, C. O., McCullough, M. E., Larson, D., & Prescott, C. A. (2003). Dimensions of religiosity and their relationship to lifetime psychiatric and substance use disorders. *American Journal of Psychiatry, 160*, 496–503. doi:10.1176/appi.ajp.160.3.496

Kim, K. (2006). Religion, body satisfaction, and dieting. *Appetite, 46*, 285–296. doi:10.1016/j.appet.2006.01.006

King, M., Marston, L., McManus, S., Brugha, T., Meltzer, H., & Bebbington, P. (2013). Religion, spirituality and mental health: Results from a national study of English households. *The British Journal of Psychiatry, 202*, 68–73. doi:10.1192/bjp.bp.112.112003

Latzer, Y., Tzischinsky, O., & Azaiza, F. (2007). Disordered eating related behaviors among Arab schoolgirls in Israel: An epidemiological study. *International Journal of Eating Disorders, 40*, 263–270. doi:10.1002/eat.20348

Lelwica, M. M. (2010). *The religion of thinness*. Carlsbad, CA: Gürze Books.

Lipsman, N., & Lozano, A. M. (2014). Targeting emotion circuits with deep brain stimulation in refractory anorexia nervosa. *Neuropsychopharmacology, 39*, 250–251. doi:10.1038/npp.2013.244

Lucas, A. R., Beard, C. M., O'Fallon, W. M., & Kurland, L. T. (1991). 50-Year trends in the incidence of anorexia nervosa in Rochester, Minn.: A population-based study. *American Journal of Psychiatry, 148*, 917–922. doi:10.1176/ajp.148.7.917

Mangweth-Matzek, B., Rupp, C. I., Hausmann, A., Assmayr, K., Mariacher, E., Kemmler, G., . . . (2006). Never too old for eating disorders or body dissatisfaction: A community study of elderly women. *International Journal of Eating Disorders, 39*, 583–586. doi:10.1002/eat.20327

Marsden, P., Karagianni, E., & Morgan, J. F. (2007). Spirituality and clinical care in eating disorders: A qualitative study. *International Journal of Eating Disorders, 40*, 7–12. doi:10.1002/eat.20333

Miller, W. R., & Thoresen, C. E. (2003). Spirituality, religion, and health: An emerging research field. *American Psychologist, 58*, 24–35. doi:10.1037/0003-066x.58.1.24

Mitchell, J. E., Erlander, M., Pyle, R. L., & Fletcher, L. A. (1990). Eating disorders, religious practices and pastoral counseling. *International Journal of Eating Disorders, 9*, 589–593. doi:10.1002/1098-108x(199009)9:5<589::aid-eat2260090517>3.0.co;2-z

Mitrany, E., Lubin, R., Chetrit, A., & Modan. B. (1995). Eating disorders among Jewish female adolescents in Israel: A five-year study. *Journal of Adolescent Health, 16*, 454–457. doi:10.1016/1054-139x(95)00005-d

Morgan, J. F., Marsden, P., & Lacey, J. H. (1999). "Spiritual starvation?": A case series concerning Christianity and eating disorders. *International Journal of Eating Disorders, 28*, 476–480. doi:10.1002/1098-108x(200012)28:4<476::aid-eat19>3.3.co;2-k

Murray, C. D., & Fox, J. (2002). Body image and prosthesis satisfaction in the lower limb amputee. *Disability and Rehabilitation, 24*, 925–931. doi:10.1080/09638280210150014

Nattiv, A., Loucks, A. B., Manore, M. M., Sanborn, C. F., Sundgot-Borgen, J., Warren, M. P., & American College of Sports Medicine. (2007). American College of Sports Medicine position stand: The female athlete triad. *Medicine and Science in Sport and Exercise, 39*, 1867–1882. doi:10.1249/mss.0b013e318149f111

Nazar, B. P., Peynenburt, V., Rhind, C., Hibbs, R., Schmidt, U., Gowers, S., . . . Treasure, J. (2017). An examination of the clinical outcomes of adolescents and young adults with broad autism spectrum traits and autism spectrum disorder and anorexia nervosa: A multi centre study. *International Journal of Eating Disorders, 51*, 174–179. doi:10.1002/eat.22823

Neumärker, K.-J. (2000). Mortality rates and causes of death. *European Eating Disorders Review, 8*, 181–187. doi:10.1002/(SICI)1099-0968(200003)8:2<181::AID-ERV336>3.0.CO;2-#

Oldershaw, A., Treasure, J., Hambrook, D., Tchanturia, K., & Schmidt, U. (2011). Is anorexia nervosa a version of autism spectrum disorder? *European Eating Disorders Review, 19*, 462–474. doi:10.1002/erv.1069

Peat, C. M., Peyerl, N. L., & Muehlenkamp, J. J. (2008). Body image and eating disorders in older adults: A review. *The Journal of General Psychology, 135*, 343–358. doi:10.3200/GENP.135.4.343-358

Petrie, T. A., & Greenleaf, C. A. (2007). Eating disorders in sport: From theory to research to intervention. In G. Tenenbaum & R. C. Eklund (Eds.), *Handbook of sport psychology* (3rd ed., pp. 352–378). Hoboken, NJ: John Wiley & Sons.

Potgieter, C., & Kahn, G. (2005). Sexual self-esteem and body image of South African spinal cord injured adolescents. *Sexuality and Disability, 23*, 1–20. doi:10.1007/s11195-004-2076-6

Preti, A., de Girolamo, G., Vilagut, G., Alonso, J., de Graaf, R., Bruffaerts, R., . . . The ESEMeD-WMH Investigators. (2009). The epidemiology of eating disorders in six European countries: Results of the ESEMeD-WHM project. *Journal of Psychiatric Research, 43*, 1125–1132. doi:10.1016/j.jpsychires.2009.04.003

Reas, D. L., & Stedal, K. (2015). Eating disorders in men aged midlife and beyond. *Maturitas, 81*, 248–255. doi:10.1016/j.maturitas.2015.03.004

Reel, J. J., & Beals, K. A. (2009). *The hidden faces of eating disorders and body image.* Sewickley, PA: American Alliance for Health, Physical Education, Recreation and Dance.

Richards, P. S., Berrett, M. E., Hardman, R. K., & Eggett, D. L. (2006). Comparative efficacy of spirituality, cognitive, and emotional support groups for treating eating disorder inpatients. *Eating Disorders, 14*, 401–415. doi:10.1080/10640260600952548

Riemann, B. C., McNally, R. J., & Meier, A. (1993). Anorexia nervosa in an elderly man. *International Journal of Eating Disorders, 14*(4), 501–504. doi:10.1002/1098-108x(199312)14:4<501::aid-eat2260140414>3.0.co;2-u

Rorty, M., Yager, J., & Rossotto, E. (1993). What and how do women recover from bulimia nervosa? The subjective appraisals of forty women recovered for a year or more. *International Journal of Eating Disorders, 14*, 249–260. doi:10.1002/1098-108X(199311)14:3<249::AID-EAT2260140303>3.0.CO;2-O

Runfola, C. D., Von Holle, A., Trace, S. E., Brownley, K. A., Hofmeier, S. M., Gagne, D. A., & Bulik, C. M. (2013). Body dissatisfaction in women across the lifespan: Results of the UNC-SELF and Gender and Body Image (GABI) studies. *European Eating Disorders Review, 21*, 52–59. doi:10.1002/erv.2201

Rybarczyk, B., Szymanski, I., & Nicholas, J. J. (2000). Limb amputation. In R. G. Fink & T. R. Elliott (Eds.), *Handbook of rehabilitation psychology* (pp. 29–47). Washington, DC: American Psychological Association.

Sandberg, M., & Spangler, D. L. (2007). Eating, substance use, and body image: A comparison of Latter-day Saint and Non-Latter-day Saint college age females. *Issues in Religion and Psychotherapy, 31*, Article 2. Available at https://scholarsarchive.byu.edu/irp/vol31/iss1/2

Scholtz, S., Hill, L. S., & Lacey, H. (2010). Eating disorders in older women: Does late onset anorexia nervosa exist? *International Journal of Eating Disorders, 43*, 393–397. doi:10.1002/eat.20704

Scleroderma Foundation. (2018). *What is scleroderma?* Retrieved from http://www.scleroderma.org/site/PageNavigator/patients_whatis.html#.Wv11AqQvyUk

Selby, C. L. B., & Reel, J. J. (2011). A coach's guide to identifying and helping athletes with eating disorders. *Journal of Sport Psychology in Action, 2,* 100–112. doi:10.1080/21520704.2011.585701

Senra, H., Oliveira, R. A., Leal, I., & Vieira, C. (2011). Beyond the body image: A qualitative study on how adults experience lower limb amputation. *Clinical Rehabilitation, 26,* 180–191. doi:10.1177/0269215511410731

Smink, F. R. E., van Hoeken, D., & Hoek. H. W. (2012). Epidemiology of eating disorders: Incidence, prevalence and mortality rates. *Current Psychiatry Reports, 14,* 406–414. doi:10.1007/s11920-012-0282-y

Smith, F. T., Hardman, R. K., Richards, P. S., & Fischer, L. (2003). Intrinsic religiousness and spiritual well-being as predictors of treatment outcome among women with eating disorders. *Eating Disorders, 11,* 15–26. doi:10.1080/10640260390167456-2199

Smolak, L., Murnen, S. K., & Ruble, A. E. (2000). Female athletes and eating problems: A meta-analysis. *International Journal of Eating Disorders, 27*(4), 371–380. doi:10.1002/(sici)1098-108x(200005)27:4<371::aid-eat1>3.0.co;2-y

Sovner, R. (1986). Limiting factors in the use of *DSM-III* criteria with mentally ill/mentally retarded persons. *Psychopharmacology Bulletin, 22,* 1055–1059.

Spangler, D. L. (2010). Heavenly bodies: Religious issues in cognitive behavioral treatment of eating disorders. *Cognitive and Behavioral Practice, 17,* 358–370. doi:10.1016/j.cbpra.2009.05.004

Spangler, D. L., & Queiroz, A. (2009). Body of faith: Religious influence on body image and eating disorders. In J. J. Reel & K. A. Beals (Eds.), *The hidden faces of eating disorders and body image* (pp. 83–102). Sewickley, PA: AAHPERD.

Sundgot-Borgen, J., & Torstveit, M. K. (2004). Prevalence of eating disorders in elite athletes is higher than in the general population. *Clinical Journal of Sport Medicine, 14,* 25–32. doi:10.1097/00042752-200401000-00005

Taleporos, G., & McCabe, M. P. (2002). Body image and physical disability—Personal perspectives. *Social Science and Medicine, 54,* 971–980. doi:10.1016/s0277-9536(01)00069-7

Thombs, B. D., Jewett, L. R., Assassi, S., Baron, M., Bartlett, S. J., Maia, A. C., . . . Khanna, D. (2012). New directions for patient-centred care in scleroderma: The Scleroderma Patient-centred Intervention Network (SPIN). *Clinical and Experimental Rheumatology, 30,* S23–S29.

Thompson, R. A., & Sherman, R. T. (1999). "Good athlete" traits and characteristics of anorexia nervosa: Are they similar? *Eating Disorders, 7,* 181–190. doi:10.1080/10640269908249284

Thompson, R. A., & Sherman, R. T. (2010). *Eating disorders in sport.* New York, NY: Routledge.

Torstveit, M. K., Rosenvinge, J. H., & Sundgot-Borgen, J. (2008). Prevalence of eating disorders and the predictive power of risk models in female elite athletes: A controlled study. *Scandinavian Journal of Medicine and Science in Sports, 18,* 108–118. doi:10.1111/j.1600-0838.2007.00657.x

Walsh, B. T. (2013). The enigmatic persistence of anorexia nervosa. *American Journal of Psychiatry, 170,* 477–484. doi:10.1176/appi.ajp.2012.12081074

Wetterhahn, K. A., Hanson, C., & Levy, C. E. (2002). Effect of participation in physical activity on body image of amputees. *American Journal of Physical Medicine & Rehabilitation, 81,* 194–201. doi:10.1097/00002060-200203000-00007

Zerbe, K. J. (2002). Eating disorders in midlife and beyond: Transition and transformation at a crucial developmental stage. *Psychoanalysis and Psychotherapy, 19,* 9–19.

Zucker, N. L., Losh, M., Bulik, C. M., LaBar, K. S., Piven, J., & Pelphrey, K. A. (2007). Anorexia nervosa and autism spectrum disorders: Guided investigation of social cognitive endophenotypes. *Psychological Bulletin, 133,* 976–1006. doi:10.1037/0033-2909.133.6.976

RISK FACTORS, CORROLATES, AND CONSEQUENCES ASSOCIATED WITH EATING DISORDERS

BIOLOGICAL AND MEDICAL FACTORS

Introduction

This is the first chapter of three that discuss the various factors that are associated in some way with eating disorders. The association may be as a risk factor, a co-occurring issue, or as a consequence of having an eating disorder. In this chapter, some of the biological and medical factors associated with eating disorders are discussed. Generally speaking, the biological factors included in this chapter are likely risk factors, meaning that they predate the onset of the disorder though that is not always clear. The medical factors by and large represent consequences or costs associated with having a particular eating disorder diagnosis.

Biological Factors

In this section, biological factors that may put an individual at risk for developing an eating disorder will be examined. Although one's age and sex are considered biological risk factors, they will not be discussed here as they were discussed earlier in Chapters 3 and 4.

Brain Function

Research in the area of how the brain may function differently in those with eating disorders has yielded some interesting results. The brain is a complex part of the human body that researchers are still trying to fully understand. What is known, however, is that there are particular structures in the brain responsible for processing different types of information and there are *neural pathways* in the brain that connect one part of the brain to another. These pathways can be more or less active in an individual depending on the purpose of the pathway and how that pathway has or has not been utilized by a particular individual. For those with eating disorders, differences in these pathways can differentiate between those with eating disorders and those without.

Friederich, Wu, Simon, and Herzog (2013) reviewed research examining brain function among those with eating disorders and reported differences with respect to fear, cognitive flexibility, and response-inhibition. Individuals diagnosed with **anorexia nervosa** were found to be more likely to react more strongly emotionally and with fear, particularly to food. That is, food was likely to evoke a highly emotional and fear-based response in the brain compared to those who did not have anorexia nervosa. When asked to perform a task that required them to be flexible in their thinking (as opposed to using rigid, black and white thinking), the area of the brain responsible for flexible thinking in those diagnosed with anorexia nervosa was more likely to be underactive, indicating that flexible thinking is more of a challenge for those with this disorder. Among those diagnosed with **bulimia nervosa**, the part of the brain responsible for producing pleasurable reactions to food was found to be underactive. This means that those with bulimia nervosa may not experience the same pleasurable feelings when tasting food compared to those without this disorder. Thus, such individuals may need more, good tasting food in order to experience some pleasure associated with eating. These same patients, when asked to perform a task requiring them to not respond, resulted in brain activity suggesting they had a more difficult time inhibiting their behavior. In terms of an eating disorder, and bulimia nervosa in particular, this means they will have a harder time inhibiting or stopping themselves from eating even if they have already eaten a substantial amount of food.

Genetics

Understanding our genetic predisposition to various disorders and diseases is an area receiving a great deal of attention with respect to medical diseases and psychiatric disorders. Although there is a growing body of research in the area of genetics and eating disorders, there continues to be much to learn with respect to which specific genes contribute to the development of a particular eating disorder. Trace, Baker, Peñas-Lledó, and Bulik (2013) conducted an extensive review of the literature in the area of genetics and eating disorders and reported that, overall, genetics may account for 40% to 60% of the explanation for why an eating disorder may exist in one person compared to another. This finding has been supported by those examining the rates of eating disorders within families, between twins, and in those who are adopted. These researchers have concluded that a significant proportion of the variance that exists among eating disorders can be explained by genetics (Yilmaz, Hardaway, & Bulik, 2015). Genetics, therefore, is a significant contributing factor in terms of whether or not someone will or will not develop an eating disorder.

With regard to specific eating disorders, research has not yet successfully identified which gene may be responsible for one eating disorder compared to another (Boraska et al., 2014; Trace et al., 2013). One explanation noted in these studies is that larger sample sizes may be required to find significant results. What geneticists have seen in their research, however, has caused them to conclude that although specific genes have not yet been matched to specific eating disorders, results of twin studies for all three disorders points to the likelihood that specific genetic factors exist but simply have not yet been identified (Boraska et al., 2014).

Medical Factors

It is not uncommon for those with an eating disorder to insist that they are okay and that they do not have a problem. Thus, it may be that the first time a patient with an eating disorder receives any kind of treatment is when medical complications associated with eating disorders arise and require treatment (Zipfel, Löwe, & Herzog, 2003). Additionally, these complications can range from the aesthetic and irritating (e.g., benign skin problems) to complications that may put the individual's life at risk (e.g., heart arrhythmias). Those who are at greatest risk for medical complications are those with anorexia nervosa who are malnourished, those with bulimia nervosa who have an extensive history of binge eating and **purging**, patients who have co-occurring medical issues such as diabetes, and those whose eating disorder behaviors may have resulted in weight fluctuations or *weight cycling* (Zipfel et al., 2003).

Medical complications are common among those diagnosed with anorexia nervosa or bulimia nervosa (Mitchell & Crow, 2010). The symptoms themselves can overlap; however, the etiology or cause of the complications arises for different reasons. For those with bulimia nervosa, the likely explanation is the frequency and method of the *compensatory behavior*, whereas for those with anorexia nervosa medical complications arise from severe malnutrition and weight loss (Mehler, Crews, & Weiner, 2004). Individuals diagnosed with anorexia nervosa will have a history of not consuming food and fluids in adequate quantities or of sufficient variety, resulting in malnutrition. The effects of malnourishing a body can be devastating and is partly why anorexia nervosa in particular has the highest mortality rate of any psychiatric illness; up to 12 times that which would be expected given the sex and age of those who die (Keel et al., 2003; Sullivan, 1995). Most of the existing knowledge on medical complications associated with eating disorders exists with the diagnoses of bulimia nervosa and anorexia nervosa. Although there are some indications that those diagnosed with **binge eating disorder** have medical complications associated with the disorder, much more research is needed in order to fully understand what these complications are (Mitchell & Crow, 2010).

Common medical consequences associated with eating disorders affect the cardiovascular, gastrointestinal, neurological, and endocrine systems in addition to consequences involving blood cells, quality of hair, nails and skin, and dehydration (National Eating Disorders Association, n.d.). Although not an exhaustive discussion of the health consequences associated with eating disorders, the sections that follow will address many of the common health-related consequences as well as some rare but serious and life-threatening disease processes.

Vital Signs and Laboratory Values

Anemia is a common problem for those with eating disorders and refers to having a low red blood cell count. Common causes of anemia include iron deficiency and vitamin deficiency, which can be found among those with any of the eating disorders. Other laboratory indicators that the body of someone with anorexia nervosa is suffering involves levels of sodium and potassium (Miller et al., 2005; Sachs & Mehler, 2016). Low sodium values are referred to as **hyponatremia**, and low potassium values are referred to as **hypokalemia**, both of which can also be found in those who abuse diuretics or engage in self-induced vomiting (Mehler, 2011). Sodium and potassium are two electrolytes that are important in keeping vital systems functioning properly, including one's cardiovascular system. Low or high levels of either can negatively affect blood pressure and muscular functioning including one's heart. The incidence of hypokalemia appears to be relatively low for those diagnosed with bulimia nervosa (less than 5%); however, when hypokalemia is present in a patient who is otherwise healthy this particular clinical finding is thought to be diagnostic of the disorder and indicates regular vomiting or abuse of diuretics (Mehler et al., 2004).

Cardiovascular

The high-mortality rate evident with anorexia nervosa can be largely explained by death by suicide; however, other deaths associated with this disorder may be the result of problems with cardiac functioning including changes to the structure of the heart itself (Mehler & Krantz, 2003). Imbalance of electrolytes can result in cardiac arrhythmia, which can include irregular heartbeat, or a heartbeat that is either too fast or too slow. When the interval between heartbeats is too long, this can disrupt the normal functioning of the heart and can lead to *ventricular arrhythmia*, which can be fatal (Mehler & Krantz, 2003; Sachs & Mehler, 2016).

Heart rate (heart beats per minute) is typically below normal among those diagnosed with eating disorders (Miller et al., 2005) and is classified as *bradycardia* when the number of heart beats per minute is less than 60. In some cases, those with anorexia nervosa can have a heart rate as low as 25 beats per minute (Mehler & Krantz, 2003). Low heart rate such as this can lead to dizziness, fatigue, and difficulty concentrating. In addition to a slower than normal heart rate, a lower than normal blood pressure can also be found among those diagnosed with an eating disorder (Miller et al., 2005). This, too, can lead to feeling lightheaded, dizzy, and the possibility of fainting. Low blood pressure may be most evident when someone goes from a sitting to standing position or from lying down to sitting up. When low blood pressure is evident in this manner it is referred to as **orthostatic hypotension** and can be caused by dehydration or anemia. Both bradycardia and hypotension are among the most common medical symptoms found in those diagnosed with anorexia nervosa (Mehler & Brown, 2015) and can occur in those with bulimia nervosa when any method of purging is used excessively (Mehler et al., 2004). Dizziness, low blood pressure, and a temporary loss of consciousness are known as *syncope*, which in addition to being a symptom of something going wrong in the body can also put the individual at risk for injury due to falls and may also mean the individual is restricted in what activities he or she can do (e.g., driving).

When syrup of ipecac is used to induce vomiting, the active ingredient that makes this happen is *emetine*, which can be highly lethal. When emetine reaches toxic levels in the body it can affect the functioning of the heart and can be fatal. Although syrup of ipecac is no longer made in the United States due, in part, to the possibility of unintentional overdosing, it is still something that can be purchased outside of the United States and therefore used to help induce vomiting (Sachs & Mehler, 2016).

Oral and Gastrointestinal Health

The health of one's oral cavity can be negatively affected by eating disorders. Negative effects can involve the appearance and functioning of the mouth and tongue, appearance and overall health of teeth and gums, and problems with the esophagus. These issues can arise as a result of repeated purging in the form of self-induced vomiting, abuse of laxatives or diuretics, or as a result of vitamin deficiencies.

Self-induced vomiting can cause a variety of medical complications that occur throughout the body, particularly the upper gastrointestinal (upper GI) system, the throat and mouth, and the eyes and nose. The stomach acid affects the throat and mouth, whereas pressure from straining and retching can result in damage to the eyes and nose. The pressure exerted in the act of vomiting can lead to small blood vessels rupturing, which can lead to visible blood in the whites of the eyes and bleeding from the nose (Sachs & Mehler, 2016). The use of laxatives, diuretics, and self-induced vomiting specifically can result in abnormalities in fluid levels and in electrolyte imbalance (Mehler, 2011; see Cardiovascular section for more information).

Erosion of tooth enamel is the most visible oral symptom of those with bulimia nervosa (Mehler et al., 2004). Thus, dental professionals have been identified as a pivotal group of professionals who are likely among the first to identify patients engaged in regular episodes of self-induced vomiting (Ashcroft & Milosevic, 2007). The erosion of the teeth themselves can have multiple causes including exposure to stomach acid from regular self-included vomiting, misuse of drinks that have carbonation and/or caffeine and that are used to increase one's energy or to reduce one's feeling of hunger, consumption of vinegar or lemon juice for the purpose of reducing one's feelings of hunger, and excessive consumption of foods or drinks high in sugar content (often consumed in those with EDs to satisfy feelings of hunger [Russo et al., 2008; Sachs & Mehler, 2016]).

Among the medical issues more likely to be found among those engaging in binge/purge cycles, particularly when self-induced vomiting is the purging method, are problems with the mouth that can be noticed as early as 6 months after self-induced vomiting begins (Mehler, 2011). *Periodontitis* is a disease of the gums that can result in inflammation of the gums and an erosion of bone in the jaw that keeps one's teeth in place. As a result, loss of teeth is possible. Redness and swelling of the gums as a result of poor oral hygiene is often found among children and adolescents who have an eating disorder, particularly when binge eating and/or purging are involved, and can lead to periodontitis (Mehler, 2011; Russo et al., 2008). Additionally, repeated self-induced vomiting can lead to other gastrointestinal issues including soreness in the throat and soreness at the corners of the mouth, which can eventually lead to scaring (Mehler, 2011), and red lesions in the mouth can form due to repeated exposure to stomach acid (Russo et al., 2008). Those diagnosed with bulimia nervosa may be more predisposed to develop *necrotizing sialometaplasia* (Russo et al., 2008), which is a lesion often found toward the back of the bottom of one's mouth. Swelling of the salivary glands is also a common symptom found among those with eating disorders (Russo et al., 2008; Sachs & Mehler, 2016).

The areas of the gastrointestinal system most affected by the symptoms associated with bulimia nervosa are the esophagus, which is what connects the throat to the stomach, and the colon which is also referred to as the large intestine (Mehler et al., 2004). In mild cases, the esophagus can become inflamed as a result of repeated self-included vomiting, and it is common for those using this particular method of purging to experience heartburn and acid reflux (Mehler, 2011; Sachs & Mehler, 2016) which may cause *hematemesis* or vomiting of blood (Robinson, 2000). In severe cases, the esophagus can rupture, which can be life threatening (Mehler, 2011; Robinson, 2000). Long-term acid reflux can also result in Barrett's esophagus, which occurs when the tissue that makes up the esophagus is replaced by tissue that is similar to that which is found in the intestines, and long-term acid reflux can result in cancer of the esophagus (i.e., esophageal adenocarcinoma; Sachs & Mehler, 2016). Chronic exposure to stomach acid can also result in changes to the vocal cords, including having a hoarse voice, a recurring cough, and pain in the throat along with difficulty swallowing (Sachs & Mehler, 2016).

Although repeated laxative use as a method to control one's weight tends not to be effective since by the time the food has made it to the bowels most of the calories consumed (up to 90%) have already been absorbed by the body (Mehler, 2011), many diagnosed with bulimia nervosa still use this for the purpose of weight control. Among those diagnosed with bulimia nervosa just over 27% have used laxatives at some point, whereas in the general population just over 4% have ever used laxatives (Mehler et al., 2004). Overuse or abuse of laxatives affects the functioning of the gastrointestinal system and can also decrease blood volume and disturb the balance of electrolytes (Mehler, 2011; Robinson, 2000; Sachs & Mehler, 2016). Repeated use of laxatives also means that the bowels will require higher and higher doses of the laxative in order to be effective. For some, this may mean using upward of 50 laxatives per day in order to get the desired effect (Mehler et al., 2004). Over a long enough period of laxative overuse the bowel is "relegated to an inert tube" (Mehler, 2011, p. 98), which is known as *cathartic colon syndrome* (Sachs & Mehler, 2016) and means that the colon is no longer able to fully process and move material as it is designed to. This results in constipation that may be difficult to treat and may require an ostomy bag or surgery to remove a portion of or the entire colon (Mehler, 2011; Robinson, 2000; Sachs & Mehler, 2016).

Although not as frequently used as laxatives some individuals, in an attempt to lower their weight, may turn to diuretics, which are designed to rid the body of fluid. Taking diuretics for the purpose of losing weight by losing "water weight" can result in a cyclical pattern of diuretic use (Mehler, 2011). Weight loss due to loss of water weight can result in dehydration of the body, which in turn causes the body to retain fluid, thereby increasing one's weight. This in turn leads to continued use of diuretics. Over time the body will routinely retain salt and water, which can lead to edema or swelling of the body's tissues, which further perpetuates the individual's desire to use diuretics (Mehler, 2011).

Vitamin deficiencies, found among those who limit the quantity and variety of food consumed, can result in *atrophic glossitis* (Russo et al., 2008), which refers to changes in the tongue's appearance. It will become smooth and shiny and may change to a darker color. Ultimately, this medical issue results in a swollen tongue that may be painful and that may interfere with eating and swallowing, likely leading to prolonged vitamin deficiency. Another indication of malnutrition found among those with anorexia nervosa is *hepatic dysfunction* or a poorly functioning liver; this can lead to liver failure that can, of course, be further complicated by the consumption of alcohol (Robinson, 2000).

Among those diagnosed with anorexia nervosa specifically, acute gastric dilation can develop and can be medically serious (Robinson, 2000). This can lead to inadequate blood supply to gastrointestinal organs such as the stomach and may be indicated by a distended or protruding abdomen and spontaneous (not self-induced) vomiting (Robinson, 2000). In severe cases of anorexia nervosa, it is possible for the pancreas, which is important for digesting food as it leaves the stomach, to become suddenly inflamed. This is known as *acute pancreatitis*, and can be life threatening (Robinson, 2000).

In a study examining binge eating disorder and gastrointestinal functioning, researchers found that binge eating disorder was associated with a number of gastrointestinal symptoms that were categorized based on whether the symptoms were associated with the upper GI system or the lower GI system (Cremonini et al., 2009). In the upper GI, those with binge eating disorder were more likely than those without binge eating disorder to experience heartburn, acid regurgitation (a symptom of acid reflux), difficulty swallowing, bloating, and pain in the upper abdominal area. Lower GI symptoms included a greater chance of diarrhea, feeling an urgent need to go to the bathroom, constipation, and feeling like one's bowels are blocked.

Neurologic

Neurological problems can arise as a result of insufficient caloric and nutritional intake. Brain atrophy can occur in patients with anorexia nervosa and in chronic, severe cases the wasting away of brain tissue is identifiable on a brain scan and may mirror the scans of someone with clinical dementia such as Alzheimer's dementia (Mehler & Brown, 2015). While many serious medical complications associated with anorexia nervosa can be reversed with weight gain, restoration of gray matter itself may not be complete. Researchers are working to determine what specific areas of the brain may be most affected by the atrophy of brain tissue (Mehler & Brown, 2015).

Other research has examined the neural circuitry in the brains of those diagnosed with eating disorders to determine if information is processed differently, which might explain food choices such as restriction of intake or binge eating. Some research has indicated that neural pathways in the brain responsible for executive functioning (e.g., decision making, processing information in working memory, and controlling behavior) or reward are activated differently in those diagnosed with anorexia nervosa compared to those without an eating disorder, which the researchers found affected food choices (Foerde, Steinglass, Shohamy, & Walsh, 2015). With regard to reward circuitry in the brain, there are multiple reward pathways that are more or less activated depending on what an individual experiences throughout the day and the degree to which that experience is rewarding to him or her. Intuitively, most of us would assume that winning would be more rewarding than losing; however, it is not quite that simple for those diagnosed with anorexia nervosa. In certain parts of the brain, those diagnosed with anorexia nervosa processed winning as a reward like others without the disorder; however, in other parts of the brain losing was processed more strongly as a reward than winning (Bischoff-Grethe et al., 2013).

Some researchers have found that systems in the brain relying on the neurotransmitter dopamine seem to be implicated in some of the symptoms seen in eating disorders. Dopamine is involved in reward- or pleasure-related pathways in the brain. Depending on how dopamine functions in the brain, someone may be more or less sensitive to rewards. For example, the brains of those diagnosed with bulimia nervosa do not respond as strongly to dopamine activated reward systems in the brain whereas those diagnosed with anorexia nervosa seem to respond more strongly (Frank, 2015). What this seems to indicate is that when it comes to food (which should activate dopamine-sensitive reward pathways in the brain) those with bulimia nervosa require more stimuli (i.e., food) to feel rewarded, whereas those with anorexia nervosa do not require as much food-related stimulation to experience a neurological reward. Perhaps adding insult to injury, not only are the dopamine pathways more sensitive to food-related stimuli in those diagnosed with anorexia nervosa, but they are also much more likely to experience anxiety or fear rather than pleasure as a result of dopamine production (Bailer et al., 2012).

Many neurological problems seem to be the result of improper nutrition, thereby making these problems neurological consequences of, rather than risk factors for, eating disorders. Some researchers, however, have found neurological markers that may precede the onset of the eating disorder, particularly anorexia nervosa, and that may be a function of changes during puberty and stress related to cultural or societal pressures (Kaye, Wierenga, Bailer, Simmons, & Bischoff-Grethe, 2013). Regardless of when any neurological symptom may arise, proper neurological functioning requires proper nutrition, which is typically severely compromised among those with eating disorders. The more seriously an individual is malnourished, the more seriously the brain and by extension the mind will be compromised, resulting in changes in mood, behavior, personality, cognitive functioning, and worsening of eating disorder symptoms (Tyson, 2010). Given the importance of a well-fed brain, it is imperative for the body to be adequately fed so that treatment addressing the psychological, physical, and interpersonal aspects of the disorder can be effective (Croll, 2010).

Endocrine System and Diabetes

When an individual with anorexia nervosa shows "classic" signs of this disorder such as a significant decrease in overall caloric intake and calories from fat, and increases the amount of exercise in which he or she engages, the individual will experience what is referred to as low energy availability. Low **energy availability** signals to the body that there may not be sufficient energy readily available to keep important bodily functions going, and as such the body attempts to adapt. Changes in levels of certain hormones, peptides, and proteins as a result of low energy availability are believed to, at least temporarily, assist the individual by helping to maintain proper blood sugar levels, and to ensure there is enough energy for the function of vital systems. In this regard, these changes are viewed as adaptive. The negative effects of these changes to endocrine functioning can lead to a decrease in bone mineral density, changes in neurocognitive functioning, and an increase in anxiety, depression, and eating disorder symptoms (Misra & Klibanski, 2014).

Another significant endocrine system issue is the loss of menstrual functioning (Miller et al., 2005), which is referred to as amenorrhea. *Amenorrhea* can refer to a postpubertal female who previously had menstrual cycles but then stopped for at least 3 months, or a postpubertal female who never started menstruating but was expected to have started. It is believed that more than 95% of all females diagnosed with anorexia nervosa experience amenorrhea (Mehler & Krantz, 2003). Among those with bulimia nervosa, amenorrhea is not likely; however, it is possible for someone with this disorder to develop infrequent menstrual cycles, which is known as *oligomenorrhea* (Mehler et al., 2004). Although the loss of one's menstrual cycle is not, in and of itself, dangerous, the fluctuation in hormones through the cycle are important for bone health.

A relatively new and disturbing trend involving the endocrine system and eating disorders is how self-administered treatment for diabetes is handled. All individuals with type 1 diabetes require insulin injections and many diagnosed with type 2 diabetes require insulin injections to remain healthy. Following through with recommended insulin injections can forestall problems associated with diabetes such as problems with the teeth and gums, skin and feet, eyes, heart, blood vessels, and kidneys (American Diabetes Association, 2010). Not effectively managing one's diabetes with prescribed insulin injections can place a patient at higher risk for stroke, heart disease, and kidney failure; reducing or omitting insulin injections also results in an increased production of urine (i.e., diuresis) and weight loss. The possibility of weight loss as a result of not taking one's insulin has led some who have been diagnosed with insulin-dependent diabetes to either omit or reduce their insulin injections, which can have serious and potentially deadly consequences (Takii et al., 2002). Additionally, the necessity for tightly controlling what one eats to help manage one's diabetes can also place someone at risk for developing symptoms related to eating disorders (e.g., avoidance of certain foods; Mehler et al., 2004).

Skeletal Health

Skeletal health refers to the strength and density of one's bones. **Osteoporosis** is a disease due to extensively weakened bones as a result of losing too much bone or the body's inability to replace or remodel one's bones. Those with osteoporosis are susceptible to bones that break more easily. **Osteopenia** is the precursor to osteoporosis and refers to bone density that is lower than it should be but not to the extent of bone density loss seen in osteoporosis. Bone mineral density is usually measured via the dual X-ray absorptiometry (DEXA) scan, and changes in bone density found in those with anorexia nervosa are likely to occur early on in the course of the disorder (Mehler & Krantz, 2003). In one study, over half of all patients diagnosed with anorexia nervosa, with an average age of 25 years old, had osteopenia and 34% had osteoporosis (Miller et al., 2005). These researchers also reported that 42% of bone fractures among this population were due to stress fractures or minor injuries that would not have otherwise resulted in a bone fracture. Another study was reported to show over 50% of those with anorexia nervosa were also diagnosed with osteoporosis (Mehler & Krantz, 2003). The likelihood that someone with anorexia nervosa will have a bone fracture at some point is three times higher than that found in the general population (Mehler & Krantz, 2003).

Factors that contribute to bone health involve maintaining a healthy diet, engaging in weight-bearing exercise, and for females having regular (i.e., once a month) menstrual cycles. If a postpubertal female does not have regular menstrual cycles there is an inverse relationship between how long a female has been without a menstrual cycle and overall bone density (Mehler & Krantz, 2003). This means the longer the period of amenorrhea the lower the density of one's bones. As noted in the section on menstrual functioning, oligomenorrhea is much more common than amenorrhea among those diagnosed with bulimia nervosa and is also specifically linked to a decline in bone health; however, the infrequency of menstrual cycles does not appear to have the same effect on bone health compared to the cessation of menses altogether. Thus, bone density among those with bulimia nervosa, without a history of anorexia nervosa, tends to be normal (Mehler et al., 2004).

Dermatologic

In those with anorexia nervosa, it is not uncommon for the skin to become dry and scaly, and sometimes have a yellowish tinge. Soft, fine hair growth referred to as *lanugo* may be visible on the face, back, and extremities, and usually diminishes with weight restoration. In addition to these changes in skin, hair loss and brittle nails are also associated with this disorder (Jagielska, Tomaszewicz-Libudzic, & Brzozowska, 2007; Mehler & Krantz, 2003).

Russell's sign refers to calluses on the back of the hand, usually the knuckles, and is typically associated with bulimia nervosa. This sign is common among those who regularly use their fingers to induce vomiting and when assessed for could lead to early identification and treatment (Glorio et al., 2000).

Males

Males diagnosed with anorexia nervosa have similar medical complications as females (with the notable exception of problems with menstruation); however, because they usually already have a lower body fat percentage than females it does not take as much weight loss for the male body to begin to burn fat instead of carbohydrates, known as *ketosis*, as well as the breaking down of protein, both of which are done when there is an inadequate nutritional supply. Males are likely to show a noticeable decline in sexual energy and sexual interest as their disorder progresses and they are likely to have a coinciding decline in serum testosterone, which can lead to a decrease in testicular size (Mehler & Brown, 2015).

Nutritional

When nutrition is inadequate, any number of issues may arise from common conditions such as dry skin and unusual hair growth to electrolyte imbalances that can affect the functioning of the heart. Dry skin can lead to cracks in the skin of the fingers and toes that bleed (Mehler & Brown, 2015). More rare conditions include scurvy (swollen and bleeding gums), which develops after prolonged vitamin C deficiency, and *pellagra*, which is the result of inadequate levels of the vitamin niacin (vitamin B) and tryptophan (an amino acid). In modern, western societies pellagra is generally found among those who are economically poor and possibly homeless, dependent on alcohol, or among those who refuse food. The symptoms that accompany pellagra include diarrhea; inflamed and itchy skin referred to as *dermatitis*; a decline in one's ability to effectively mentally process information, referred to as *dementia*; and if the vitamin deficiency is not treated, death is the final outcome. The most common and often the first sign of those with pellagra who are also diagnosed with anorexia nervosa are changes to the skin (Prousky, 2003). These changes include patchy redness of the skin, swelling of the tongue, and a sore mouth. Although only a handful of cases of pellagra in those diagnosed with anorexia nervosa are known, it is possible that the disease is underdiagnosed as the symptoms of pellagra are similar to or the same as some symptoms of anorexia nervosa (Jagielska et al., 2007).

Conclusion

There are a multitude of biological and medical factors associated with eating disorders. Some of these factors help to explain why an eating disorder might develop to begin with, whereas many others are serious consequences of being chronically malnourished or using dangerous weight control methods. Understanding biologically related risk factors can help illuminate the complexity of these disorders and the notion that the development of these disorders is beyond an individual's control. Similarly, being aware of the medically related consequences of having an eating disorder can help to dispel the notion that eating disorders are simply severe forms of dieting.

References

American Diabetes Association. (2010). *Skipping insulin injections—What are the risk factors?* Retrieved from http://www.diabetes.org/newsroom/press-releases/2010/skipping-insulin-injections.html

Ashcroft, A., & Milosevic, A. (2007). The eating disorders: 2. Behavioral and dental management. *Dental Update, 34*, 619–620. doi:10.12968/denu.2007.34.10.612

Bailer, U. F., Narendran, R., Frankle, W. G., Himes, M. L., Duvvuri, V., Mathis, C. A., . . . Kaye, W. H. (2012). Amphetamine induced dopamine release increases anxiety in individuals recovered from anorexia nervosa. *International Journal of Eating Disorders, 45*, 263–271. doi:10.1002/eat.20937

Bischoff-Grethe, A., McCurdy, D., Grenesko-Stevens, E., Irvine, L. E., Wagner, A., Yau, W. Y., . . . Kay, W. H. (2013). Altered brain response to reward and punishment in adolescents with anorexia nervosa. *Psychiatry Research, 214*, 331–340. doi:10.1016/j.pscychresns.2013.07.004

Boraska, V., Franklin, C. S., Floyd, J. A. B., Thornton, L. M., Huckins, L. M., Southam, L., . . . Bulik, C. M. (2014). A genome-wide associate study of anorexia nervosa. *Molecular Psychiatry, 19*, 1085–1094. doi:10.1038/mp.2013.187

Cremonini, F., Camilleri, M., Clark, M. M., Beebe, T. J., Locke, G. R., Zinsmeister, A. R., . . . Talley, N. J. (2009). Associations among binge eating behavior patterns and gastrointestinal symptoms: A population-based study. *International Journal of Obesity, 33*, 342–353. doi:10.1038/ijo.2008.272

Croll, J. K. (2010). Nutritional impact on the recovery process. In M. Maine, B. H. McGilley, & D. W. Bunnell (Eds.), *Treatment of eating disorders: Bridging the research-practice gap* (pp. 127–142). San Diego, CA: Academic Press.

Foerde, K., Steinglass, J., Shohamy, D., & Walsh, B. T. (2015). Neural mechanisms supporting maladaptive food choices in anorexia nervosa. *Nature Neuroscience, 18*, 1571–1573. doi:10.1038/nn.4136

Frank, G. K. W. (2015). Advances from neuroimaging studies in eating disorders. *CNS Spectrums, 20*, 391–400. doi:10.1017/S1092852915000012

Friederich, H., Wu, M., Simon, J. J., & Herzog, W. (2013). Neurocircuit function in eating disorders. *International Journal of Eating Disorders, 46*, 425–432. doi:10.1002/eat.22099

Glorio, R., Allevato, M., De Pablo, A., Abbruzzese, M., Carmona, L., Savarin, M., . . . Woscoff, A. (2000). Prevalence of cutaneous manifestations in 200 patients with eating disorders. *International Journal of Dermatology, 39*, 348–353. doi:10.1046/j.1365-4362.2000.00924.x

Jagielska, G., Tomaszewicz-Libudzic, C. E., & Brzozowska, A. (2007). Pellagra: A rare complication of anorexia nervosa. *European Child & Adolescent Psychiatry, 16*, 417–420. doi:10.1007/s00787-007-0613-4

Kaye, W. H., Wierenga, C. E., Bailer, U. F., Simmons, A. N., & Bischoff-Grethe, A. (2013). Nothing tastes as good as skinny feels: The neurobiology of anorexia nervosa. *Trends in Neuroscience, 36*, 110–120. doi:10.1016/j.tins.2013.01.003

Keel, P. K., Dorer, D., Eddy, K., Franko, D., Charatan, D., & Herzog, D. (2003). Predictors of mortality in eating disorders. *Archives of General Psychiatry, 60,* 179–183. doi:10.1001/archpsyc.60.2.179

Keel, P. K., & Forney, K. J. (2013). Psychosocial risk factors for eating disorders. *International Journal of Eating Disorders, 46,* 433–439. doi:10.1002/eat.22094

Mehler, P. S. (2011). Medical complications of bulimia nervosa and their treatments. *International Journal of Eating Disorders, 44,* 95–104. doi:10.1002/eat.20825

Mehler, P. S., & Brown, C. (2015). Anorexia nervosa—medical complications. *Journal of Eating Disorders, 3,* 1–8. doi:10.1186/s40337-015-0040-8

Mehler, P. S., Crews, C., & Weiner, K. (2004). Bulimia: Medical complications. *Journal of Women's Health, 13,* 668–675. doi:10.1089/jwh.2004.13.668

Mehler, P. S., & Krantz, M. (2003). Anorexia nervosa: Medical issues. *Journal of Women's Health, 12,* 331–340. doi:10.1089/154099903765448844

Miller, K. K., Grinspoon, S. K., Ciampa, J., Hier, J., Herzog, D., & Klibanski, A. (2005). Medical findings in outpatients with anorexia nervosa. *Archives of Internal Medicine, 165,* 561–566. doi:10.1001/archinte.165.5.561

Misra, M., & Klibanski, A. (2014). Endocrine consequences of anorexia nervosa. *Lancet Diabetes & Endocrinology, 2,* 581–592. doi:10.1016/S2213-8587(13)70180-3

Mitchell, J. E., & Crow, S. J. (2010). Medical comorbidities of eating disorders. In W. S. Agras (Ed.), *The Oxford handbook of eating disorders* (pp. 259–266). New York, NY: Oxford University Press.

National Eating Disorders Association. (n.d.). Common health consequences of eating disorders. Retrieved from https://www.nationaleatingdisorders.org/health-consequences

Prousky, J. E. (2003). Pellagra may be a rare secondary complication of anorexia nervosa: A systematic review of the literature. *Alternative Medicine Review, 8,* 180–185.

Robinson, P. H. (2000). The gastrointestinal tract in eating disorders. *European Eating Disorders Review, 8,* 88–97. doi:10.1002/(SICI)1099-0968(200003)8:2<88::AID-ERV344>3.0.CO;2-R

Russo, L. L., Campisi, G., Di Fede, O., Di Liberto, C., Panzarella, V., & Musio, L. L. (2008). Oral manifestations of eating disorders: A critical review. *Oral Diseases, 14,* 479–484. doi:10.1111/j.1601-0825.2007.01422.x

Sachs, K., & Mehler, P. S. (2016). Medical complications of bulimia nervosa and their treatments. *Eating and Weight Disorders, 21,* 13–18. doi:10.1007/s40519-015-0201-4

Sullivan, P. (1995). Mortality in anorexia nervosa. *American Journal of Psychiatry, 152,* 1073–1074. doi:10.1176/ajp.152.7.1073

Takii, M., Uchigata, Y., Nozaki, T., Nishikata, H., Kawai, K., Komaki, G., . . . Kubok, C. (2002). Classification of type 1 diabetic females with bulimia nervosa into subgroups according to purging behavior. *Diabetes Care, 25,* 1571–1575. doi:10.2337/diacare.25.9.1571

Trace, S. E., Baker, J. H., Peñas-Lledó, E., & Bulik, C. M. (2013). The genetics of eating disorders. *Annual Review of Clinical Psychology, 9,* 589–620. doi:10.1146/annurev-clinpsy-050212-185546

Tyson, E. P. (2010). Medical assessment of eating disorders. In M. Maine, B. H. McGilley, & D. W. Bunnell (Eds.), *Treatment of eating disorders: Bridging the research-practice gap* (pp. 89–110). San Diego, CA: Academic Press.

Yilmaz, Z., Hardaway, J. A., & Bulik, C. M. (2015). Genetics and epigenetics of eating disorders. *Advances in Genomics and Genetics, 5,* 131–150. doi:10.2147/AGG.S55776

Zipfel, S., Löwe, B., & Herzog, W. (2003). Medical complications. In J. Treasure, U. Schmidt, & van Furth, E. (Eds.), *Handbook of eating disorders* (2nd ed., pp. 169–190). West Sussex, UK: Wiley. doi:10.1002/0470013443.ch10

PSYCHOLOGICAL FACTORS

Introduction

Psychological factors involve internal experiences that an individual has. In this context, these internal experiences will revolve around one's perception about body weight, shape, and size; other mental health issues in addition to an eating disorder; personality characteristics; and the degree to which an individual has control over his or her emotions and behaviors. There are a multitude of psychological factors that can affect the development of, maintenance of, or recovery from an eating disorder. What follows is a description of some of these factors.

Weight Concerns

Concern about how much one weighs is commonly associated with eating disorders. This may manifest in some by their desire to lose weight, to maintain the weight they already have, or the fear of gaining weight at all. Generally weight concerns such as these are most strongly associated with females as they attempt to achieve the **thin ideal**, whereas males usually strive for building and maintaining muscle mass to fit the **muscular ideal** (Selby, 2017). In their review of studies examining the relationship between having concerns about one's weight and the development of an eating disorder, Keel and Forney (2013) reported that as weight concerns increase the rates of eating disorders also increase. Additionally, they reported that when weight concerns decline, which often happens with age, eating disorder diagnoses also decline. Although Keel and Forney identified weight concerns as "one of the most robust predictors of eating disorders" (p. 436) based on the studies they reviewed, they also noted that weight concern is but a small factor in the overall picture in terms of what puts one person at greater risk for developing an eating disorder over another (see Chapters 5 and 7).

An element of having weight concerns involves the degree to which one internalizes the ideal set by a particular culture. Internalization refers to a process by which someone experiences the opinions, expectations, and ideals set by others and takes them on as his or her own. Thin-ideal internalization refers to the extent to which an individual, usually a female, has identified with or internalized the thin ideal. Practically speaking, what this means is that such a person believes that being thin is an ideal that should be pursued. Thin-ideal internalization has been routinely linked to eating disorders (Keel & Forney, 2013; Striegel-Moore & Bulik, 2007; Van Diest & Perez, 2013). Similarly, a drive for muscularity has been regularly associated with eating disorders as well (Brennan, Craig, & Thompson, 2012; Rodgers, Ganchou, Franko, & Chabrol, 2012). What may make people particularly vulnerable to internalizing harmful ideals such as the thin- or muscular-ideal is a concept referred to as *self-concept clarity*.

Self-concept clarity was identified and defined in the 1990s as "the extent to which the contents of an individual's self-concept (e.g., perceived personal attributes) are clearly and confidently defined, internally consistent, and temporally stable" (Campbell et al., 1996, p. 141). This construct has been linked to psychological constructs such as self-esteem (Blazek & Besta, 2012; Campbell et al., 1996), meaning of life (Blazek & Besta, 2012), and thin-ideal internalization (Vartanian & Dey, 2013). A lack of self-concept clarity leaves individuals vulnerable to the influences and standards of others; thus, those low in self-concept clarity will look to others to determine what should or should not be valued. Research has indicated that low self-concept clarity can lead individuals to compare their appearance to others' and to ultimately internalize the current standard of female attractiveness: the thin ideal (Vartanian & Dey, 2013).

Body dissatisfaction, which has been found to be one of the strongest predictors of eating disorders (Stice, Marti, & Durant, 2011), is another element of weight concerns; however, that will be discussed more fully in the section on Personality Factors.

▦ Comorbid Psychiatric Disorders

Other psychiatric disorders are often diagnosed along with eating disorders (Hudson, Hiripi, Pope, & Kessler, 2007). As many as 70% of those diagnosed with an eating disorder will also be diagnosed with another mental health disorder, the most common falling in the categories of mood disorders and anxiety disorders (Grilo, White, & Masheb, 2009; Keski-Rahkonen & Mustelin, 2016) with mood disorders more commonly found among those with an eating disorder compared to those without one (Godart et al., 2015). Specific disorders that are often diagnosed along with an eating disorder include Major Depressive Disorder (i.e., depression), Generalized Anxiety Disorder, Obsessive-Compulsive Disorder, and Specific Phobias. In some cases a Substance Use Disorder (e.g., Alcohol Use Disorder) is also diagnosed.

A study examining unhealthy weight control behaviors among adolescents, which included behaviors such as **purging** and use of diet pills, found that females in comparison to males were more likely to engage in these unhealthy behaviors (Stephen, Rose, Kenney, Rosselli-Navarra, & Weissman, 2014). Moreover, they found that these behaviors were associated with depression symptoms in addition to factors such as low self-esteem and delinquency. Depression among those with **anorexia nervosa** has been hypothesized to be due in part to food restriction and significant weight loss, which leads to a multitude of changes in the body including hormonal changes and changes in how the brain metabolizes energy (Grachev, 2016). Reestablishing normal eating patterns may have the effect of reducing depressive as well as anxiety symptoms (Sala et al., 2011). Recent research in this area has found that other mental health concerns may differ depending on the Cerniglia et al. (2017) found that adolescents diagnosed with anorexia nervosa displayed high scores for symptoms related to depression, anxiety, obsessive-compulsive disorder, and high levels of hostility. Adolescents diagnosed with **bulimia nervosa** scored higher on items reflecting phobia-related anxiety and somatization (symptoms without a medical cause). Those diagnosed with **binge eating disorder** reported having interpersonal sensitivity and psychoticism which may reflect feelings of social alienation rather than true psychosis.

Obsessive-compulsiveness is another trait often linked to eating disorders and shares characteristics of perfectionism (Cassin & von Ranson, 2005; Cederlöf et al., 2015; van Passel et al., 2016). Obsessive-compulsive disorder (OCD) is generally characterized by an individual experiencing intrusive thoughts (obsessions) about which he or she does not have any control and that are distressing. Additionally, the individual typically engages in ritualistic behaviors (compulsions) designed to reduce the distress that accompanies the obsessions. Rigid behavior patterns and inflexible thinking are believed to be shared characteristics of OCD and anorexia nervosa and inflexible thinking specifically may be an important factor in maintaining both disorders (van Passel et al., 2016). Some studies have found that the co-occurrence of these two disorders is significant and therefore not likely due to chance (e.g., Cederlöf et al., 2015; Torresen et al., 2013; van Passel et al., 2016).

Substance use is also common among those diagnosed with eating disorders. Nearly 25% of adolescents diagnosed with Anorexia Nervosa also reported using substances, and nearly 50% and 29% of those diagnosed with Bulimia Nervosa and *eating disorder not otherwise specified* (EDNOS; the *DSM-IV* diagnosis that included individuals with binge eating disorder), respectively, reported using substances (Mann et al., 2014)

Personality Disorders

Personality disorders have often been associated with eating disorders and are believed to be the most commonly occurring comorbid diagnosis (Cassin & von Ranson, 2005). Moreover, personality disorder diagnoses are thought to precede the development of an eating disorder as personality disorders are believed to have their beginnings in early childhood (Sansone & Sansone, 2011). The addition of personality disorders to the diagnostic picture may in part account for why eating disorders are so difficult to treat. There may be, however, some differences between males and females when it comes to which personality disorders are diagnosed.

Personality disorders are organized by category or "clusters" based on the shared traits among them. There are three clusters (American Psychiatric Association [APA], 2013): *Cluster A*, which includes the personality disorders with odd or eccentric traits; *Cluster B*, which includes the personality disorders characterized by dramatic, emotional, and erratic behavioral traits; and *Cluster C*, which is characterized by anxious and fearful traits. Many individuals with eating disorders also have a personality disorder diagnosis that is likely to fall under Cluster B or Cluster C (Satir, Thompson-Brenner, Boisseau, & Crisafulli, 2009).

Reas, Ro, Karterud, Hummelen, and Pedersen (2013) found that there was a greater risk for a personality disorder diagnosis among female patients with eating disorders compared to men and that specific eating disorders are more likely to be linked to specific personality disorder diagnoses among women. Overall for the men, there was a relatively low rate of patients included in this study who were diagnosed with both an eating disorder and a personality disorder; however, in other studies, males with eating disorders have been found to have a higher rate of the borderline personality disorder diagnosis (e.g., Chen, McCloskey, Michelson, Gordon, & Coccaro, 2011). Reas et al. reported not only a higher rate of personality disorder diagnoses among women with an eating disorder diagnosis but they were also able to identify to some extent which personality disorder diagnoses are more likely to be associated with which eating disorder diagnosis. The previously used diagnostic category of EDNOS (APA, 2000) included what is now diagnosed as Binge Eating Disorder (BED) as well as versions of bulimia nervosa and anorexia nervosa that did not quite meet all of the criteria for those diagnoses. As such, the researchers noted that they were not able to discern which presentation of symptoms was present among those diagnosed with EDNOS. It is interesting, however, that women diagnosed with EDNOS were more likely to also be diagnosed with the Cluster C diagnoses of avoidant personality disorder, dependent personality disorder, and obsessive-compulsive personality disorder, the Cluster B diagnosis of Borderline Personality Disorder, and Personality Disorder not Otherwise Specified (similar to EDNOS, this diagnosis indicates that individuals clearly meet the criteria for a personality disorder but their symptoms are such that they do not fit neatly into a specific personality disorder diagnosis).

The picture is quite different for those diagnosed with bulimia nervosa or anorexia Nervosa. Reas et al. (2013) found that women diagnosed with Bulimia Nervosa were more likely to also have the diagnosis of Avoidant Personality Disorder or Borderline Personality Disorder. Women diagnosed with Anorexia Nervosa were most likely to have the personality disorder diagnosis of Obsessive-Compulsive Personality Disorder. As many as 47% of women with anorexia nervosa have also been found to be diagnosed with a wider range of personality disorders, and in some cases more than one personality disorder, including obsessive-compulsive personality disorder, Paranoid Personality Disorder, Dependent Personality Disorder, Avoidant Personality Disorder, and Borderline Personality Disorder (Pham-Scottez et al., 2012). Others have found that the type of anorexia nervosa may indicate which personality disorder diagnosis is most likely. Obsessive-compulsive personality disorder, for example, may be more common among those with the restricting-type of anorexia nervosa, whereas those diagnosed with the binge eating purging type may be more likely to be diagnosed with borderline personality disorder (Sansone, Levitt, & Sansone, 2005). Sansone et al. also found that the restricting subtype was also associated with avoidant personality disorder, borderline personality disorder, and dependent personality disorder. Avoidant and dependent personality disorders were also found among those with the binge eating/purging subtype along with histrionic personality disorder (a Cluster B disorder)

Personality Factors

Personality refers to the typical way we think, feel, and interact with ourselves and the world around us. Although some aspects of our personality may change as we age or experience significant life events, other aspects of our personality may persist over time. Some personality traits that have been linked to eating disorders include negative emotionality, perfectionism, low self-directedness, low cooperativeness, drive for thinness, obsessive-compulsive traits, and poor awareness of the changes that occur in one's body, self-esteem and impulsivity (e.g., Cassin & von Ranson, 2005; Dawe & Loxton, 2004; Lilenfeld, Wonderlich, Riso, Crosby, & Mitchell, 2006; Mitchell, Wolf, Reardon, & Miller, 2014). Some personality traits may be risk factors preceding the development of an eating disorder, whereas others may be consequences of having developed an eating disorder. It is not always clear-cut in terms of when a factor may come before or follow an eating disorder (Lilenfeld et al., 2006). Given this confusion, others have suggested that personality traits ought to be considered as part of the diagnosis of eating disorders themselves (Cassin & von Ranson, 2005).

Two personality traits connected to eating disorders are negative emotionality and perfectionism. *Negative emotionality* can reflect things such as being highly critical of one's self, overall dissatisfaction with life, and low self-esteem (Keel & Forney, 2013), whereas *perfectionism* refers to a drive for flawlessness. Elements of negative emotionality and perfectionism have historically and recently been linked to eating disorder psychopathology (Cassin & von Ranson, 2005; Fairburn, Cooper, Doll, & Welch, 1999; Fairburn, Welch, Doll, Davies, & O'Connor, 1997; Franco-Paredes, Mancilla-Díaz, Vázquez-Arévalo, López-Aguilar, & Álvarez-Rayón, 2005; Slof-Op't Landt, Claes, & van Furth, 2016; Stice, 2002; Wade, O'Shea, & Shafran, 2016). Negative emotionality or negative affect has been found to not only be an important factor related to eating disorders in general, but has been specifically identified as a factor that may serve to help perpetuate an eating disorder that already exists (Stice, 2002).

Perfectionism has received abundant empirical attention with studies linking a high degree of perfectionism to eating disorders, particularly anorexia nervosa (e.g., Claes, Mitchell, & Vandereycken, 2012; Dakanalis et al., 2014). Studies on perfectionism have suggested that there may be healthy and unhealthy versions of this particular trait, including the notion that perfectionism may not be a unidimensional construct but multidimensional including influences from one's self and others (Franco-Paredes et al., 2005; Slof-Op't Landt et al., 2016). An examination of healthy and unhealthy perfectionism revealed that unhealthy perfectionism was found to be a predictor of eating disorder symptoms compared to healthy perfectionism (Slof-Op't Landt et al., 2016). Additional research in this area confirmed the connection between perfectionism and eating disorders but noted that the presence of anxiety partially explains this relationship, indicating that perfectionism *and* the presence of anxiety together help to predict the presence of eating disorder symptoms (Egan et al., 2013).

Other researchers set out to determine if perfectionism can be manufactured within study participants and if so whether this would predict the development of eating disorder symptoms (Boone, Soenens, Vansteenkiste, & Braet, 2012). They reported that in the 24 hours following experimentally induced perfectionism study participants were more likely to engage in dietary restraint and binge eating behaviors compared to those who experienced the nonperfectionism conditions. While perfectionism seems to play a significant role in explaining eating disorder symptoms, others have suggested that self-criticism rather than perfectionism may play a more important role.

Ferreira, Pinto-Gouveia, and Duarte (2014) examined the relationship between self-criticism, perfectionism, and eating disorders. They also examined these factors in terms of how depression and body dissatisfaction may be involved. Overall, they found that the impact of self-criticism seemed to outweigh the impact of perfectionism. Although being critical of one's self was connected to the desire to be perceived as perfect by other people, self-criticism affected feelings of body dissatisfaction and depression to a much greater degree than perfectionism. More importantly, Ferreira et al. found that perceiving one's self as inadequate and lesser than explained the severity of eating disorder symptoms, whereas perfectionism did not. This means that the more highly critical someone with an eating disorder is of himself or herself, the more severe the individual's eating disorder symptoms. Furthermore, they found that the impact of self-criticism on the severity of eating disorder symptoms was independent of any other factors they examined. That is, eating disorder symptoms are going to be more severe in those who are self-critical regardless of whether or not they are also depressed or are also experiencing body dissatisfaction. Overall, these results led the authors to conclude that a "self-to-self critic relationship is key in eating disorders" (p. 417). The findings related to self-criticism and its connection with perfectionism seem to reflect the idea that self-imposed standards rather than societal pressures for perfectionism have been found to be stronger among those with eating disorders (Lampard, Byrne, McLean, & Fursland, 2012).

Costa, Marôco, Gouveia, and Ferreira (2016) examined individuals diagnosed with an eating disorder and conceptualized perfectionism in terms of the version of one's self that they see as "ideal." When this perfect version of themselves is compared to who they actually are, the result is that they view who they actually are in a negative way (i.e., they are highly self-critical), encompassing a view that they are inferior to the ideal version of themselves, which further leads to negative emotions including depression. Thus, the presentation of a perfect version of themselves is believed to be an attempt to showcase a more positive version of themselves and may help them manage some social interactions, but ultimately does not help them with regard to having symptoms related to depression.

Behavioral and Emotional Control

Claes et al. (2012) examined the differences that seem to exist between eating disorders when it comes to how much control an individual may have over his or her behaviors (i.e., restrictive eating, binge eating, and purging). Perhaps unsurprisingly, they found those diagnosed with anorexia nervosa exhibited overcontrol of their behaviors, which may be seen in perfectionism and obsessive-compulsiveness, whereas those diagnosed with bulimia nervosa demonstrated an undercontrolling of their behavior, which can be seen in impulsivity and difficulty inhibiting their behaviors. Behaviors reflecting a lack of control include binge eating behaviors, purging behaviors, and excessive exercising. Although these behaviors are considered to be undesirable and potentially harmful, they are also believed to be among the strategies used to regulate and cope with unwelcome emotional experiences (Anestis, Smith, Fink, & Joiner, 2009; Smyth et al., 2007; Svaldi, Griepenstroh, Tuschen-Caffier, & Ehring, 2012; Wild et al., 2007).

Impulsivity is another personality trait and behavioral control issue that has been linked to eating disorders (Dawe & Loxton, 2004; Wonderlich, Connolly, & Stice, 2004). Impulsivity refers to the tendency to act without thinking, particularly of potential consequences of one's actions. Although impulsivity has been connected to eating disorders, it is possible that this trait is more reflective of anxiety rather than the eating disorder specifically (Boisseau et al., 2012).

Svaldi et al. (2012) examined the extent to which difficulties in regulating one's emotions, or emotional control, were specific to eating disorders or whether it is found among myriad diagnoses. Findings indicated that those diagnosed with an eating disorder had more significant problems regulating their emotions in comparison to those who did not have a mental health diagnosis; however, when compared to those diagnosed with borderline personality disorder or major depressive disorder, there were very few differences. This led researchers to conclude that emotional regulation difficulties, while highly likely to be present among those with an eating disorder, do not differentiate eating disorders from at least some other mental illnesses. Svaldi et al. reported that those with an eating disorder diagnosis displayed a greater degree of emotional intensity, had a more difficult time accepting their emotional experiences, had greater difficulty in accurately identifying the presence of a particular emotional experience, and had the tendency to use maladaptive efforts to regulate their emotional experiences. These findings were particularly true of those diagnosed with anorexia nervosa and bulimia nervosa. Those diagnosed with binge eating disorder also showed greater difficulties in regulating their emotions compared to those without a mental health diagnosis, but were also shown to be slightly more effective at regulating their emotions overall compared to the other two eating disorder diagnoses.

Conclusion

The psychological factors presented in this chapter, though not comprehensive, paint a picture that reveals the complex nature of eating disorders. Although many people think eating disorders are purely about food, the myriad psychological factors associated with eating disorders indicate that there is much going on within a person with such a diagnosis to state that eating disorders reflect an issue with one particular thing. Some of the factors here may predate, coexist with, or may be the result of the eating disorder itself. Regardless of when these psychological factors emerge, they clearly impact the overall well-being of the individual dealing with them.

References

American Psychiatric Association. (2000). *Diagnostic and statistical manual of mental disorders* (4th ed., Text Rev.). Washington, DC: Author.

American Psychiatric Association. (2013). *Diagnostic and statistical manual of mental disorders* (5th ed.). Washington, DC: Author.

Anestis, M. D., Smith, A. R., Fink, E. L., & Joiner, T. E. (2009). Dysregulated eating and distress: Examining the specific role of negative urgency in a clinical sample. *Cognitive Therapy Research, 33*, 390–397. doi:10.1007/s10608-008-9201-2

Blazek, M., & Besta, T. (2012). Self-concept clarity and religious orientations: Prediction of purpose in life and self-esteem. *Journal of Religious Health, 51*, 947–960. doi:10.1007/s10943-010-9407-y

Boisseau, C. L., Thompson-Brenner, H., Caldwell-Harris, C., Pratt, E., Farchione, T., & Barlow, D. H. (2012). Behavioral and cognitive impulsivity in obsessive-compulsive disorder and eating disorders. *Psychiatry Research, 200*, 1062–1066. doi:10.1016/j.psychres.2012.06.010

Boone, L., Soenens, B., Vansteenkiste, M., & Braet, C. (2012). Is there a perfectionism in each of us? An experimental study on perfectionism and eating disorder symptoms. *Appetite, 59*, 531–540. doi:10.1016/j.appet.2012.06.015

Brennan, D. J., Craig, S. L., & Thompson, D. E. A. (2012). Factors associated with a drive for muscularity among gay and bisexual men. *Culture, Health & Sexuality, 14*, 1–15. doi:10.1080/13691058.2011.619578

Campbell, J. D., Trapnell, P. D., Heine, S. J., Katz, I. M., Lavallee, L. F., & Lehman, D. R. (1996). Self-concept clarity: Measurement, personality correlates, and cultural boundaries. *Journal of Personality and Social Psychology, 70*, 141–156. doi:10.1037/0022-3514.70.1.141

Cassin, S., & von Ranson, K. M. (2005). Personality and eating disorders: A decade in review. *Clinical Psychology Review, 25*, 895–916. doi:10.1016/j.cpr.2005.04.012

Cederlöf, M., Thornton, L. M., Baker, J., Lichtenstein, P., Larsson, H., Rück, C., . . . Mataix-Cols, D. (2015). Etiological overlap between obsessive-compulsive disorder and anorexia nervosa: A longitudinal cohort, multigenerational family and twin study. *World Psychiatry, 14*, 333–338. doi:10.1002/wps.20251

Cerniglia, L., Cimino, S., Tafà, M., Marzilli, E., Ballarotto, G., & Bracaglia, F. (2017). Family profiles in eating disorders: Family functioning and psychopathology. *Psychology Research and Behavior Management, 10*, 305–312. doi:10.2147/PRBM.S145463

Chen, E. Y., McCloskey, M. S., Michelson, S., Gordon, K. H., & Coccaro, E. (2011). Characterizing eating disorders in a personality disorders sample. *Psychiatry Research, 185*, 427–432. doi:10.1016/j.psychres.2010.07.002

Claes, L., Mitchell, J. E., & Vandereycken, W. (2012). Out of control? Inhibition processes in eating disorders from a personality and cognitive perspective. *International Journal of Eating Disorders, 45*, 407–414. doi:10.1002/eat.20966

Costa, J., Marôco, J., Gouveia, J. P., & Ferreira, C. (2016). Shame, self-criticism, perfectionistic self-presentation and depression in eating disorders. *International Journal of Psychology and Psychological Therapy, 16*, 315–328.

Dakanalis, A., Timko, C. A., Zanetti, M. A., Rinaldi, L., Prunas, A., Carrà, G., . . . Clerici, M. (2014). Attachment insecurities, maladaptive perfectionism, and eating disorder symptoms: A latent mediated and moderated structural equation modeling analysis across diagnostic groups. *Psychiatry Research, 215*, 176–184. doi:10.1016/j.psychres.2013.10.039

Dawe, S., & Loxton, N. (2004). The role of impulsivity in the development of substance use and eating disorders. *Neuroscience and Biobehavioral Reviews, 28*, 343–351. doi:10.1016/j.neubiorev.2004.03.007

Egan, S. J., Watson, H. J., Kane, R. T., McEvoy, P., Fursland, A., & Nathan, P. R. (2013). Anxiety as a mediator between perfectionism and eating disorders. *Cognitive Therapy and Research, 37*, 905–913. doi:10.1007/s10608-012-9516-x

Fairburn, C. G., Cooper, Z., Doll, H. A., & Welch, S. L. (1999). Risk factors for anorexia nervosa: Three integrated case-control comparisons. *Archives of General Psychiatry, 56*, 468–476. doi:10.1001/archpsyc.56.5.468

Fairburn, C. G., Welch, S. L., Doll, H. A., Davies, B. A., & O'Connor, M. E. (1997). Risk factors for bulimia nervosa. A community-based case-control study. *Archives of General Psychiatry, 54*, 509–517. doi:10.1001/archpsyc.1997.01830180015003

Ferreira, C., Pinto-Gouveia, J., & Duarte, C. (2014). Self-criticism, perfectionism and eating disorders: The effect of depression and body dissatisfaction. *International Journal of Psychology and Psychological Therapy, 14*, 409–420.

Franco-Paredes, K., Mancilla-Díaz, J. M., Vázquez-Arévalo, R., López-Aguilar, X., & Álvarez-Rayón, G. (2005). Perfectionism and eating disorders: A review of the literature. *European Eating Disorders Review, 13*, 61–70. doi:10.1002/erv.605

Godart, N., Radon, L., Curt, F., Duclos, J., Perdereau, F., Lang, F., . . . Flament, M. F. (2015). Mood disorders in eating disorder patients: Prevalence and chronology of ONSET. *Journal of Affective Disorders, 185*, 115–122. doi:10.1016/j.jad.2015.06.039

Grachev, V. V. (2016). Depressive states at the stage of manifest clinical signs of anorexia nervosa in adolescents. *Neuroscience and Behavioral Physiology, 46*, 348–353. doi:10.1007/s11055-016-0240-y

Grilo, C. M., White, M. A., & Masheb, R. M. (2009). *DSM-IV* psychiatric disorder comorbidity and its correlates with binge eating disorder. *International Journal of Eating Disorders, 42*, 228–234. doi:10.1002/eat.20599

Hudson, J. I., Hiripi, E., Pope, H. G., & Kessler, R. C. (2007). The prevalence and correlates of eating disorders in the National Comorbidity Survey Replication. *Biological Psychiatry, 61*, 348–358. doi:10.1016/j.biopsych.2006.03.040

Keel, P. K., & Forney, K. J. (2013). Psychosocial risk factors for eating disorders. *International Journal of Eating Disorders, 46*, 433–439. doi:10.1002/eat.22094

Keski-Rahkonen, A., & Mustelin, L. (2016). Epidemiology of eating disorders in Europe: Prevalence, incidence, comorbidity, course, consequences, and risk factors. *Current Opinion in Psychiatry, 29*, 340–345. doi:10.1097/YCO.0000000000000278

Lampard, A. M., Byrne, S. M., McLean, N., & Fursland, A. (2012). The eating disorder inventory-2 perfectionism scale: Factor structure and associations with dietary restraint and weight and shape concern in eating disorders. *Eating Behaviors, 13*, 49–53. doi:10.1016/j.eatbeh.2011.09.007

Lilenfeld, L. R. R., Wonderlich, S. A., Riso, L. P., Crosby, R., & Mitchell, J. (2006). Eating disorders and personality: A methodological and empirical review. *Clinical Psychology Review, 26*, 299–320. doi:10.1016/j.cpr.2005.10.003

Mann, A. P., Accurso, E. C., Stiles-Shields, C., Capra, L., Labuschagne, Z., Karnik, N. S., . . . Le Grange, D. (2014). Factors associated with substance use and adolescents with eating disorders. *Journal of Adolescent Health, 55*, 182–187. doi:10.1016/j.jadohealth.2014.01.015

Mitchell, K. S., Wolf, E. J., Reardon, A. F., & Miller, M. W. (2014). Association of eating disorder symptoms with internalizing and externalizing dimensions of psychopathology among men and women. *International Journal of Eating Disorders, 47*, 860–869. doi:10.1002/eat.22300

Pham-Scottez, A., Huas, C., Perez-Diaz, F., Nordon, C., Divac, S., Dardennes, R., . . . Rouillon, F. (2012). Why do people with eating disorders drop out from inpatient treatment?: The role of personality factors. *The Journal of Nervous and Mental Disease, 200*, 807–813. doi:10.1097/NMD.0b013e318266bbba

Reas, D. L., Rø, Ø., Karterud, S., Hummelen, B., & Pedersen, G. (2013). Eating disorders in a large clinical sample of men and women with personality disorders. *International Journal of Eating Disorders, 46*, 801–809.doi:10.1002/eat.22176

Rodgers, R. F., Ganchou, C., Franko, D. L., & Chabrol, H. (2012). Drive for muscularity and disordered eating among French adolescent boys: A sociocultural model. *Body Image, 9*, 318–323. doi:10.1016/j.bodyim.2012.03.002

Sala, L., Mirabel-Sarron, C., Gorwood, P., Pham-Scottez, P., Blanchet, A., & Rouillon, F. (2011). The level of associated depression and anxiety traits improves during weight regain in eating disorder patients. *Eating and Weight Disorders, 16*, e280–e284. doi:10.1007/BF03327473

Sansone, R. A., Levitt, J. L., & Sansone, L. A. (2005). The prevalence of personality disorders among those with eating disorders. *Eating Disorders, 13*, 7–21. doi:10.1080/10640260590893593

Sansone, R. A., & Sansone, L. A. (2011). Personality pathology and its influence on eating disorders. *Innovations in Clinical Neuroscience, 8*, 14–18.

Satir, D. A., Thompson-Brenner, H., Boisseau, C. L., & Crisafulli, M. A. (2009). Countertransference reactions to adolescents with eating disorders: Relationship to clinician and patient factors. *International Journal of Eating Disorders, 42*, 511–521. doi:10.1002/eat.20650

Selby, C. L. B. (2017). *The body size and health debate.* Santa Barbara, CA: Greenwood.

Slof-Op't Landt, M. C. T., Claes, L., & van Furth, E. F. (2016). Classifying eating disorders based on "healthy" and "unhealthy" perfectionism and impulsivity. *International Journal of Eating Disorders, 49*, 673–680. doi:10.1002/eat.22557

Smyth, J. M., Wonderlich, S. A., Heron, K. E., Sliwinski, M. J., Crosby, R. D., Mitchell, J. E., . . . Engel, S. G. (2007). Daily and momentary mood and stress are associated with binge eating and vomiting in bulimia nervosa patients in the natural environment. *Journal of Consulting and Clinical Psychology, 75*, 629–638. doi:10.1037/0022-006X.75.4.629

Stephen, E. M., Rose, J. S., Kenney, L., Rosselli-Navarra, F., & Weissman, R. S. (2014). Prevalence and correlates of unhealthy weight control behaviors: Findings from the national longitudinal study of adolescent health. *Journal of Eating Disorders, 2*, 1–9. doi:10.1186/2050-2974-2-1

Stice, E. (2002). Risk and maintenance factors for eating pathology: A meta-analytic review. *Psychological Bulletin, 128*, 825–848. doi:10.1037/0033-2909.128.5.825

Stice, E., Marti, C. N., & Durant, S. (2011). Risk factors for onset of eating disorders: Evidence of multiple risk pathways from an 8-year prospective study. *Behaviour Research and Therapy, 49*, 622–627. doi:10.1016/j.brat.2011.06.009

Striegel-Moore, R. H., & Bulik, C. M. (2007). Risk factors for eating disorders. *American Psychologist, 62*, 181–198. doi:10.1037/0003-066X.62.3.181

Svaldi, J., Griepenstroh, J., Tuschen-Caffier, B., & Ehring, T. (2012). Emotion regulation deficits in eating disorders: A marker of eating pathology or general psychopathology? *Psychiatry Research, 197*, 103–111. doi:10.1016/j.psychres.2011.11.009

Torresan, R. C., Ramos-Cerqueira, A. T., Shavitt, R. G., do Rosario, M. C., de Mathis, M. A., Miguel, E. C., & Torres, A. R. (2013). Symptom dimensions, clinical course and comorbidity in men and women with obsessive-compulsive disorder. *Psychiatry Research, 209*, 186–195. doi:10.1016/j.psychres.2012.12.006

Van Diest, A. M. K., & Perez, M. (2013). Exploring the integration of thin-ideal internalization and self-objectification in the prevention of eating disorders. *Body Image, 10*, 16–25. doi:10.1016/j.bodyim.2012.10.004

van Passel, B., Danner, U., Dingemans, A., van Furth, E., Sternheim, L., van Elburg, A., . . . Cath, D. (2016). Cognitive remediation therapy (CRT) as a treatment enhancer of eating disorders and obsessive compulsive disorders: Study protocol for a randomized controlled trial. *BMC Psychiatry, 16*, 393. doi:10.1186/s12888-016-1109-x

Vartanian, L. R., & Dey, S. (2013). Self-concept clarity, thin-ideal internalization, and appearance-related social comparison as predictors of body dissatisfaction. *Body Image, 10*, 495–500. doi:10.1016/j.bodyim.2013.05.004

Wade, T. D., O'Shea, A., & Shafran, R. (2016). Perfectionism and eating disorders. In F. M. Sirois & D. S. Molnar (Eds.), *Perfectionism, health, & well-being* (pp. 205–222). Cham, Switzerland: Springer International.

Wild, B., Eichler, M., Feiler, S., Friederich, H. C., Hartmann, M., Herzog, W., . . . Zipfel, S. (2007). Dynamic analysis of electronic diary data of obese patients with and without binge eating disorder. *Psychotherapy and Psychosomatics, 76*, 250–252. doi:10.1159/000101505

Wonderlich, S. A., Connolly, K. M., & Stice, E. (2004). Impulsivity as a risk factor for eating disorder behavior: Assessment implications with adolescents. *International Journal of Eating Disorders, 36*, 172–182. doi:10.1002/eat.20033

INTERPERSONAL AND SOCIOCULTURAL FACTORS

Introduction

Multiple interpersonal and sociocultural factors can have a negative influence on eating disorder behaviors and related concerns. Some factors associated with family, peers, and the media, when examined together, have been found to result in a higher degree of body dissatisfaction and a greater likelihood of how much control over food intake someone is exerting (Dunkley, Wertheim, & Paxton, 2001). This chapter will examine some of the influences found among interpersonal factors, including peers and family, and sociocultural influences including mass media, social media, and video games.

Interpersonal Factors

Disconnection from important others such as peers and family can put individuals at risk for developing a variety of issues. Disconnection from others often results in feelings of loneliness that have been identified as an important contributing factor to eating disorders (Levine, 2012). Teasing and bullying by those most important to us contributes to feeling disconnected from others, feeling lonely, and can put individuals at greater risk for eating disorder-related behaviors in addition to depression, anxiety, and a decrease in self-esteem (Libbey, Story, Neumark-Sztainer, & Boutelle, 2008). A discussion of factors related to peer relationships and family relationships as they relate to eating disorders follows.

Peers

Peer relationships in addition to relationships with parents have been shown to contribute to body dissatisfaction and eating disorder-related behaviors (Eisenberg, Neumark-Sztainer, Story, & Perry, 2005; Marcos, Sebastián, Aubalat, Ausina, & Treasure,

2013), particularly if the nature of the communication involves the importance of being thin and being critical of one's appearance (Linville, Stice, Gau, & O'Neil, 2011; Vincent & McCabe, 2000). These and other relationships, however, when appropriately supportive, have also been shown to be critical to an individual's recovery process (Marcos & Cantero, 2009) (see Chapter 12).

Keel and Forney (2013) identified peer relationships as "self-selected environments" for adolescents and that these relationships can directly impact the risk an adolescent may have for developing an eating disorder. Since we tend to gravitate toward those who share similar interests and characteristics, if those interests and characteristics are known risk factors for eating disorders (e.g., perfectionism, drive for thinness) then peer relationships may unintentionally place someone at even greater risk. By contrast, the reverse is true. If peer relationships are selected based on shared interests and characteristics that are not linked to eating disorder risk, then peer relationships may serve as a buffer against developing an eating disorder. Thus, who we are influences who we select as friends rather than our friends influencing who we are; however, once we have selected our friends they are in a position to influence the behaviors we engage in, which can include eating disorder behaviors (Zalta & Keel, 2006).

Studies that examined friendship influence on eating disorder behaviors over several years revealed that when friends dieted there was a greater chance of body dissatisfaction, drive for thinness, and engaging in eating disorder behaviors designed to control one's weight (Eisenberg & Neumark-Sztainer, 2010; Keel, Forney, Brown, & Heatherton, 2013; Paxton, Eisenberg, & Neumark-Sztainer, 2006). For women, but not men, the behaviors of one's college roommate affected women's own behavior in the long term. When women had a college roommate who dieted, they were more likely to have a higher drive to be thin, and to be engaged in eating disorder-related behaviors up to a decade later (Keel et al., 2013).

The effects of the media will be discussed in greater detail in the section "Sociocultural Factors"; however, despite the extensive research demonstrating the impact that media (e.g., television, social media) has on individuals' views of themselves and the behaviors in which they engage, peer relationships may very-well trump some of those effects. An examination of the effects of social media use, television viewing, and the degree to which adolescents felt competitive with their peers revealed that peer competition had a greater influence on factors such as overall life-satisfaction, body dissatisfaction, and eating disorder-related behaviors than the forms of media investigated. Exposure to social media was found to exacerbate peer competition but that peer competition itself had a more direct impact on adolescent perceptions and behaviors (Ferguson, Muñoz, Garza, & Galindo, 2014). Similarly, researchers have found that *how* individuals use Facebook, including using it as a platform for social comparison with peers, is more predictive of eating disorder-related behavior than use of Facebook alone (Mabe, Forney, & Keel, 2014).

Linville, Brown, Sturm, and McDougal (2012) examined how social support may help or hinder the recovery process in women. They found that helping processes that benefitted women in their recovery involved feeling connected to others, having close relationships, hearing supportive comments, having friends who were empathic, and feeling compassion from others. Processes that interfered with successful recovery included comments that trivialized what they were going through, too much attention given to food and eating, avoiding talking about the eating disorder, feeling isolated, feeling stereotyped or stigmatized by others, and hearing hurtful comments about their weight.

Family

There is more than one way to think about families in the context of eating disorders. One involves the degree to which family members may affect or otherwise influence someone who has an eating disorder, and another is in terms of the impact the eating disorder has on family members themselves. Research has suggested that problems within the family and the expression of negative emotions could be a factor in the development of eating disorders and may have an effect on the eating disorder itself. Additionally, problems in the family that predate the onset of an eating disorder will likely be exacerbated by the presence of the disorder (Hooper & Williams, 2011).

Young women diagnosed with eating disorders have been found to have significant family problems related to mental health, problem solving, clarity of role expectations, ability of family members to respond to one another with appropriate feelings, and overall functioning (McGrane & Carr, 2002). The quality of the relationships between family members may have an effect on how serious an eating disorder in the family may be. For example, a child with an eating disorder may experience more significant and severe symptoms if his or her relationship with one or both parents is difficult (Amianto, Abbate-Daga, Morando, Sobrero, & Fassino, 2011), and if the relationship between the mother and father themselves is strained (Latzer, Lavee, & Gal, 2009). Additionally, some personality traits that may negatively impact the quality of relationships in general found in parents have been linked to the child's own personality and eating disorder behaviors (Amianto, Ercole, Marzola, Daga, & Fassino, 2015).

Family or parental dysfunction has been routinely linked to eating disorders (Berge, Loth, Hanson, Croll, & Neumark-Sztainer, 2012; Berge et al., 2014; Cerniglia et al., 2017; Federico, 2015; Le Grange, Lock, Loeb, & Nicholls, 2010; Wenzlaff, Schmidt, Brauhardt, & Hilbert, 2016). Factors such as poor communication, avoidance of conflict, and inappropriately high dependence on family members was linked to behaviors related to eating disorders (Berge et al., 2014). Moreover, increasing severity of eating disorder symptoms occurred as family dysfunction increased (Wisotsky et al., 2003). Recently, researchers have found that family dysfunction may vary based on which eating disorder diagnosis is present within the family.

Cerniglia et al. (2017) studied patients with an eating disorder and their families to determine if problematic family characteristics might vary based on which eating disorder diagnosis a child in the family had. Overall, they found that they were able to generate disorder-specific family profiles, all of which were different from what is known to reflect healthy family functioning (e.g., high cohesion and flexibility, low **enmeshment** and rigidity). When **anorexia nervosa** was the diagnosis of an adolescent family member, there was low satisfaction within the family itself as well as problems with maintaining boundaries between family members and difficulty of the family to tolerate conflict. In families with a child diagnosed with **bulimia nervosa**, the families were identified as being more chaotic than families with a child with anorexia nervosa. They also reported that such families were less flexible and less cohesive in comparison to the other two family profiles. Finally, in families where a child had a **binge eating disorder** diagnosis, families were rated as having better cohesion and flexibility scores compared to the other two family profiles but were also described as being too enmeshed and as having poor communication.

These family profiles were also connected to the nature of the symptoms experienced by the family member diagnosed with an eating disorder (Cerniglia et al., 2017). When anorexia nervosa was the diagnosis, the individual was likely to experience greater degrees of somatization if the family was high in rigidity; however, when the family was highly enmeshed there were greater levels of anxiety in the family member with anorexia nervosa. Those diagnosed with bulimia nervosa in families characterized by rigidity were more likely to experience depression; however, if the family had poor communication and/or there were low levels of family satisfaction, then the adolescent was more likely to be more interpersonally sensitive, which reflects feelings of inferiority and inadequacy when comparing themselves to others. Adolescents with a diagnosis of binge eating disorder in families characterized by rigidity were likely to experience higher levels of interpersonal sensitivity.

Among parents who have a child with an eating disorder, mothers and fathers are both impacted but in ways that differ from one another (Anastasiadou, Sepulveda, Parks, Cuellar-Flores, & Graell, 2016). Mothers of individuals with eating disorders are more likely to report feeling high levels of anxiety and being more emotionally overinvolved or enmeshed with their child than fathers. They were also more likely to be aware of both their positive and negative reactions to their child and in regards to the process of being a caretaker of that child. Fathers also reported feeling anxiety but were also more likely to accommodate eating disorder behaviors in their child compared to mothers. These experiences not only illustrate the effects an eating disorder may have on loved ones, particularly parents, but also partially explain the severity of the eating disorder itself. That is, even though the reactions reported by mothers and fathers may exist because their child has an eating disorder, the fact that the parents have these reactions negatively impacts the child and his or her eating disorder symptoms, making them worse (Ravi, Forsberg, Fitzpatrick, & Lock, 2009; Treasure & Schmidt, 2013).

There is often a heavy burden associated with providing care for an individual with an eating disorder (Ágh et al., 2016; Padierna et al., 2013), and family members caring for individuals with anorexia nervosa specifically were more likely to be depressed and anxious, have a higher chance of divorce, and experience a high degree of burden (Padierna et al., 2013; Zabala, Macdonald, & Treasure, 2009). These findings are important not only in terms of the reported distress from caregivers, but when compared to those caring for someone with psychosis (e.g., schizophrenia) the levels of anxiety, depression, and burden experienced by caregivers of those with anorexia nervosa was higher (Zabala et al., 2009). The anxiety and depression experienced by caregivers is likely a result of the burden of providing care while the experience of anxiety and depression itself likely influences how the burden is perceived.

Those with higher levels of depression or anxiety are more likely to perceive a greater burden compared to those without or with lower levels of depression or anxiety even if the objective burden is the same (Padierna et al., 2013). A higher degree of burden was also experienced in caregivers who had a lower level of education and when the family member diagnosed with an eating disorder had a low quality of life. This burden was reported in terms of degree of tension and worry about the family member, particularly with respect to the family member's health, their future, their treatment, and the degree of tension in the relationship itself. Padierna et al. (2013) also found that burden was noticeable among caregivers based on the degree to which regular family functioning had been disrupted due to the need to highly focus on helping the family member eat and ensuring that they followed treatment recommendations. These findings represent what these researchers called "objective burden," but they also noted that these families reported high levels of "subjective burden," which simply refers to the caregivers' personal experience of the amount of burden with which they are trying to cope. Padierna et al. concluded by stating that the degree of burden reported by family member caregivers is directly related to how they perceive the symptoms of the family member with an eating disorder.

Attachment

Attachment refers to the emotional connection or bond that exists between a parent and child and can range from satisfactory or secure to unsatisfactory or insecure. Ainsworth and colleagues (1978) developed a method of studying infants and the degree to which they were attached or psychologically and emotionally bonded with their primary caretaker, which at the time would predominantly have been the child's mother. The method they devised was called the "strange situation" and involved various combinations of the child, the child's mother, and a stranger in a room together. Ainsworth was primarily focused on how the baby responded to the mother when she returned after the baby had been alone or with a stranger for a few minutes. Based on their observations, Ainsworth and colleagues identified three distinct attachment patterns: secure, anxious-avoidant, and anxious-ambivalent. The last two patterns are considered insecure forms of attachment.

Securely attached children were observed to be comfortable exploring their surroundings when their primary caretaker was present, would interact with the stranger in the room, and would show distress when their primary caretaker left. Upon her return, infants would be happy to see the primary caretaker. Anxious-ambivalent attachment (a form of insecure attachment) was observed in infants who did not explore their surroundings very much, were cautious around strangers, and showed a high level of distress when the primary caretaker left the room. Upon the caretaker's return, infants were likely to display ambivalence toward her in the form of anger or helplessness. Finally, the anxious-avoidant attachment (another form of insecure attachment) was observed in infants who seemed to avoid their primary caretaker both while in the room with the caretaker and upon her return after leaving the room. These infants were also not likely to explore their surroundings regardless of who was in the room with them. Although these infants appeared to not be in distress, Ainsworth and colleagues hypothesized that their indifference was a protective mechanism or a mask to hide their distress.

All three attachment styles are believed to reflect the degree to which the child has had his or her basic needs met by the caretaker (Ainsworth, Blehar, Waters, & Wall, 1978). Securely attached children have consistently had their needs met (though not perfectly), which results in the infant knowing he or she can count on the primary caretaker to be there when needed. The anxious-ambivalent attachment style is believed to reflect caretaking that has been unpredictable, and the infant's reaction of anger or helplessness when the caregiver returns is believed to be a way for the infant to keep the caregiver around, thereby taking control of the situation to try to ensure his or her needs will be met. Finally, the anxious-avoidant attachment style is believed to reflect the experience that the infant's needs will not be met and that no matter what the infant does he or she will not get what is needed.

Insecure attachment styles have been found among those diagnosed with eating disorders (Caglar-Nazali et al., 2014; Tasca & Balfour, 2014). Tasca and Balfour (2014) reviewed 50 studies that examined eating disorders in adults and attachment style. They specifically looked at how well individuals are able to regulate their affect, how they relate to others, the degree to which they are able to reasonably talk about their most important (i.e., attachment) relationships without becoming overwhelmed emotionally or cognitively, how well they are able to recognize that their internal experiences are separate from others, and the degree to which they could recognize that their internal experiences influence their behaviors. Overall, Tasca and Balfour found those diagnosed with an eating disorder were more likely to have one of the two types of insecure attachment compared to those without an eating disorder diagnosis and were more likely to have difficulty separating their own internal experiences from that of others. Additionally, those with an eating disorder diagnosis were found to be more likely to either overcontrol or undercontrol their affective experiences. Interpersonally, their review revealed that those with an eating disorder diagnosis may have a stronger need for approval and a higher fear of abandonment, particularly if the need for approval from others is high. Collectively, these experiences may impact how severe the individual's eating disorder symptoms are.

Not all who have an insecure attachment style ultimately develop an eating disorder. Some researchers have noted that certain psychological factors (see Chapter 6) may have an influence. Dakanalis et al. (2015) noted that high degrees of perfectionism were not only related to eating disorders but that problematic forms of perfectionism helped to explain the relationship between an insecure attachment style and eating disorders. Thus, while insecure attachment styles have been connected with eating disorders (Caglar-Nazali et al., 2013; Tasca & Balfour, 2014), it is possible that the presence and nature of an individual's perfectionism may explain why some insecurely attached individuals do develop an eating disorder whereas others do not.

Sociocultural Factors

Some of the factors associated with eating disorders, particularly the drive for thinness, tend to be more pronounced in cultures in which food is plentiful, whereas in cultures in which food is less abundant a larger body size is more highly valued (Polivy & Herman, 2002). Sociocultural factors include those things that an individual is exposed to as he or she relates to the society or culture in which he or she exists. For some, the society and cultural expectations may be protective factors keeping the eating disorder and related symptoms at bay, whereas for others society and cultural prescriptions may overtly support or even glamorize eating disorder symptomology.

Mass Media (television, magazines)

Mass media is considered to be a factor to which many if not most people in westernized societies are exposed on a daily basis and that is used in a variety of ways including for entertainment, to educate one's self, and as an outlet to explore who one is as an individual (Levine & Murnen, 2009). Of course, mass media is not necessarily something we use solely for our own purposes since one major reason the various forms of media exist is as a means of mass marketing, including selling the ideal image of beauty (Ballentine & Ogle, 2005).

In terms of media exposure for children and adolescents, the Council on Communications and Media of the American Academy of Pediatrics has published two articles addressing media in general and digital media in particular. In their statement on media in general, the Council on Communications and Media (2013) stated its concerns about the amount of time children and adolescents spend consuming media and their subsequent exposure to violence, sexually themed images, substance use, and so on. They also stated that media can be used for prosocial efforts designed to educate, teach empathy, expand comfort with racial and ethnic diversity, and so on. As digital media has gained widespread use, the American Academy of Pediatrics published a second statement reflecting similar ideas to that on media in general (Chassiakos et al., 2016). This paper stated that digital media can be beneficial in ways similar to that of traditional forms of media, but can be harmful in ways potentially unique to this form of media: sleep and attention problems, higher rates of depression, exposure to inappropriate or inaccurate information, and problems with privacy and **confidentiality**.

Exposure to mass media that frequently portrays images of the ideal body type (for females and males) are believed to facilitate the development of body dissatisfaction. When body dissatisfaction develops individuals are more likely to experience negative emotions, a decrease in self-esteem, self-objectification, dieting, and may ultimately develop eating disorder symptoms (Agliata & Tantleff-Dunn, 2004; Bartlett, Vowels, & Saucier, 2008; Cramblitt & Pritchard, 2013; Dakanalis et al., 2015; Fernandez & Pritchard, 2012; Grabe, Ward, & Hyde, 2008; Hausenblas et al., 2013; Levine & Harrison, 2004; Stice, Ziemba, Margolis, & Flick, 1996). Additional research has revealed that long-term exposure to media images that feature the thin-ideal does not automatically result in long-term negative effects (Stice, Spangler, & Agras, 2001). In fact, these findings revealed that those who are vulnerable to such images are more likely to experience negative effects over the long term. Factors that create vulnerability for some adolescent females include the degree to which they feel pressure to be thin, have existing body dissatisfaction, and have poor social support. The degree to which someone internalizes the thin-ideal (see Chapter 6) is the link between exposure to fashion magazines and how strongly someone pursues becoming thin (Saito, 2017). Thus, making appearance-based comparisons between one's self and those portrayed in the media has been connected to internalization of the thin ideal (Van Vonderen & Kinnally, 2012); however, internalization of sex-specific body ideals may not impact males and females the same way. Internalization of the muscular ideal for males has been hypothesized to not have as strong an impact as internalization of the thin ideal for females (Levine & Chapman, 2010).

The concern about the impact of media on children and adolescents is reflected in the Policy Statement produced by the Council on Communications and Media (2013) of the American Academy of Pediatrics. This statement acknowledges the prominence of media including "new media" (e.g., cell phones, social media) in children's' lives and recommends that specific questions about a child's media use be asked at every well-child visit and that all households should have a plan regarding how much media a child should be exposed to daily and where media devices should exist (e.g., living room, a child's bedroom, etc.). There is much to be said about the role media may play in the development of an eating disorder. Western media in particular may play a significant role. Interestingly, despite the concern about the effect media may have on children, it is possible that children in the age range of 3 to 6 years old are not negatively impacted by appearance-related media (Hayes & Tantleff-Dunn, 2010).

Most girls aged 3 to 6 were satisfied with how they looked; however, those who did report having concerns about their body (i.e., they worry about becoming fat or they would change something about their body) did not feel worse after having been exposed to appearance-related media (Hayes & Tantleff-Dunn, 2010). The thinking is that rather than comparing themselves to characters or images that have the ideal **body image**, they identify with their favorite characters and therefore do not see them as a standard by which to compare themselves. This seems to change around age 6 when children this age are more likely to be dissatisfied with their bodies with a preference for a body that is thinner than what they have (Dittmar, Halliwell, & Ive, 2006; Dohnt & Tiggemann, 2006).

One of the most interesting studies to examine the effect of western media on the development of eating disorder symptoms was conducted in the late 1990s. This study examined the prevalence of eating disorder symptomology before and after the introduction of western media to adolescent girls living in Fiji (Becker, Burwell, Gilman, Herzog, & Hamburg, 2002). The authors noted that Fiji historically has a low-prevalence rate of eating disorders, has a culture that values a larger body size, and the particular province of Fiji they studied until the mid-1990s did not have television. The percentage of high scores among Fijian girls on a questionnaire designed to measure eating disorder symptoms more than doubled from 1995 to 1998. In particular, there was a significant increase in symptoms such as self-induced vomiting and dieting behaviors. They also found that attitudes toward dieting in general, weight loss, and appearance shifted after the introduction of television, indicating that more Fijian girls valued dieting and weight loss, and a thinner body size. Many years later, Becker et al. (2011) returned to Fiji and found that exposure to social media was also associated with eating disorder-related behaviors.

Similar findings were identified in the Czech Republic, which transitioned from a "socialist Eastern Block country to a western-type democracy" (Pavlova, Uher, Dragomircka, & Papezova, 2010, p. 541) and saw a significant increase in hospitalizations for eating disorders throughout the 1990s. This leads the authors to conclude that eating disorders are influenced by changes that occur in the culture of a country. Other studies have linked the occurrence of eating disorders in non-Western countries to many substantial influences including exposure to mass media (Becker et al., 2011; Eddy, Hennessey, & Thompson-Brenner, 2007). Other evidence indicates that the influence of mass media in Western societies may not affect all races the same and that Black adults specifically have been shown to be less likely to compare themselves to those portrayed in the media and were less aware of the ideal body type portrayed in the media (Quick & Byrd-Bredbenner, 2014).

Interestingly, another examination of the literature confirmed that mass media has an impact on eating disorder symptoms but that the influence is not equal between bulimia nervosa and anorexia nervosa. Bulimia nervosa was found to be more closely tied to cultural influences such as exposure to mass media that perpetuate the thin ideal than anorexia nervosa (Keel & Klump, 2003).

Web-Based Media (websites, social media)

Exposure to web-based media and its effect on factors related to eating disorders is a relatively new area of study. Given the findings associated with mass media exposure and its effects on factors such as body dissatisfaction, drive for thinness, and eating disorder symptoms specifically, it is not surprising that research on exposure to web-based media has yielded similar results (e.g., Becker et al., 2011; Mabe et al., 2014; Tiggemann & Slater, 2013). The use of the Internet in general has been shown to affect the degree to which adolescent girls internalize the thin-ideal, monitor their body and have concern about how it looks to others, and the drive to become thin (Tiggemann & Slater, 2013). Extensive use of the social media platform Facebook, in particular, has been connected with a higher rate of eating disorder-related behaviors, body image concern, the perpetuation of weight concerns, thin-ideal internalization, drive for thinness, self-objectification, and temporary feelings of anxiety (Mabe et al., 2014; Meier & Gray, 2014; Stronge et al., 2015; Tiggemann & Slater, 2013). This seems to be the case, however, depending on *how* the social media platform is used (e.g., making appearance-based comparisons) (Fardouly, Diedrichs, Vartanian, & Halliwell, 2015; Fardouly & Vartanian, 2016; Meier & Gray, 2014).

Along with the proliferation of social media platforms has been an emergence of websites that have a pro-eating disorder message, which is viewed as an "alternative lifestyle" rather than a mental health disorder (Chancellor, Pater, Clear, Gilbert, & De Choudhury, 2016). Websites that encourage bulimia-related behavior are called "pro-mia" or "e-mia" sites, and those that encourage anorexia-related behavior are called "pro-ana" or "e-ana" websites. Overall, these sites encourage users to try eating disorder behaviors related to anorexia nervosa and bulimia nervosa such as fasting or vomiting to attain a thin body, and they post images of thin, often emaciated women as "thinspiration" or "thinspo" (Borzekowski, Schenk, Wilson, & Peebles, 2010). Some social media platforms such as Instagram® have taken steps to prevent individuals from using search terms that will land users on pro-eating disorder websites; however, owners of such websites have changed the search terminology to ensure those who want to consume such sites can still find them (Chancellor et al., 2016). Perhaps not surprisingly, websites with a pro-eating disorder focus have been found to be associated with body dissatisfaction, dieting behavior, lower quality of life, negative affect, and eating disorder-related behaviors (Peebles et al., 2012; Rodgers, Lowy, Halperin, & Franko, 2016).

Video Games

A final sociocultural factor that has been found to negatively impact males and females is video games. Despite a lot of negative press regarding video games (e.g., many are too violent), some researchers have stated that there are many benefits of video game playing including benefits associated with play in general, and benefits associated with more efficient cognitive processing and creativity (Granic, Lobel, & Engels, 2014). Others have grown concerned about how people are graphically represented in many games and have found, at least for female characters, that characters created to look as graphically realistic as possible are generally thinner than the average female (Martins, Williams, Harrison, & Ratan, 2009). Others found that in comparison to male characters, female characters were more likely to have an unrealistic body and were more likely to be sexualized

(Downs & Smith, 2010). A great deal of research has been devoted to how female characters are portrayed in video games, particularly with respect to role type, body shape, and sexualization (e.g., Behm-Morawitz & Mastro, 2009; Miller & Summers, 2007); however, both males and females have been found to experience negative effects of playing video games that unrealistically represent male and female body types, which tend to be thin and curvy for females (Martins et al., 2009) and hyper-masculine for males (Sylvia, King, & Morse, 2014). For example, after playing a video game for 15 minutes that featured male characters representing the muscular ideal or characters that represented the thin ideal, both males and females reported feeling worse about their bodies (Bartlett & Harris, 2008), and men who played a realistic video game depicting the hyper-masculine body type reported greater body dissatisfaction (Sylvia et al., 2014).

Conclusion

A number of factors can contribute to the development of eating disorders. Interpersonal relationships in the form of friendships and relationships with family members can influence how someone views his or her body and the degree to which he or she desires to pursue the thin ideal. By contrast, when these relationships are more supportive, they can be a buffer against other factors that may contribute to the development of an eating disorder. Sociocultural factors, too, have been implicated in the development of eating disorders. Mass media, social media, and video games have all been found to negatively impact body image perception in both males and females.

References

Ágh, T., Kovács, G., Supina, D., Pawaskar, M., Herman, B. K., & Vokó, Z., . . . Sheehand, D. V. (2016). A systematic review of the health-related quality of life and economic burden of anorexia nervosa, bulimia nervosa, and binge eating disorder. *Eating and Weight Disorders, 21*, 353–364. doi:10.1007/s40519-016-0264-x

Agliata, D., & Tantleff-Dunn, S. (2004). The impact of media exposure on males' body image. *Journal of Social and Clinical Psychology, 23*, 7–22. doi:10.1521/jscp.23.1.7.26988

Ainsworth, M. D. S., Blehar, M. C., Waters, E., & Wall, S. (1978). *Patterns of attachment: A psychological study of the strange situation.* Hillsdale, NJ: Earlbaum.

Amianto, F., Abbate-Daga, G., Morando, S., Sobrero, C., & Fassino, S. (2011). Personality development characteristics of women with anorexia nervosa, their healthy siblings and healthy controls: What prevents and what relates to psychopathology? *Psychiatry Research, 187*, 401–408. doi:10.1016/j.psychres.2010.10.028

Amianto, F., Ercole, R., Marzola, E., Daga, G. A., & Fassino, S. (2015). Parents' personality clusters and eating disordered daughters' personality psychopathology. *Psychiatry Research, 230*, 19–27. doi:10.1016/j.psychres.2015.07.048

Anastasiadou, D., Sepulveda, A. R., Parks, M., Cuellar-Flores, I., & Graell, M. (2016). The relationship between dysfunctional family patterns and symptom severity among adolescent patients with eating disorders: A gender-specific approach. *Women & Health, 56*, 695–712. doi:10.1080/03630242.2015.1118728

Ballentine, L. W., & Ogle, J. P. (2005). The making and unmaking of body problems in *Seventeen* magazine, 1992–2003. *Family and Consumer Sciences Research Journal, 33*, 281–307. doi:10.1177/1077727X04274114

Bartlett, C. P., & Harris, R. J. (2008). The impact of body emphasizing video games on body image concerns in men and women. *Sex Roles, 59*, 586–601. doi:10.1007/s11199-008-9457-8

Bartlett, C. P., Vowels, C. L., & Saucier, D. A. (2008). Meta-analyses of the effects of media images on men's body-image concerns. *Journal of Social and Clinical Psychology, 27*, 279–310. doi:10.1521/jscp.2008.27.3.279

Becker, A. E., Burwell, R. A., Gilman, S. E., Herzog, D. B., & Hamburg, P. (2002). Eating behaviours and attitudes following prolonged exposure to television among ethnic Fijian adolescent girls. *British Journal of Psychiatry, 180*, 509–514. doi:10.1192/bjp.180.6.509

Becker, A. E., Fay, K. E., Agnew-Blais, J., Khan, A. N., Stiegel-Moore, R. H., & Gilman, S. E. (2011). Social network media exposure and adolescent eating pathology in Fiji. *British Journal of Psychiatry, 198*, 43–50. doi:10.1192/bjp.bp.110.078675

Behm-Morawitz, E., & Mastro, D. (2009). The effects of the sexualization of female video game characters on gender stereotyping and female self-concept. *Sex Roles, 61*, 808–823. doi:10.1007/s11199-009-9683-8

Berge, J. M., Loth, K., Hanson, C., Croll, J., & Neumark-Sztainer, D. (2012). Family life cycle transitions and the onset of eating disorders: A retrospective grounded theory approach. *Journal of Clinical Nursing, 21*, 1355–1363. doi:10.1111/j.1365-2702.2011.03762.x

Berge, J. M., Wall, M., Larson, N., Eisenbert, M. E., Loth, K. A., & Neumark-Sztainer, D. (2014). The unique and additive associations of family functioning and parenting practices with disordered eating behaviors in diverse adolescents. *Journal of Behavioral Medicine, 37*, 205–217. doi:10.1007/s10865-012-9478-1

Borzekowski, D. L. G., Schenk, S., Wilson, J. L., & Peebles, R. (2010). e-Ana and e-Mia: A content analysis of pro-eating disorder websites. *American Journal of Public Health, 100*, 1526–1534. doi:10.2105/AJPH.2009.172700

Caglar-Nazali, H. P., Corfield, F., Cardi, V., Ambwani, S., Leppanen, J., Olabintan, O., . . . Treasure, J. (2014). A systematic review and meta-analysis of 'Systems for Social Processes' in eating disorders. *Neuroscience and Biobehavioral Reviews, 42*, 55–92. doi:10.1016/j.neubiorev.2013.12.002

Cerniglia, L., Cimino, S., Tafà, M., Marzilli, E., Ballarotto, G., & Bracaglia, F. (2017). Family profiles in eating disorders: Family functioning and psychopathology. *Psychology Research and Behavior Management, 10*, 305–312. doi:10.2147/PRBM.S145463

Chancellor, S., Pater, J. A., Clear, T., Gilbert, E., & De Choudhury, M. (2016). #thyghgapp: *Instagram content moderation and lexical variation in pro-eating disorder communities. Proceedings from CSCW '16: Computer-Supported Cooperative Work & Social Computing.* New York, NY: Association for Computing Machinery.

Chassiakos, Y. R., Radesky, J., Christakis, D., Moreno, M. A. Cross, C., FAAP, & Council on Communications and Media. (2016). Children and adolescents and digital media. *Pediatrics, 138*, e1–e18. doi:10.1542/peds.2016-2593

Council on Communications and Media. (2013). Children, adolescents, and the media. *Pediatrics, 132*, 958–961. doi:10.1542/peds.2013-2656

Cramblitt, B., & Pritchard, M. (2013). Media's influence on the drive for muscularity in undergraduates. *Eating Behaviors, 14*, 441–446. doi:10.1016/j.eatbeh.2013.08.003

Dakanalis, A., Carrà, G., Calogero, R., Fida, R., Clerici, M., & Zanetti, M. A., . . . Riva, G. (2015). The developmental effects of media-ideal internalization and self-objectification processes on adolescents' negative body-feelings, dietary restraint, and binge eating. *European Child and Adolescent Psychiatry, 24*, 997–1010. doi:10.1007/s00787-014-0649-1

Dittmar, H., Halliwell, E., & Ive, S. (2006). Does Barbie make girls want to be thin? The effect of experimental exposure to images of dolls on the body image of 5- to 8-year old girls. *Developmental Psychology, 42*, 283–292. doi:10.1037/0012-1649.42.2.283

Dohnt, H., & Tiggemann, M. (2006). Body image concerns in young girls: The role of peers and media prior to adolescence. *Journal of Youth and Adolescence, 35*, 141–151. doi:10.1007/s10964-005-9020-7

Downs, E., & Smith, S. L. (2010). Keeping abreast of hypersexuality: A video game character analysis. *Sex Roles, 62*, 721–733. doi:10.1007/s11199-009-9637-1

Dunkley, T. L., Wertheim, E. H., & Paxton, S. J. (2001). Examination of a model of multiple sociocultural influences on adolescent girls' body dissatisfaction and dietary restraint. *Adolescence, 36*, 265–279.

Eddy, K. T., Hennessey M., & Thompson-Brenner H. (2007). Eating pathology in East African women: The role of media exposure and globalization. *Journal of Nervous and Mental Disorders, 195*, 196–202. doi:10.1097/01.nmd.0000243922.49394.7d

Eisenberg, M. E., & Neumark-Sztainer, D. (2010). Friends' dieting and disordered eating behaviors among adolescents five years later: Findings from project EAT. *Journal of Adolescent Health, 47*, 67–73. doi:10.1016/j.jadohealth.2009.12.030

Eisenberg, M. E., Neumark-Sztainer, D., Story, M., & Perry, C. (2005). The role of social norms and friends' influences on unhealthy weight-control behaviors among adolescent girls. *Social Science & Medicine, 60*, 1165–1173. doi:10.1016/j.socscimed.2004.06.055

Fardouly, J., Diedrichs, P. C., Vartanian, L., & Halliwell, E. (2015). Social comparisons on social media: The impact of Facebook on young women's body image concerns and mood. *Body Image, 13*, 38–45. doi:10.1016/j.bodyim.2014.12.002

Fardouly, J., & Vartanian, L. R. (2016). Social media and body image concerns: Current research and future directions. *Current Opinion in Psychology, 9*, 1–5. doi:10.1016/j.copsyc.2015.09.005

Federico, A. (2015). Parents' personality clusters and eating disordered daughters' personality and psychopathology. *Psychiatry Research, 230*, 19–27. doi:10.1016/j.psychres.2015.07.048

Ferguson, C. J., Muñoz, M. E., Garza, A., & Galindo, M. (2014). Concurrent and prospective analyses of peer, television and social media influences on body dissatisfaction, eating disorder symptoms and life satisfaction in adolescent girls. *Journal of Youth and Adolescence, 43*, 1–14. doi:10.1007/s10964-012-9898-9

Fernandez, S., & Pritchard, M. (2012). Relationships between social self-esteem, media influence and drive for thinness. *Eating Behaviors, 13*, 321–325. doi:10.1016/j.eatbeh.2012.05.004

Grabe, S., Ward, L. M., & Hyde, J. S. (2008). The role of media in body image concerns among women: A meta-analysis of experimental and correlational studies. *Psychological Bulletin, 134*, 460–476. doi:10.1037/0033-2909.134.3.460

Granic, I., Lobel, A., & Engels, R. C. M. E. (2014). The benefits of playing video games. *American Psychologist, 69*, 66–78. doi:10.1037/a0034857

Hausenblas, H. A., Campbell, A., Menzel, J. E., Doughty, J., Levine, M., & Thompson, J. K. (2013). Media effects of experimental presentation of the ideal physique on eating disorder symptoms: A meta-analysis of laboratory studies. *Clinical Psychology Review, 33*, 168–181. doi:10.1016/j.cpr.2012.10.011

Hayes, S., & Tantleff-Dunn, S. (2010). Am I too fat to be a princess? Examining the effects of popular children's media on young girls' body image. *British Journal of Developmental Psychology, 28*, 413–426. doi:10.1348/026151009X424240

Hooper, B., & Williams, E. B., (2011). Anorexia–Too complex an issue to simply blame mums. *Nutrition Bulletin, 36*, 216–220. doi:10.1111/j.1467-3010.2011.01893.x

Keel, P. D., & Forney, K. F. (2013). Psychosocial risk factors for eating disorders. *International Journal of Eating Disorders, 46*, 433–439. doi:10.1002/eat.22094

Keel, P. K., Forney, K. J., Brown, T. A., & Heatherton, T. F. (2013). Influence of college peers on disordered eating in women and men at 10-year follow-up. *Journal of Abnormal Psychology, 122*, 105–110. doi:10.1037/a0030081

Keel, P. K., & Klump, K. L. (2003). Are eating disorders culture-bound syndromes? Implications for conceptualizing their etiology. *Psychological Bulletin, 129*, 747–769. doi:10.1037/0033-2909.129.5.747

Latzer, Y., Lavee, Y., & Gal, S. (2009). Marital and parent-child relationships in families with daughters who have eating disorders. *Journal of Family Issues, 30*, 1201–1220. doi:10.1177/0192513X09334599

Le Grange, D., Lock, J., Loeb, K., & Nicholls, D. (2010). Academy for Eating Disorders position paper: The role of the family in eating disorders. *International Journal of Eating Disorders, 43*, 1–5. doi:10.1002/eat.20751

Levine, M. P. (2012). Loneliness and eating disorders. *The Journal of Psychology: Interdisciplinary and Applied, 146*, 243–257. doi:10.1080/00223980.2011.606435

Levine, M. P., & Chapman, K. (2010). Media influences on body image. In T. F. Cash & L. Smolak (Eds.), *Body image: A handbook of science, practice & prevention* (pp. 101–109). New York, NY: Guilford Press.

Levine, M. P., & Harrison, K. (2004). Media's role in the perpetuation and prevention of negative body image and disordered eating. In J. K. Thompson (Ed.), *Handbook of eating disorders & obesity* (pp. 695–717). Hoboken, NJ: John Wiley & Sons.

Levine, M. P., & Murnen, S. K. (2009). "Everybody knows that mass media are/are not [*pick one*] a cause of eating disorders": A critical review of evidence for a causal link between media, negative body image, and disordered eating in females. *Journal of Social and Clinical Psychology, 28*, 9–42. doi:10.1521/jscp.2009.28.1.9

Libbey, H. P., Story, M. T., Neumark-Sztainer, D. R., & Boutelle, K. N. (2008). Teasing, disordered eating behaviors, and psychological morbidities among overweight adolescents. *Obesity, 16*, S24–S29. doi:10.1038/oby.2008.455

Linville, D., Brown, T., Sturm, K., & McDougal, T. (2012). Eating disorders and social support: Perspectives of recovered individuals. *Eating Disorders, 20*, 216–231. doi:10.1080/10640266.2012.668480

Linville, D., Stice, E., Gau, J., & O'Neil, M. (2011). Parent and peer influences on increases in adolescent eating disorder risk factors and symptoms: A 3-year prospective study. *International Journal of Eating Disorders, 44*, 745–751. doi:10.1002/eat.20907

Mabe, A. G., Forney, K. J., & Keel, P. K. (2014). Do you "like" my photo? Facebook use maintains eating disorder risk. *International Journal of Eating Disorders, 47*, 516–523. doi:10.1002/eat.22254

Marcos, Y. Q., & Cantero, C. (2009). Assessment of social support dimensions in patients with eating disorders. *Spanish Journal of Psychology, 12*, 226–235. doi:10.1017/S1138741600001633

Marcos, Y. Q., Sebastián, M. J. Q., Aubalat, L. P., Ausina, J. B., & Treasure, J. (2013). Peer and family influence in eating disorders: A meta-analysis. *European Psychiatry, 28*, 199–206. doi:10.1016/j.eurpsy.2012.03.005

Martins, N., Williams, D. C., Harrison, K., & Ratan, R. A. (2009). A content analysis of body imagery in video games. *Sex Roles, 61*, 824–836. doi:10.1007/s11199-009-9682-9

McGrane, D., & Carr, A. (2002). Young women at risk for eating disorders: Perceived family dysfunction and parental psychological problems. *Contemporary Family Therapy, 24*, 385–395. doi:10.1023/A: 1015359610774

Meier, E. P., & Gray, J. (2014). Facebook photo activity associated with body image disturbance in adolescent girls. *Cyberpsychology, Behavior, and Social Networking, 17*, 199–206. doi:10.1089/cyber.2013.0305

Miller, M. K., & Summers, A. (2007). Gender differences in video games characters' roles, appearances, and attire as portrayed in video game magazines. *Sex Roles, 57*, 733–742. doi:10.1007/s11199-007-9307-0

Padierna, A., Martín, J., Aguirre, U., González, N., Muñoz, P., & Quintana, J. M. (2013). Burden of caregiving amongst family caregivers of patients with eating disorders. *Social Psychiatry and Psychiatric Epidemiology, 48*, 151–161. doi:10.1007/s00127-012-0525-6

Pavlova, B., Uher, R., Dragomirecka, E., & Papezova, H. (2010). Trends in hospital admissions for eating disorders in a country undergoing a socio-cultural transition, the Czech Republic 1981–2005. *Social Psychiatry and Psychiatric Epidemiology, 45*, 541–550. doi:10.1007/s00127-009-0092-7

Paxton, S. J., Eisenberg, M. E., & Neumark-Sztainer, D. (2006). Prospective predictors of body dissatisfaction in adolescent girls and boys: A five-year longitudinal study. *Developmental Psychology, 42*, 888–899. doi:10.1037/0012-1649.42.5.888

Peebles, R., Wilson, J. L., Litt, I. F., Hardy, K. K., Lock, J. D., & Mann, J. D., . . . Borzekowski, D. L. G. (2012). Disordered eating in a digital age: Eating behaviors, health, and quality of life in users of websites with pro-eating disorder content. *Journal of Medical Internet Research, 14*, e148. doi:10.2196/jmir.2023

Polivy, J., & Herman, C. P. (2002). Causes of eating disorders. *Annual Review of Psychology, 53*, 187–213. doi:10.1146/annurev.psych.53.100901.135103

Quick, V. M., & Byrd-Bredbenner, C. (2014). Disordered eating, socio-cultural media influencers, body image, and psychological factors among a racially/ethnically diverse population of college women. *Eating Behaviors, 15*, 37–41. doi:10.1016/j.eatbeh.2013.10.005

Ravi, S., Forsberg, S., Fitzpatrick, K., & Lock, J. (2009). Is there a relationship between parental self-reported psychopathology and symptoms severity in adolescents with anorexia nervosa? *Eating Disorders, 17*, 63–71. doi:10.1080/10640260802570122

Rodgers, R. F., Lowy, A. S., Halperin, D. M., & Franko, D. L. (2016). A meta-analysis examining the influence of pro-eating disorder websites on body image and eating pathology. *European Eating Disorders Review, 24*, 3–8. doi:10.1002/erv.2390

Saito, S. (2017). Media exposure and thin-ideal internalization in the drive for thinness in Japanese women. *Communication Research Reports, 34*, 89–97. doi:10.1080/08824096.2016.1224174

Stice, E., Spangler, D., & Agras, W. S. (2001). Exposure to media-portrayed thin-ideal images adversely affects vulnerable girls: A longitudinal experiment. *Journal of Social and Clinical Psychology, 20*, 270–288. doi:10.1521/jscp.20.3.270.22309

Stice, E., Ziemba, C., Margolis, J., & Flick, P. (1996). The dual pathway model differentiates bulimics, subclinical bulimics, and controls: Testing the continuity hypothesis. *Behavior Therapy, 27*, 531–549. doi:10.1016/S0005-7894(96)80042-6

Stronge, S., Greaves, L. M., Milojev, P., West-Newman, T., Barlow, F. K., & Sibley, C. G. (2015). Facebook is linked to body dissatisfaction: Comparing users and non-users. *Sex Roles, 73*, 200–213. doi:10.1007/s11199-015-0517-6

Sylvia, A., King, T. K., & Morse, B. J. (2014). Virtual ideals: The effect of video game play on male body image. *Computers in Human Behavior, 37*, 183–188. doi:10.1016/j.chb.2014.04.029

Tasca, G. A., & Balfour, L. (2014). Attachment and eating disorders: A review of current research. *International Journal of Eating Disorders, 47*, 710–717. doi:10.1002/eat.22302

Tiggemann, M., & Slater, A. (2013). NetGirls: The Internet, Facebook, and body image concern in adolescent girls. *International Journal of Eating Disorders, 46*, 630–633. doi:10.1002/eat.22141

Treasure, J., & Schmidt, U. (2013). The cognitive-interpersonal maintenance model of anorexia nervosa revisited: A summary of the evidence of cognitive, socio-emotional and interpersonal predisposing and perpetuating factors. *Journal of Eating Disorders, 1*, 1–13. doi:10.1186/2050-2974-1-13

Van Vonderen, K. E., & Kinnally, W. (2012). Media effects on body image: Examining media exposure in the broader context of internal and other social factors. *American Communication Journal, 14*, 41–57.

Vincent, M. A., & McCabe, M. P. (2000). Gender differences among adolescents in family, and peer influences on body dissatisfaction, weight loss, and binge eating behaviors. *Journal of Youth and Adolescence, 29*, 205–221. doi:10.1023/A: 1005156616173

Wenzlaff, A., Schmidt, R., Brauhardt, A., & Hilbert, A. (2016). Family functioning in adolescents with binge-eating disorder. *European Eating Disorders Review, 24*, 430–433. doi:10.1002/erv.2462

Wisotsky, W., Dancyger, I., Fornari, V., Katz, J., Wisotsky, W. L., & Swencionis, C. (2003). The relationship between eating pathology and perceived family functioning in eating disorder patients in a day treatment program. *Eating Disorders, 11*, 89–99. doi:10.1080/10640260390199280

Zabala, M. J., Macdonald, P., & Treasure, J. (2009). Appraisal of caregiving burden, expressed emotion and psychological distress in families of people with eating disorders: A systematic review. *European Eating Disorders Review, 17*, 338–349. doi:10.1002/erv.925

Zalta, A. K., & Keel, P. K. (2006). Peer influence on bulimic symptoms in college students. *Journal of Abnormal Psychology, 115*, 185–189. doi:10.1037/0021-843X.115.1.185

III

IDENTIFYING AND REFERRING THOSE WHO ARE AT RISK

SCREENING AND ASSESSMENT

▨ Introduction

Although the terms *screening* and *assessment* are used interchangeably by some, they are two different processes that serve two different purposes. The process of screening is typically a much briefer process than that which is involved in an assessment process. Screening involves gathering limited information, usually through a brief set of questions designed to pickup on specific symptoms that may indicate there is a problem. In this regard, screening serves the purpose of determining whether or not an assessment is warranted. Most screening tools have instructions that include something like if a person answers "yes" to two or more questions then a more thorough assessment should be conducted. An assessment serves the purpose of gathering more detailed information about symptoms and other indicators of a particular problem. As a result, the assessment process takes time and often multiple assessment tools to get enough information. The information gathered during an assessment not only helps to confirm or rule out a particular diagnosis but it can also help with treatment planning if there is a diagnosis.

With regards to eating disorders specifically, there are multiple screening tools that can be used to help determine if someone shows signs of an eating disorder, thereby warranting a more formal assessment. Likewise, there are multiple assessment tools designed to confirm the diagnosis, determine the severity of the symptoms, and help inform the type and mode of treatment (see Chapter 12). Some commonly used screening and assessment tools for eating disorders are briefly summarized in the sections that follow.

▨ Screening

Eating Attitudes Test

The eating attitudes test (EAT; Garner & Garfinkel, 1979) was originally designed as a 40-item self-report measure that was subsequently shortened to 26 items

(Garner, Olmsted, Bohr, & Garfinkel, 1982). This was done after a factor analysis confirmed that the final 26 items sufficiently captured the symptoms measured in the original version and provided an indication of whether or not an eating disorder might be present. A score of 20 or more on this test indicates that a formal assessment for an eating disorder should be conducted. Scores less than 20 may still indicate that there is a problem.

Bulimia Test-Revised

The bulimia test-revised (BULIT-R; Thelen, Farmer, Wonderlich, & Smith, 1991) is a 36-item self-report measure specifically designed to screen for symptoms related to bulimia nervosa. This measure has been found to align strongly with the criteria for bulimia nervosa as outlined in the fourth edition of the *Diagnostic and Statistical Manual of Mental Disorders* (Thelen, Mintz, & Vander Wal, 1996). Scores on this instrument range from 28 to 140; the higher the score, the more severe the symptoms.

SCOFF SCREENING TOOL

The SCOFF (Morgan, Reid, & Lacey, 1999) screening tool is one of the briefest screening tools for eating disorders and is commonly used. It consists of five questions. Each letter in the acronym SCOFF represents a primary element associated with eating disorders. The questions are

>   S Do you make yourself **S**ick because you feel uncomfortably full?
>
>   C Do you worry you have lost **C**ontrol over how much you eat?
>
>   O Have you recently lost more than **O**ne stone (6.35 kg or 14 lb) in a 3-month period?
>
>   F Do you believe yourself to be **F**at when others say you are too thin?
>
>   F Would you say **F**ood dominates your life?

The recommendation for this screening tool is that if someone answers "yes" to two or more of the questions then the individual should be referred for a more thorough assessment. The SCOFF has only been validated for use with adults and is recommended for use in clinical settings (Bermudez et al., 2016). Despite this tool only having been studied for use with adults, it is frequently used among pediatric medical providers (Campbell & Peebles, 2014). Although it is brief, the SCOFF has been found to align well with the *DSM-IV* clinical interview (Hill, Reid, Morgan, & Lacey, 2010), which is used for the purpose of determining which *DSM* diagnosis is appropriate. The SCOFF has been found to be an effective screening tool when delivered orally or in written format with the possibility that respondents might be more inclined to endorse items when filling out the questionnaire version compared to answering questions directly to an interviewer (Perry et al., 2002).

Screen for Disordered Eating

The screen for disordered eating (SED; Maguen et al., 2018) is a five-item screening tool developed to provide an effective instrument for primary care providers that would capture **binge eating disorder** in addition to **anorexia nervosa** and **bulimia nervosa**. Each item was pulled from one of five other eating disorder or general health-related instruments. The SED was also reportedly designed to "strike a balance" (p. 24) between missing patients with eating disorders or falsely identifying patients who did not have eating disorders.

Comparison of Screening Tools

Some screening tools have been compared to determine if any are more effective than others in detecting eating disorder pathology. The SCOFF has been studied in comparison to the EAT with results indicating that the shorter SCOFF was highly correlated to items on the longer EAT, suggesting that if brevity is important the SCOFF may be as effective at detecting eating disorder pathology as the EAT (Noma et al., 2006). The study also revealed, however, that the SCOFF may not be as sensitive at detecting anorexia nervosa based on the weight item (item number 3—the O item in the SCOFF). The authors suggested that this item could be improved by revising it from its current form asking about weight loss to asking about having low body weight.

The SCOFF has also been compared to the EDE-Q (see Assessment section). The EDE-Q was found to be more sensitive in its ability to detect eating pathology; however, it was noted that because the SCOFF is easy to use and does not take much time to administer it may be a preferred screening tool in a variety of settings where time may be limited (Hill, Reid, Morgan, & Lacey, 2010; Mond et al., 2008). Finally, the SED was compared to the SCOFF and the eating disorder screen for primary care (EDS-PC; Cotton, Ball, & Robinson, 2003). The SED was found to be more effective than the SCOFF in accurately identifying those who had an eating disorder, and was more effective than the EDS-PC in accurately identifying those who did not have an eating disorder (Maguen et al., 2018).

Preparticipation Screening for Athletes

Since athletes may be at greater risk for developing an eating disorder (Sundgot-Borgen & Torstveit, 2004), some have recommended that a standard part of any preparticipation screening should include a screening for eating disorders (Thompson & Sherman, 2010). All competitive athletes in school (secondary and postsecondary) should complete a preparticipation physical prior to competing in sport. A highly utilized tool for middle school athletes through collegiate athletics is the *PPE: Preparticipation Physical Evaluation* in its fourth edition (Bernhardt, Roberts, American Academy of Family Physicians [AAFP], & American Academy of Pediatrics [AAP], 2010), which includes questions related to eating disorders. The *Female Athlete Triad Coalition* recommends 11 specific questions that should be included as part of any preparticipation examination (De Souza et al., 2014). Regardless of the preparticipation screening used, the intent is to ensure that the athlete is physically well enough to handle the rigors of practice and competition, as well as to identify anything that may place him or her at risk for developing medical or mental health issues. Not all schools, however, adequately screen for eating disorders and related symptoms (Mencias, Noon, & Hoch, 2012) despite the fact that screening tools have been found to be effective in identifying eating disorders in athletes (Wagner, Erickson, Tierney, Houston, & Bacon, 2016).

▒ Assessment

Eating disorders can be considered **biopsychosocial** disorders requiring an assessment that addresses all aspects of an eating disorder (Matytsina, Greydanus,

Babenko-Sorocopud, & Matytsina, 2014). Typically, any assessment begins with a description of the current concerns as well as a thorough history of the problem. Depending on who the patient is, as well as his or her degree of motivation for being there, the patient himself or herself may provide the information. Alternatively, a family member or friend may provide the information. Regardless, it can be helpful to get information at the initial assessment from someone else who knows the person well and who knows about the ways in which he or she has been struggling. Starting with a question about why the person is at the appointment that day can be helpful as the patient's response may reveal a good deal about his or her motivation for treatment and overall attitude about being there (Katzman & Steinegger, 2013). A complete and thorough assessment of vital signs, history of eating behaviors, attitudes and thoughts about food and eating, assessment of other psychiatric problems, and assessment of any family history of eating disorders, the family's views about eating, weight and exercise, and the like can take several hours (American Psychiatric Association [APA], 2006) but is important to develop a clear picture of what is going on with a patient and how he or she is affected...

Initial Assessment

The overall assessment of the patient and his or her eating disorder may be structured or semistructured. A *structured* assessment has a list of questions that are asked in a particular order. The assessment contains only those questions and the patient's answers to them. A *semistructured* assessment includes a list of questions that must be asked but allows the interviewer to ask follow-up questions or questions that are not included in the assessment itself. Regardless of the specific type of assessment used, most generally agree that establishing a good rapport with the patient and his or her family (if they are involved) is critical (APA, 2006; Katzman & Steinegger, 2013; Peterson, 2005). Peterson (2005) noted that connecting with patients who have an eating disorder can be challenging since in some cases they do not want to be in treatment or may be in denial that there is a problem (Schoen et al., 2012; see Chapter 10).

Beyond assessing for specific behaviors that may be related to an eating disorder, an initial assessment often includes a family history of eating disorders and other psychiatric illnesses, the patient's history of other psychiatric illnesses (it is common for patients to have a **comorbid diagnosis** and/or a diagnosis that preceded the eating disorder [Grilo, White, & Masheb, 2009; Hudson, Hiripi, Pope, & Kessler, 2007; Keski-Rahkonen & Mustelin, 2016]), the nature and quality of the relationships the patient has with friends and family members, what it was like for the individual growing up, and a mental status exam (Katzman & Steinegger, 2013). Initial assessment in a medical setting will include assessing vital signs, food and fluid intake, medical signs of problems such as edema, gastrointestinal symptoms, and cardiac distress (APA, 2006).

Medical Assessment

Given the severity of many medical complications associated with eating disorders (see Chapter 5), it is recommended that a thorough medical evaluation is conducted, particularly for those with anorexia nervosa and those who frequently vomit or use laxatives or diuretics (Glover & Sharma, 2012). Moreover, the medical assessment is important for determining how serious the eating disorder is which can, in turn, determine what level of care is required (Glover & Sharma, 2012; see Chapter 12). Such an assessment should include full blood count, an electrocardiogram (ECG) for all individuals diagnosed with anorexia nervosa and other eating disorder patients with evidence of electrolyte deficiencies, and a dual-energy X-ray absorptiometry (DEXA) scan to measure bone mineral density in those with chronic anorexia nervosa (Zipfel, Löwe, & Herzog, 2003). Moreover, primary care providers need to be cognizant of symptoms that may appear to be related to an eating disorder but may in fact be the result of another medical condition (Katzman, Kanbur, & Steinegger, 2010).

The Academy for Eating Disorder's Medical Care Standards Committee created a document entitled *Eating Disorders: A Guide to Medical Care* (Bermudez et al., 2016), which outlines the severity of eating disorders, medical signs that someone might have an eating disorder, what a comprehensive medical assessment should include, and recommendations for when a patient may require a higher level of care, including how to prevent **refeeding syndrome**. The document also includes the recommendation that medical specialty providers "maintain a high index of suspicion for EDs" (Bermudez et al., 2016, p. 15) along with knowing signs and symptoms of patients who may have been appropriately referred to them for a medical problem that may have its origins in an eating disorder. These specialty providers include cardiologists, emergency room providers, endocrinologists, gastroenterologists, OB/GYN providers, psychiatrists, and pediatricians.

Tyson (2010) warns that eating disorders are "wolves in sheep's clothing" (p. 90) as it is common for individuals with eating disorders to deny that anything is wrong (Schoen et al., 2012) and may even appear to be functioning at a very high level. However, beneath the surface someone with an eating disorder may be close to death or have a severe medical complication that may permanently affect one's mind and/or body. Thus, a thorough understanding and assessment of those showing signs of an eating disorder (see Chapter 2) is imperative.

When conducting a medical assessment, it is important for healthcare professionals to gather information regarding medical history, and, through a physical examination, determine what diagnosis is appropriate. Additionally, it is important for the assessor to determine if there are any medical symptoms that are not part of, but rather the result of, the patient's eating disorder (Katzman & Steinegger, 2013). Areas of focus for the physical examination would include a general assessment of the patient's body (e.g., is the patient emaciated, is the patient dehydrated, have there been weight fluctuations) along with specific examination of the head, ears, nose and throat, heart, abdomen, skin, muscle tone, and brain functioning (Katzman & Steinegger, 2013; see Chapter 5).

Psychological Assessment

Assessment for an eating disorder outside of the context of a medical professional's office is likely to include one or more tools designed specifically to reveal eating disorder symptoms and to make a formal diagnosis. The use of assessment tools that have been empirically validated and widely used can aid clinicians in their development of treatment plans as well as provide data on treatment progress and outcome (Anderson, Lundgren, Shapiro, & Paulosky, 2004). Although this chapter is focused on screening and assessment as it specifically relates to eating disorder symptoms, it is recommended that a thorough assessment of an individual includes an assessment for other psychiatric illnesses as well (Andrews, 2012). A brief description of widely used eating disorder assessment tools follows.

Eating Disorder Examination

The eating disorder examination (EDE; Cooper & Fairburn, 1987; Fairburn & Cooper, 1993; Fairburn, Cooper, & O'Connor, 2008) is a semistructured interview assessment that has been extensively studied and that has been identified as among the best, most effective tools to assess for eating disorders (Wilfley, Schwartz, Spurrell, & Fairburn, 2000). It was developed for use with adults but has since been adapted for use with children and adolescents (Bryant-Waugh, Cooper, Taylor, & Lask, 1996). This tool, as well as the self-report version (the EDE-Q), is designed to detect eating disorder behaviors, including the severity of these behaviors, which can inform a formal diagnosis.

Eating Disorder Examination—Questionnaire

The eating disorder examination—questionnaire (EDE-Q; Fairburn & Beglin, 1994) is a 33-item self-report assessment tool based on the semistructured interview version of the EDE. It has been identified as being particularly useful when assessing for binge eating disorder (Wilson, 1993). The EDE and the EDE-Q do not, however, completely align in terms of what is assessed, and therefore the EDE-Q may not be as effective at assessing more complicated presentations of eating disorders (Carter, Aimé, & Mills, 2001). A 12-item short version of the EDE-Q was developed called the eating disorder examination—questionnaire short (EDE-QS; Gideon et al., 2016) and was found to be similar in effectiveness as the EDE-Q.

Eating Disorder Inventory-3

The eating disorder inventory-3 (EDI; Garner & Olmsted, 1984; Garner, Olmsted, & Polivy, 1983) is a 91-item self-report questionnaire designed to measure symptoms reflective of an eating disorder; it also includes items believed to detect other psychological processes associated with eating disorders (e.g., perfectionism, interpersonal distrust). The original EDI included eight subscales and the revised EDI-2 (Garner, 1991) added three additional subscales. The newest version, EDI-3 (Garner, 2004), includes a total of 12 subscales. Those subscales are: drive for thinness, bulimia, body dissatisfaction, low self-esteem, personal alienation, interpersonal insecurity, interpersonal alienation, interoceptive deficits, emotional dysregulation, perfectionism, asceticism, and maturity fears.

Eating Disorder Questionnaire

The eating disorder questionnaire (EDQ; Mitchell, Hatsukami, Eckert, & Pyle, 1985) is a self-report questionnaire that includes 16 parts: demographic information, weight history, dieting behavior, binge eating behavior, weight control behavior, exercise, menstrual history, history of abuse, psychiatric history, medical history, chemical use history, family members, family medical and psychiatric history, medication history, social history, and medical checklist. It is designed to detect symptoms of anorexia nervosa, bulimia nervosa, and binge eating disorder.

Binge Eating Scale

The binge eating scale (BES; Gormally, Black, Daston, & Rardin, 1982) is a self-report questionnaire that includes 16 items designed to assess symptoms of binge eating and their severity. Questions address behaviors associated with binge eating (e.g., eating when bored) and cognitive elements associated with binge eating (e.g., feeling out of control).

Eating Disorders Assessment for DSM-5

The eating disorders assessment for *DSM-5* (EDA-5; Sysko et al., 2015) was specifically developed to assess feeding and eating disorders as they are defined in the *DSM-5* (APA, 2013). The developers compared the EDA-5 to the EDE and clinical interview by doctoral level clinicians revealing that results of the EDA-5 were similar to those found via the EDE and the clinical interview. This suggests that the EDA-5 is likely as effective at assessing individuals for the presence of anorexia nervosa, bulimia nervosa, and binge eating disorder as the other two methods.

Child-Oriented Assessment and Screening Tools

The assessments noted earlier are generally acceptable for use with adults and adolescents. Some assessments, however, were specifically designed for use with children, many of which are adaptations of assessments identified earlier (Nicholson, 2013). These assessments include the EDE, which has been adapted for use with children and adolescents; the child eating disorder examination (ChEDE; Bryant-Waugh et al., 1996); the EDE-Q, which has been normed for children as young as 12; the Eating Disorder Inventory for Children (EDI-C; Franko et al., 2004; the EDI-3 has been adapted for use with adolescents as young as 13); the children's eating attitudes test (ChEAT; Maloney, McGuire, & Daniels, 1988); and the kid's eating disorder survey (KEDS; Childress, Brewerton, Hodges, & Jarrell, 1993). When using any assessment tool, it is important to ensure that it has been designed and approved for use with the age of the patient being assessed.

Nutritional Assessment

The Academy of Nutrition and Dietetics (formerly the American Dietetic Association [ADA]) stated it is their position "that nutrition intervention, including nutrition counseling by a registered dietitian, is an essential component of the team treatment of patients with anorexia nervosa, bulimia nervosa, and other eating disorders during assessment and treatment across the continuum of care" (ADA, 2011, p. 1236). The information gathered by a registered dietitian can supplement and enhance the information gathered via other forms of assessment and can aid in treatment planning.

The position statement of the ADA (2011) provides specific recommendations with regard to what should be included in a thorough nutrition assessment, nutrition intervention, monitoring and evaluating nutrition, information to be shared with the multidisciplinary treatment team (see Chapter 12), and the importance of advanced training for working with individuals with eating disorders. Registered dietitians can also gather information about food history, which may be more valuable than information related to current food intake (Wilson, Grilo, & Vitousek, 2007). They can also assess readiness for change, which is often low for those with lower weights (Geller, Cassin, Brown, & Srikameswaran, 2009).

Family Assessment

Involvement of family for children and adolescents is important in the treatment process, and, for those who are married, involvement of a spouse or partner may be important as well (APA, 2006). This seems to be particularly the case for adolescents with anorexia nervosa who are in the early stages of the disorder, whereas for those with a later onset or who are in later stages of their eating disorder, the effectiveness of family involvement in treatment is less promising (Downs & Blow, 2013). Weaver and Liebman (2011) indicate that an assessment of patients and families that encourages successful engagement in the treatment process is critical for a favorable outcome. Family members are able to provide information that may illuminate contributing factors to the onset of the eating disorders, including any factors that may interfere with the treatment and recovery process (APA, 2006).

An additional way family members are assessed has to do with the needs they may have as they cope with a family member with an eating disorder, as well as in terms of the needs they have in the context of providing care to the family member (Treasure et al., 2008). In the context of what the family needs, what is reported to be of significant importance is helping family members understand the impact that the eating disorder has on how the family functions, including what changes have been made to accommodate the eating disorder, rather than on determining how the eating disorder developed in the first place (Whitney & Eisler, 2005).

Conclusion

Screening for and assessment of eating disorders have distinct but highly important roles. Several screening tools have been developed that effectively detect when someone may have or may be at risk for developing an eating disorder. When such a detection is made, a thorough assessment must be conducted to confirm whether or not an eating disorder diagnosis is warranted. A thorough evaluation includes a medical assessment, psychological assessment, nutritional assessment, and family assessment. Each can provide invaluable information that can aid in the diagnosis and treatment of someone with an eating disorder.

References

American Dietetic Association. (2011). Position of the American Dietetic Association: Nutrition intervention in the treatment of eating disorders. *Journal of the American Dietetic Association, 111*, 1236–1241. doi:10.1016/j.jada.2011.06.016

American Psychiatric Association. (2006). *Practice guideline for the treatment of patients with eating disorders* (3rd ed.). Washington, DC: Author.

American Psychiatric Association. (2013). *Diagnostic and statistical manual of mental disorders* (5th ed.). Washington, DC: Author.

Anderson, D. A., Lundgren, J. D., Shapiro, J. R., & Paulosky, C. A. (2004). Assessment of eating disorders: Review and recommendations for clinical use. *Behavior Modification, 28*, 763–782. doi:10.1177/0145445503259851

Andrews, H. (2012). The assessment of mental state, psychiatric risk and co-morbidity in eating disorders. In J. R. E. Fox & K. P. Goss (Eds.), *Eating and its disorders* (pp. 11–27). New York, NY: John Wiley & Sons.

Bermudez, O., Devlin, M., Dooley-Hash, S., Guarda, A., Katzman, D. K., Madden, S., . . . Waterhous, T. (2016). *Eating disorders: A guide to medical care* (3rd ed.). Reston, VA: Academy for Eating Disorders.

Bernhardt, D. T., Roberts, W. O., American Academy of Family Physicians, & American Academy of Pediatrics. (2010). *PPE: Preparticipation physical evaluation* (4th ed.). Elk Grove Village, IL: American Academy of Pediatrics.

Bryant-Waugh, R. J., Cooper, P. J., Taylor, C. L., & Lask, B. D. (1996). The use of the eating disorder examination with children: A pilot study. *International Journal of Eating Disorders, 19*, 391–397. doi:10.1002/(SICI)1098-108X(199605)19:4<391::AID-EAT6>3.0.CO;2-G

Campbell, K., & Peebles, R. (2014). Eating disorders in children and adolescents: State of the art review. *Pediatrics, 134*, 582–592. doi:10.1542/peds.2014-0194

Carter, J. C., Aimé, A. A., & Mills, J. S. (2001). Assessment of bulimia nervosa: A comparison of interview and self-report questionnaire methods. *International Journal of Eating Disorders, 30*, 187–192. doi:10.1002/eat.1071

Childress, A. C., Brewerton, T. D., Hodges, E. L., & Jarrell, M. P. (1993). The kids' eating disorders survey (KEDS): A study of middle school students. *Journal of the American Academy of Child Adolescent Psychiatry, 32*, 843–850. doi:10.1097/00004583-199307000-00021

Cooper, Z., & Fairburn, C. G. (1987). The eating disorder examination: A semi-structured interview for the assessment of the specific psychopathology of eating disorders. *International Journal of Eating Disorders, 6*, 1–8. doi:10.1002/1098-108X(198701)6:1<1::AID-EAT2260060102>3.0.CO;2-9

Cotton, M. A., Ball, C., & Robinson, P. (2003). Four simple questions can help screen for eating disorders. *Journal of General Internal Medicine, 18*, 53–56. doi:10.1046/j.1525-1497.2003.20374.x

De Souza, M. J., Nattiv, A., Joy, E., Misra, M., Williams, N. I., Mallinson, R. J., . . . Expert Panel. (2014). 2014 Female Athlete Triad Coalition Consensus Statement on treatment and return to play of the female athlete triad: 1st International Conference held in San Francisco, California, May 2012 and 2nd International Conference held in Indianapolis, Indiana, May 2013. *British Journal of Sport Medicine, 48*, 289–308. doi:10.1136/bjsports-2013-093218

Downs, K. J., & Blow, A. J. (2013). A substantive and methodological review of family-based treatment for eating disorders: The last 25 years of research. *Journal of Family Therapy, 35*, 3–28. doi:10.1111/j.1467-6427.2011.00566.x

Fairburn, C. G., & Beglin, S. J. (1994). Assessment of eating disorders: Interview of self-report questionnaire? *International Journal of Eating Disorders, 16*, 363–370. doi:10.1002/1098-108X(199412)16:4<363::AID-EAT2260160405>3.0.CO;2-#.

Fairburn, C. G., & Cooper, Z. (1993). The eating disorder examination. In C. G. Fairburn & G. T. Wilson (Eds.), *Binge eating: Nature, assessment and treatment* (12th ed., pp. 317–360). New York, NY: Guilford Press.

Fairburn, C. G., Cooper, Z., & O'Connor, M. (2008). Eating disorder examination. In C. G. Fairburn (Ed.), *Cognitive behavior therapy and eating disorders* (16th ed., pp. 265–308). New York, NY: Guilford Press.

Franko, D. L., Striegel-Moore, R., Barton, B. A., Schumann, B. C., Garner, D. M., Daniels, S. R., . . . Crawford, P. B. (2004). Measuring eating concerns in Black and White adolescent girls. *International Journal of Eating Disorders, 35*, 179–189. doi:10.1002/eat.10251

Garner, D. M. (1991). *Eating disorder inventory—2 manual*. Odessa, FL: Psychological Assessment Resources.

Garner, D. M. (2004). *Eating disorder inventory—3*. Lutz, FL: Psychological Assessment Resources.

Garner, D. M., & Garfinkel, P. E. (1979). The eating attitudes test: An index of the symptoms of anorexia nervosa. *Psychological Medicine, 9*, 273–279. doi:10.1017/S0033291700030762

Garner, D. M., & Olmsted, M. P. (1984). *The eating disorder inventory manual*. Odessa, FL: Psychological Assessment Resources.

Garner, D. M., Olmsted, M. P., Bohr, Y., & Garfinkel, P. E. (1982). The eating attitudes test: Psychometric features and clinical correlates. *Psychological Medicine, 12*, 871–878. doi:10.1017/S0033291700049163

Garner, D. M., Olmsted, M. P., & Polivy, J. (1983). The eating disorder inventory: A measure of cognitive-behavioral dimensions of anorexia nervosa and bulimia nervosa. In P. L. Darby, P. E. Garfinkel, D. M. Garner, & D. V. Coscina (Eds.), *Anorexia nervosa: Recent developments in research* (pp. 173–184). New York, NY: Alan R. Liss.

Geller, J., Cassin, S. E., Brown, K. E., & Srikameswaran, S. (2009). Factors associated with improvements in readiness for change: Low vs. normal BMI eating disorders. *International Journal for Eating Disorders, 42*, 40–46. doi:10.1002/eat.20574

Gideon, N., Hawkes, N., Mond, J., Saunders, R., Tchanturia, K., & Serpell, L. (2016). Development and psychometric validation of the EDE-QS, a 12 item short form of the eating disorder examination questionnaire (EDE-Q). *PLOS ONE, 11*, e0152744. doi:10.1371/journal.pone.0152744

Glover, T., & Sharma, S. (2012). Physiological assessment of eating disorders. In J. R. E. Fox & K. P. Goss (Eds.), *Eating and its disorders* (pp. 42–60). New York, NY: John Wiley & Sons.

Gormally, J., Black, S., Daston, S., & Rardin, D. (1982). The assessment of binge eating severity among obese persons. *Addictive Behaviors, 7*, 47–55. doi:10.1016/0306-4603(82)90024-7

Grilo, C. M., White, M. A., & Masheb, R. M. (2009). *DSM-IV* psychiatric disorder comorbidity and its correlates in binge eating disorder. *International Journal of Eating Disorders, 42*, 228–234. doi:10.1002/eat.20599

Hill, L. S., Reid, F., Morgan, J. F., & Lacey, J. H. (2010). SCOFF, the development of an eating disorder screening questionnaire. *International Journal of Eating Disorders, 43*, 344–351. doi:10.1002/eat.20679

Hudson, J. I., Hiripi, E., Pope, H. G., & Kessler, R. C. (2007). The prevalence and correlates of eating disorders in the national comorbidity survey replication. *Biological Psychiatry, 61*, 348–358. doi:10.1016/j.biopsych.2006.03.040

Katzman, D., Kanbur, N. O., & Steinegger, C. M. (2010). Medical screening and management of eating disorders in adolescents. In W. S. Agras (Ed.), *The Oxford handbook of eating disorders* (pp. 267–291). New York, NY: Oxford University Press.

Katzman, D., & Steinegger, C. (2013). Physical assessment. In B. Lask & R. Bryant-Waugh (Eds.), *Eating disorders in childhood and adolescence* (4th ed., pp. 77–104). New York, NY: Routledge.

Keski-Rahkonen, A., & Mustelin, L. (2016). Epidemiology of eating disorders in Europe: Prevalence, incidence, comorbidity, course, consequences, and risk factors. *Current Opinion in Psychiatry, 29*, 340–345. doi:10.1097/YCO.0000000000000278

Maguen, S., Hebenstreit, C., Li, Y., Dinh, J. V., Donalson, R., Dalton, S., . . . Masheb, R. (2018). Screen for disordered eating: Improving the accuracy of eating disorder screening in primary care. *General Hospital Psychiatry, 50*, 20–25. doi:10.1016/j.genhosppsych.2017.09.004

Maloney, M. J., McGuire, J. B., & Daniels, S. R. (1988). Reliability testing of a children's version of the eating attitudes test. *Journal of the American Academy of Child and Adolescent Psychiatry, 27*, 541–543. doi:10.1097/00004583-198809000-00004

Matytsina, L., Greydanus, D. E., Babenko-Sorocopud, I. V., & Matytsina, L. (2014). Anorexia nervosa in adolescence: Current concepts of medical and psychological assessment and management. *International Journal of Child and Adolescent Health, 7*, 167–181. doi:10.1097/JSM.0b013e3182425aee

Mencias, T., Noon, M., & Hoch, A. Z. (2012). Female athlete triad screening in National Collegiate Athlete Association Division I athletes: Is the preparticipation evaluation form effective? *Clinical Journal of Sport Medicine, 22*, 122–125. doi:10.1097/JSM.0b013e3182425aee

Mitchell, J. E., Hatsukami, D., Eckert, E., & Pyle, R. (1985). Eating disorders questionnaire. *Psychopharmacology Bulletin, 21,* 1025–1043.

Mond, J. M., Myers, T. C., Crosby, R. D., Hay, P. J., Rodgers, B., Morgan, J. F., . . . Mitchell, J. E. (2008). Screening for eating disorders in primary care: EDE-Q versus SCOFF. *Behaviour Research and Therapy, 46,* 612–622. doi:0.1016/j.brat.2008.02.003

Morgan, J. F., Reid, F., & Lacey, J. H. (1999). The SCOFF questionnaire: Assessment of a new screening tool for eating disorders. *British Medical Journal, 319,* 1467–1648. doi:10.1136/bmj.319.7223.1467

Nicholson, J. (2013). Psychological assessment. In B. Lask & R. Bryant-Waugh (Eds.), *Eating disorders in childhood and adolescence* (4th ed., pp. 105–124). New York, NY: Taylor & Francis.

Noma, S., Nakai, Y., Hamagaki, S., Uehara, M., Hayashi, A., & Hayashi, T. (2006). Comparison between the SCOFF questionnaire and the eating attitude test in patients with eating disorders. *International Journal of Psychiatry in Clinical Practice, 10,* 27–32. doi:10.1080/13651500500305275

Perry, L., Morgan, J., Reid, F., Brunton, J., O'Brien, A., Luck, A., & Lacey, H. (2002). Screening for symptoms of eating disorders: Reliability of the SCOFF screening tool with written compared to oral delivery. *International Journal of Eating Disorders, 32,* 466–472. doi:10.1002/eat.10093

Peterson, C. B. (2005). Conducting the diagnostic interview. In J. E. Mitchell & C. B. Peterson (Eds.), *Assessment of eating disorders* (pp. 32–58). New York, NY: Guilford Press.

Schoen, E. G., Lee, S., Skow, C., Greenberg, S. T., Bell, A. S., Wiese, J. E., & Martens, J. K. (2012). A retrospective look at the internal help-seeking process in young women with eating disorders. *Eating Disorders, 20,* 14–30. doi:10.1080/10640266.2012.635560

Sundgot-Borgen, J., & Torstveit, M. K. (2004). Prevalence of eating disorders in elite athletes is higher than in the general population. *Clinical Journal of Sport Medicine, 14,* 25–32. doi:10.1097/00042752-200401000-00005

Sysko, R., Glasofer, D. R., Hidebrandt, T., Klimek, P., Mitchell, J. E., Berg, K. C., . . . Walsh, B. T. (2015). The eating disorder assessment for *DSM-5* (EDA-5): Development and validation of a structured interview for feeding and eating disorders. *International Journal of Eating Disorders, 48,* 452–463. doi:10.1002/eat.22388

Thelen, M. H., Farmer, J., Wonderlich, S., & Smith, M. (1991). A revision of the bulimia test: The BULIT-R. *Psychological Assessment, 3,* 119–124. doi:10.1037//1040-3590.3.1.119

Thelen, M. H., Mintz, L. B., & Vander Wal, J. S. (1996). The bulimia test-revised: Validation with *DSM-IV* criteria for bulimia nervosa. *Psychological Assessment, 8,* 219–221. doi:10.1037/1040-3590.8.2.219

Thompson, R. A., & Sherman, R. (2010). *Eating disorders in sport.* New York, NY: Routledge.

Treasure, J., Sepulveda, A. R., MacDonald, P., Whitaker, W., Lopez, C., Zabala, M., . . . Todd, G. (2008). The assessment of the family of people with eating disorders. *European Eating Disorders Review, 16,* 247–255. doi:10.1002/erv.859

Tyson, E. P. (2010). Medical assessment of eating disorders. In M. Maine, B. H. McGilley, & D. W. Bunnell (Eds.), *Treatment of eating disorders: Bridging the research-practice gap* (pp. 89–110). San Diego, CA: Academic Press.

Wagner, A. J., Erickson, C. D., Tierney, D. K., Houston, M. N., & Bacon, C. E. W. (2016). The diagnostic accuracy of screening tools to detect eating disorders in female athletes. *Journal of Sport Rehabilitation, 25,* 395–398. doi:10.1123/jsr.2014-0337

Whitney, J., & Eisler, I. (2005). Theoretical and empirical models around caring for someone with an eating disorder: The reorganization of family life and interpersonal maintenance factors. *Journal of Mental Health,14,* 575–585. doi:10.1080/09638230500347889

Weaver, L., & Liebman, R. (2011). Assessment of anorexia nervosa in children and adolescence. *Current Psychiatry Reports, 12*, 93–98. doi:10.1007/s11920-010-0174-y

Wilfley, D. E., Schwartz, M. B., Spurrell, E. B., & Fairburn, C. G. (2000). Using the eating disorder examination to identify the specific psychopathology of binge eating disorder. *International Journal of Eating Disorders, 27*, 259–269. doi:10.1002/(SICI) 1098-108X(200004)27:3<259::AID-EAT2>3.0.CO;2-G

Wilson, G. T. (1993). Assessment of binge eating. In C. G. Fairburn & G. T. Wilson (Eds.), *Binge eating: Nature, assessment, and treatment* (pp. 227–249). New York, NY: Guilford Press.

Wilson, G. T., Grilo, C. M., & Vitousek, K. M. (2007). Psychological treatment for eating disorders. *American Journal of Psychology, 62*, 199–216. doi:10.1037/0003-066X.62.3.199

Zipfel, S., Löwe, B., & Herzog, W. (2003). Medical complications. In J. Treasure, U. Schmidt, & van Furth, E. (Eds.), *Handbook of eating disorders* (2nd ed., pp. 169–190). West Sussex, UK: John Wiley & Sons.

MAKING AN EFFECTIVE REFERRAL

Introduction

Many individuals with eating disorders will not self-refer for treatment or seek an evaluation; therefore, the ability of friends, family, and others to recognize signs and symptoms of an eating disorder is crucial (Fairburn, 2002). This chapter includes a discussion of the role various individuals can play in the identification and referral of someone suspected of having an eating disorder, what happens after a referral is made, and what can be done to increase the chances that an individual will follow-through on a referral.

First Line of Defense

Although primary care providers (PCPs) are in a position to be among the first to identify an eating disorder, these conditions are often underdiagnosed by PCPs, resulting in no treatment or delayed treatment (Campbell & Peebles, 2014; Flahavan, 2006). This may be due to the fact that many physicians feel underprepared to identify and intervene with patients with eating disorders (Linville, Benton, O'Neil, & Sturm, 2010). Dentists and oral hygienists are also often in a position to identify eating disorders early based on the health of a patient's gums, mouth, and teeth (Johansson, Norring, Unell, & Johansson, 2012); however, they may or may not feel comfortable broaching the subject with their patients. Thus, important members of the first line of defense usually include nonprofessionals.

Since family, friends, coaches, teachers, and colleagues in the workplace spend a lot of time with one another, these individuals are often in an excellent position to notice signs and symptoms of an eating disorder (see Chapter 2). One of the leading eating disorder organizations in the United States, the National Eating Disorders Association (NEDA), developed several toolkits designed to help inform those who have regular contact with individuals at greatest risk for developing an eating disorder: adolescents.

The recommendations the toolkits provide can help inform individuals how to recognize eating disorders and intervene with adolescents and other age groups.

Parents and Other Family Members

The first Parent Toolkit was published by NEDA in 2008 with the most recent version published 7 years later (2015b). This toolkit includes information about eating disorders, supporting a loved one, treatment information, dealing with insurance, and information to help parents understand the neurobiology of eating disorders (i.e., what is happening in the brain). The "supporting a loved one" section of the toolkit provides advice on how to talk with someone who needs an assessment or treatment for an eating disorder. The items they recommend are:

> Clear both of your schedules and set up a quiet place to talk.
> Be prepared for denial and anger.
> Don't expect insight or buy-in.
> Stay focused on what you need to do.
> Seek a second opinion.
> Remind your child that life will be there after recovery.
> Use whatever leverage you have.
> Set your own boundaries.
> Seek to be involved with the child's treatment.
> Keep lines of communication open. (NEDA, 2015b, pp. 18–19)

As can be gleaned from this list, encouraging a child or adolescent to seek treatment is not necessarily straightforward or easy. It is not uncommon, for example, for someone with an eating disorder to deny that there is a problem and to insist that he or she is fine, thereby delaying treatment (Schoen et al., 2012). In another section of this toolkit, NEDA indicates that persistence in encouraging a loved one to get help is important. An eating disorder is sometimes personified and talked about as if it is its own person (Bowlby, Anderson, Hall, & Willingham, 2015). As such, it (the eating disorder) can offer up a litany of excuses for why now is not a good time to get help, or it will offer a promise to agree to get help at some point, just not right now. One way to help work around the eating disorder's wish to not receive treatment is to "(a)lly with the part of them that wants to get well" (NEDA, 2015b, p. 17) and to routinely talk with the loved one about why he or she wants to get well. Eating disorders end up taking quite a bit away from the individual diagnosed with one (see Chapters 5–77); thus, it can be important to note the ways in which the eating disorder has prevented the loved one from pursuing the things he or she wants to pursue, or the ways in which the eating disorder has not allowed the loved one to be who he or she wants to be.

Teachers and Other School Personnel

Educators and other school personnel are also in a position to be among the first to know about or to be informed about a problem that may indicate the presence of an eating disorder. Research has indicated that screening for eating disorders is a cost-effective endeavor on par with screenings for other medical issues such as hypertension (Wright,

Austin, Noh, Jiang, & Sonneville, 2014; see Chapter 8). Thus, it is important for school personnel to specifically screen for eating disorders or, alternatively, to recognize their signs and symptoms (see Chapter 2) and to develop a protocol for handling such concerns about students. NEDA (2015a) developed the *Educator Toolkit* to help school personnel identify eating disorder symptoms that are likely to be noticeable in a school setting, and to develop strategies for assisting students who may have or are at risk for developing an eating disorder. This toolkit also provides specific advice for various personnel such as school psychologists, school nurses, and coaches (see Coaches and Athletic Trainers section). The *Educator Toolkit* provides an example of a Student Assistance Program information form (pp. 19–21) which could be included as part of a formal school protocol for how to handle situations in which a student may be at risk for an eating disorder.

One of the issues unique to a school setting is that a nonfamily member may be the first to identify that a student is showing signs of an eating disorder. The school nurse, for example, spends a significant amount of time attending to the mental health needs of students by offering brief interventions and making referrals to outside providers (Bohnenkamp, Stephan, & Bobo, 2015). In many cases, when eating disorders are identified or suspected an offer of help may be rejected by primary caretakers (Rees & Clark-Stone, 2006). To help with this the *Educator Toolkit* (NEDA, 2015a) provides advice for effective ways to communicate with parents and guardians.

Recommendations include being aware of potential issues that may affect how a phone call or in-person conversation may go. These include things such as considering the student's culture, the nature of his or her relationship with family members, and other social issues that may be impacting the student, all of which may make a conversation with parents or guardians more or less difficult. It is possible that not only will the student pushback by saying there is not a problem or that he or she does not want the school personnel to contact his or her family member, but the family member may also be resistant to the idea that the child may have a mental health concern. Regardless of the openness with which a family member may approach such a conversation, the toolkit recommends expressing concern and empathy while patiently listening to what the family member(s) have to say, and also being respectfully firm with one's concern about the seriousness of his or her concerns. A critical element of such a conversation also includes having a list of qualified, community-based healthcare professionals available to provide to the family member(s). Finally, the toolkit provides guidance regarding conversations that are not going well (e.g., the family member is angry that someone has reached out with this concern and is not receptive to information or advice). The toolkit indicates that persisting in a conversation that is not productive or amicable can ultimately harm any possibility of a future conversation when the family member(s) have had a chance to digest the information they received from the school. Thus, the recommendation is to acknowledge that the conversation and topic are difficult to discuss, to provide reassurance that school personnel are available for future conversations, and that they will check in with them again in the near future to offer assistance or answer any questions.

Coaches and Athletic Trainers

In many cases, athletes may be more at risk for developing an eating disorder than the general population (Sundgot-Borgen & Torstveit, 2004), and if left undetected and untreated the eating disorder will eventually negatively impact performance (El Ghoch, Soave, Calugi, & Grave, 2013). Using a preparticipation screening tool designed to screen for eating disorders is considered to be the standard of practice (Bernhardt, Roberts, & American Academy of Family Physicians, American Academy of Pediatrics, 2010; see Chapter 8). Once identified, an athlete should be referred to a multidisciplinary treatment team with expertise in eating disorders and sport (Joy, Kussman, & Nattiv, 2016). Whether or not a preparticipation screening tool reveals a risk for an eating disorder in a student–athlete, it is important for school personnel, particularly coaches and athletic trainers, to have a good working knowledge of the signs and symptoms of eating disorders, particularly as they relate to athletes (see Chapter 4).

The *Coaches & Trainers Toolkit* (NEDA, n.d.-a) was developed in recognition of the fact that for many students coaches and athletic trainers may be in a position to identify signs and symptoms of an eating disorder before other school personnel may. This toolkit includes signs and symptoms that may be particularly evident in an athletic setting and includes signs such as longer recovery times, frequent muscle strains or fractures, struggling to taper or take a day off, training above and beyond what is expected or recommended, and so on. This toolkit also provides information about the **female athlete triad**, which includes low bone mineral density, energy deficiency (e.g., not eating enough given the demands of the sport), and menstrual disturbances. The idea is that if one element of the triad is detected then the other two should be assessed to determine not only if an eating disorder is present (which is not always the case) but also what consequences of not consuming enough calories may be present (see Chapter 5). It is important to note that, although the female athlete triad was developed to help identify female athletes who may be putting their bodies at risk for serious medical issues, the fact is that male athletes who are not sufficiently fueling their bodies are also at risk for many of the same problems (e.g., electrolyte imbalance, low blood pressure, dehydration, etc.).

In addition to including basic information about eating disorders, how eating disorders may be evident in a sport setting, and how to encourage healthy eating and prevent an eating disorder, the *Coaches & Trainers Toolkit* also provides recommendations for coaches and athletic trainers in terms of how to intervene effectively with an athlete. Many of these recommendations apply to anyone in a position to intervene with an individual suspected of showing signs of an eating disorder. These recommendations include finding a private place to talk with the athlete, refraining from judging or criticizing what the athlete says, expecting denial or anger, and encouraging the athlete to seek treatment. What is unique to the athletic setting is whether or not the athlete should participate in sport due to medical reasons or for lack of treatment compliance (International Olympic Committee Medical Commission, 2005). Restrictions with respect to practice or competition are not uncommon and in some cases the recommendation may be for the athlete to cease all physical activity until his or her weight is restored or other eating disorder behaviors (e.g., **purging**) are under control. Although a coach or athletic trainer is not part of the treatment team, these individuals are important resources in the athlete's recovery process (Thompson & Sherman, 2010). The toolkit recommends that coaches and athletic trainers consult with treatment team members, follow recommendations, and share as much information as possible (as allowed by **confidentiality**). By doing so, athletic personnel communicate clearly to the athlete that his or her health and well-being are top priority and that they will follow the recommendations of the treating healthcare providers.

The *Coaches & Trainer's Toolkit* concludes by providing stories from a variety of personnel including coaches and psychologists regarding their interactions with athletes with eating disorders. Such stories can provide valuable information and perspective for those unsure of what to expect, how to handle their athlete, and how to manage the impact the athlete's concerns may have on all involved, including teammates.

Employers

Because eating disorders by their very nature are secretive, it can be difficult to identify an eating disorder in any setting including in the workplace (Anderson, Lundgren, & Morier, 2004). Although work itself is not necessarily a cause of an eating disorder, job-related stress can be significant and may exacerbate eating disorder symptoms.

Although adolescents and young adults in middle school through college are at higher risk for developing an eating disorder than any other age group (see Chapter 3) it is possible that an eating disorder may develop or become evident on the job regardless of whether the employee is a new hire or someone who has spent the better part of his or her career with a company. To aid employers in their efforts to support a healthy workplace NEDA (n.d.-b) recently developed the *Eating Disorders in the Workplace* toolkit (this toolkit was not among the first toolkits developed by NEDA nor was it available when previous revisions of those toolkits were published). This toolkit is much more brief in comparison to the other toolkits (the *Parent Toolkit* is 76 pages and the *Eating Disorders in the Workplace* toolkit is 4 pages) and serves as a resource for human resource departments and other offices in an organization that may address wellness among employees. This toolkit provides links to resources for more information about eating disorders, a screening tool that can be made available to employees, and what impact an eating disorder can have in the workplace. There are also recommendations for how colleagues or bosses can express concern about a particular employee.

The *Eating Disorders in the Workplace* toolkit also provides specific recommendations regarding wellness programs that are common at many companies. Recommendations include things like avoiding wellness programs that focus on weight or weight loss, and not including programs that might encourage employees to compete based on how much weight they lose. Such competition-based programs often require weigh-ins, which are not recommended.

▨ What Happens When a Referral Is Made?

When a referral is made, and the individual who is referred for treatment for an eating disorder follows through with that referral, the first thing that will occur is confirmation that an eating disorder diagnosis is appropriate (see Chapter 8). If such a diagnosis is confirmed, the patient will ultimately receive treatment from a group of multidisciplinary professionals who may or may not work at the same healthcare agency (see Chapter 12). When a referral is made to a primary care provider or a licensed mental health professional and a diagnosis of an eating disorder is confirmed, the minimum standard of care is that the individual will receive treatment from a medical professional, a mental health professional, and a registered dietitian (American Psychiatric Association, 2006). The amount of contact that the patient may have with each professional will vary based on the nature of the services provided, the severity of the eating disorder, and the degree to which medical complications are evident and require urgent attention.

The individual to whom the referral is made may or may not have any expertise in eating disorders. For example, the person being referred may feel more comfortable having what is likely to be a difficult conversation with the primary care provider with whom he or she already has a relationship. In this case, the professional will most likely seek out someone in the local area who does specialize in the treatment of eating disorders and refer the patient to that individual to confirm the diagnosis (see Chapter 8), and to make recommendations for how to proceed from there.

If the patient and/or his or her family (if the patient is a minor) provides permission to do so, the professional providing ongoing treatment may inform the person who made the referral (e.g., school counselor, coach, boss) that the patient has in fact followed through on the referral and is actively seeking treatment at that time. Depending on who made the referral, that may be the extent of his or her contact with the treatment team members; however, in the case where the individual in question may find that his or her school, work, or athletic performance is affected, relevant personnel may not only be continuously informed about the patient's progress but also informed about accommodations for school (and potentially work) and recommendations for participation in athletics. In cases where the eating disorder is severe and requires a higher level of care (see Chapter 12) that may take the student out of school, various school personnel will be informed about this and will be highly involved in helping the patient transition back to school life when he or she is discharged from the treatment program.

How Can One Increase the Chances That There Will Be Follow Through on the Referral?

One of the things that is repeatedly recommended when intervening or confronting someone who may have an eating disorder is to express a caring concern for the individual's well-being (American Psychiatric Association, 2006; NEDA, n.d.-c; Schoen et al., 2012; Selby & Reel, 2011). Concern can be expressed in terms of the individual's mental health and physical well-being. Although the person making the referral may strongly suspect an eating disorder, ultimately only a licensed professional can make such a diagnosis, which is why it is important to stick with one's own observations and specific concerns (National Eating Disorders Association, n.d.-c; Selby & Reel, 2011). For example, a coach may say something like "I have noticed that you don't seem to have the same energy level at practice that you usually do and that your times have been dropping in competition. I have also noticed that you're not eating much when we have team dinners." A teacher may say something like "I have noticed that you seem distracted in class quite a bit and at lunch time when I'm in the cafeteria I have noticed that you often throw away most of your food. I am really worried about you and I am concerned that something may be wrong." Sticking to "I" statements and specific, observed behavior keeps the referring individual out of the trap of expressing vague concerns that can be more easily dismissed and explained away (NEDA, n.d.-c). This does not mean that the student would not attempt to deflect concern or dismiss the concern as unwarranted; however, having specific observations can help to illustrate why the teacher, coach, or other is so concerned and why they will reach out to the student's parent/legal guardian even if the student does not want them to.

Despite expressing caring concern when talking with someone suspected of having an eating disorder, it may also take the individual experiencing a great deal of emotional distress and health-related concerns that are connected to the eating disorder before they are ready to seek treatment (Regan, Cachelin, & Minnick, 2017; Schoen et al., 2012). Other barriers to seeking treatment have been identified as certain personality traits of the individual, beliefs about their health, their emotional experiences, stigma, misperceptions by healthcare providers about eating disorders, and denial of the problem (Schoen et al., 2012; Thompson & Park, 2016).

Conclusion

Having a conversation about concern regarding an eating disorder is truly not easy, particularly if there is concern about alienating the individual or worry that one's concerns may be overblown. Such concerns are why having resources such as the various toolkits developed by NEDA can be invaluable when someone does not know how to start a conversation or how to handle the conversation should it start to go badly.

References

American Psychiatric Association. (2006). *Practice guideline for the treatment of patients with eating disorders* (3rd ed.). Washington, DC: Author.

Anderson, D. A., Lundgren, J. D., & Morier, R. G. (2004). Eating disorders. In J. C. Thomas & M. Hersen (Eds.), *Psychopathology in the workplace: Recognition and adaptation* (pp. 187–199). New York, NY: Brunner-Routledge.

Bernhardt, D. T., Roberts, W. O., & American Academy of Family Physicians, American Academy of Pediatrics. (2010). *PPE: Preparticipation physical evaluation* (4th ed.). Elk Grove Village, IL: American Academy of Pediatrics.

Bohnenkamp, J. H., Stephan, S. H., & Bobo, N. (2015). Supporting student mental health: The role of the school nurse in coordinated school mental health care. *Psychology in the Schools, 52,* 714–727. doi:10.1002/pits.21851

Bowlby, C. G., Anderson, T. L., Hall, M. E. L., & Willingham, M. M. (2015). Recovered professionals exploring eating disorder recovery: A qualitative investigation of meaning. *Clinical Social Work Journal, 43,* 1–10. doi:10.1007/s10615-012-0423-0

Campbell, K., & Peebles, R. (2014). Eating disorders in children and adolescents: State of the art review. *Pediatrics, 134,* 582–592. doi:10.1542/peds.2014-0194

El Ghoch, M., Soave, F., Calugi, S., & Grave, R. D. (2013). Eating disorders, physical fitness and sport performance: A systematic review. *Nutrients, 5,* 140–160. doi:10.3390/nu5125140

Fairburn, C. (2002). The eating disorders: Anorexia nervosa and bulimia nervosa. In J. Mann & S. Truswell (Eds.), *Essentials of human nutrition* (2nd ed., pp. 371–380). New York, NY: Oxford University Press.

Flahavan, C. (2006). Detection, assessment and management of eating disorders; how involved are GPs? *Irish Journal of Psychological Medicine, 23,* 96–99. doi:10.1017/S079096670000971X

International Olympic Committee Medical Commission. (2005). *Position stand: The female athlete triad.* Retrieved from https://www.olympic.org/news/ioc-consensus-statement-on-the-female-athlete-triad

Johansson, A-K., Norring, C., Unell L., & Johansson, A. (2012). Eating disorders and oral health: A matched case-control study. *European Journal of Oral Science, 120*, 61–68. doi:10.1111/j.1600-0722.2011.00922.x

Joy, E., Kussman, A., & Nattiv, A. (2016). 2016 update on eating disorders in athletes: A comprehensive narrative review with a focus on clinical assessment and management. *British Journal of Sports Medicine, 50*, 154–162. doi:10.1136/bjsports-2015-095735

Linville, D., Benton, A., O'Neil, M., & Sturm, K. (2010). Medical providers' screening, training and intervention practices for eating disorders. *Eating Disorders, 18*, 110–131. doi:10.1080/10640260903585532

National Eating Disorders Association. (n.d.-a). *Coach & athletic trainer toolkit.* Retrieved from https://www.nationaleatingdisorders.org/sites/default/files/nedaw18/3.%20Coachand TrainerToolkit%20-%20Copy.pdf

National Eating Disorders Association. (n.d.-b). *Eating disorders in the workplace.* Retrieved from https://www.nationaleatingdisorders.org/sites/default/files/nedaw18/workplace_guide_web _UPDATE.pdf

National Eating Disorders Association. (n.d.-c). *How to help a loved one.* Retrieved from https://www.nationaleatingdisorders.org/learn/help/caregivers

National Eating Disorders Association. (2015a). *Educator toolkit.* New York, NY: Author.

National Eating Disorders Association. (2015b). *Parent toolkit* (3rd ed.). New York, NY: Author.

Rees, L., & Clark-Stone, S. (2006). Can collaboration between education and health professionals improve the identification and referral of young people with eating disorders in schools? A pilot study. *Journal of Adolescence, 29*, 137–151. doi:10.1016/j.adolescence.2005.08.017

Regan, P., Cachelin, F. M., & Minnick, A. M. (2017). Initial treatment seeking from professional health care providers for eating disorders: A review and synthesis of potential barriers to and facilitators of "first contact." *International Journal of Eating Disorders, 50*, 190–209. doi:10.1002/eat.22683

Schoen, E. G., Lee, S., Skow, C., Greenberg, S. T., Bell, A. S., Wiese, J. E., & Martens, J. K. (2012). A retrospective look at the internal help-seeking process in young women with eating disorders. *Eating Disorders, 20*, 14–30. doi:10.1080/10640266.2012.635560

Selby, C. L. B., & Reel, J. J. (2011). A coach's guide to identifying and helping athletes with eating disorders. *Journal of Sport Psychology in Action, 2*, 100–112. doi:10.1080/21520704.2011.585701

Sundgot-Borgen, J., & Torstveit, M. K. (2004). Prevalence of eating disorders in elite athletes is higher than in the general population. *Clinical Journal of Sport Medicine, 14*, 25–32. doi:10.1097/00042752-200401000-00005

Thompson, C., & Park, S. (2016). Barriers to access and utilization of eating disorder treatment among women. *Archives of Women's Mental Health, 19*, 753–760. doi:10.1007/s00737-016 -0618-4

Thompson, R. A., & Sherman, R. T. (2010). *Eating disorders in sport.* New York, NY: Routledge.

Wright, D. R., Austin, S., Noh, L., Jiang, Y., & Sonneville, K. R. (2014). The cost-effectiveness of school-based eating disorder screening. *American Journal of Public Health, 104*, 1774–1782. doi:10.2105/AJPH.2014.302018

IDENTIFYING AND MANAGING REACTIONS TO INDIVIDUALS WITH EATING DISORDERS

Introduction

Eating disorders are complex and difficult to treat. One of the most significant reasons for difficulty with respect to treatment is not only the degree to which these disorders can be life threatening, but perhaps more significantly, the degree to which the eating disorder fights tooth and nail to ensure its survival. In other contexts, this ferocity to defend one's self can be seen as a virtue and something to be admired. In the context of an eating disorder, however, the degree to which the eating disorder, and the part of the individual that needs the disorder and fights to keep it, can result in a wide range of emotional reactions from others. These can include feelings of frustration, sadness, confusion, coercion, disgust or revulsion, devaluation, hopelessness, love, anger, rage, pity, sorrow, hate, worry, feeling of being manipulated, resignation, and surrender (Abbate-Daga, Amianto, Delsedime, De-Bacco, & Fassino, 2013; Betan, Heim, Conklin, & Westen, 2005; Colli et al., 2015; Golan, Yaroslavski, & Stein, 2011; Land, 2004; Matusek & Wright, 2010; McEneaney, 2007; Walker & Lloyd, 2011). These and other reactions, while certainly understandable, can interfere with the process of recovery regardless of whether these reactions are felt by family and friends or treatment providers. Generally speaking, emotional reactions of this type and in the context of helping someone recover from an eating disorder are referred to as **countertransference** reactions.

Countertransference

Emotional reactions, emotional responses, and countertransference are terms that can be used interchangeably (Colli et al., 2015). Understanding that these reactions are real, powerful, and can interfere with treatment has led some to suggest that the therapist's countertransference reactions, specifically, should become a significant part of effective treatment (Tobin, 2012; Zerbe, 2008). Some things signaling that a reaction one is having to someone with an eating disorder is actually a countertransference reaction include things such as anxiety, envy, dread, confusion, rage, shame, fatigue or other body-related symptoms, disorientation, and violence (Grotstein, 1981). Clinicians have been found to have negative attitudes toward those diagnosed with an eating disorder and these reactions are felt more strongly among less experienced clinicians (Thompson-Brenner, Satir, Franko, & Herzog, 2012). Thus, developing a greater understanding of how these reactions can impact treatment and how to support clinicians who are struggling to work effectively with patients with eating disorders is important.

Countertransference is usually discussed in the context of client/patient and health-care provider. Indeed, the origins of this concept are found in the work of Sigmund Freud and his work on psychoanalysis. The concept of "transference" was something he identified as being critical to the process of psychoanalysis. Transference refers to the patient's undeserved and unconscious emotional reactions to the analyst. In other words, the patient's feelings toward and about the analyst were believed to be about the patient and his or her relationship with someone important to him or her (usually a parent), not his or her relationship with the analyst. Countertransference, by contrast, is essentially the reverse. Countertransference involves the undeserved and unconscious emotional reactions the analyst has about the patient that have to do more with the analyst than the patient. In his work in 1910, Freud stated that countertransference "arises in the physician as a result of the patient's influence on his unconscious feelings, and have nearly come to the point of requiring the physician to recognize and overcome this counter-transference in himself" (p. 289). Erlichman (1998), a psychoanalytically trained therapist, said this about countertransference:

> . . . I have grown to understand countertransference, as many others do, as the totality of the experiences I have in my role as a therapist: all my feelings, thoughts, memories, actions, and reactions, consciously or unconsciously determined, which are generated in the therapy process. (p. 289)

The implication of both Freud's (1910) and Erlichman's (1998) statements is that the helping professional has feelings he or she is not aware of that are inadvertently triggered by the patient. Ultimately what this means is that whatever reactions the professional has about the patient and his or her behaviors are likely reactions that the professional must address on his or her own since they are the professional's problem and not necessarily something to be processed within the patient–professional relationship. Recognizing, understanding, and managing one's countertransference reactions are the responsibilities of the professional; however, those reactions can be instructive and ultimately useful for the professional in his or her work with the patient. The harm of countertransference reactions comes from not recognizing them, not managing them, and ultimately acting them out with the patient.

As previously noted, in the context of eating disorders one's reaction to someone with an eating disorder can vary widely from sadness to rage. Not managing such reactions can interfere with one's ability to effectively assist the individual with an eating disorder. Although countertransference is usually discussed in the context of, and understood as being part of, the patient–helper relationship, others in a relationship with someone with an eating disorder—such as family, friends, and romantic partners—can have such reactions as well. Thus, understanding what countertransference is and how it can help or harm one's relationship with the person with an eating disorder will ultimately benefit both people in the relationship.

In the context of countertransference felt in relationship with an individual diagnosed with an eating disorder, Erlichman (1998) said the following:

> *Eating disorders can induce strange and curious countertransference responses, and for that reason many therapists, veterans, and energetic new-comers alike, choose not to work with this population. The countertransference reactions and memories induced in treatment are frequently too difficult to tolerate. The profound pain that patients unravel is sometimes like balls of yarn that have been tied so tightly that fingers hurt loosening the knots and tangles that have laced together over the years. The mix of reported trauma . . . is so perplexing that it is hard for a therapist to determine what to explore or how to resolve the many complexities that often present simultaneously. Therapists can leave sessions confused, angry, and frustrated. Their feelings often reflect, through conscious and unconscious identifications, the patient's own intense struggles, and it is risky to assume that the credentials of the therapist are in effect a grant of immunity from the personal struggles that may result from working with such difficult cases. (pp. 289–290)*

Indeed, even well-trained, highly experienced healthcare providers are not immune to the effects of their patients, which give rise to a wide range of thoughts and emotions, many of which can be intensely experienced and overwhelming in their impact.

In addition to Erlichman's (1998) description, emotional reactions to patients with an eating disorder have also been described as like being on a roller coaster ride due in part to the potential life and death nature of the disorders as well as accompanying psychological disorders that complicate the diagnostic and treatment picture (Beale, Cole, Hillege, McMaster, & Nagy, 2004; Walker & Lloyd, 2011). The predominant emotional reaction to patients with eating disorders is typically negative. That is, more likely than not, what is felt by professionals and anyone else in a position of providing support are feelings such as anger, frustration, confusion, rage, and the like. One facet that may explain predominantly negative reactions is the notion that despite being informed about or knowing that eating disorders have a genetic component, many people still endorse the idea that eating disorders are within a person's control, further fueling the social stigma associated with this and other mental illnesses (Angermeyer et al., 2013). Thus, if you believe someone can stop his or her eating disorder behaviors at any time if he or she really wants to, then when the individual does not do so it appears as if he or she is choosing to be obstinate or is choosing behaviors that may ultimately cause serious harm or death.

Countertransference as a Barrier in the Treatment Relationship and Recovery Process

Countertransference reactions have the possibility of hindering treatment outcomes (Abbate-Daga et al., 2013) even when they are considered "positive" reactions (e.g., warmth and protective). The therapist, instead of reflecting on the nature of the work in each session, becomes more reactionary and may misperceive his or her patient's behaviors as well as misperceive who the patient is as an individual (Walker & Lloyd, 2011). When treatment providers fail to recognize their countertransference reactions or feel like they need to bring those reactions into the therapy setting, the risk becomes making treatment about the provider's own issues, avoiding difficult topics that may be critical for the patient's recovery process, and reenacting some element of his or her own life that makes the treatment provider feel important (D. Bunnell, personal communication, May 7, 2009).

In their examination of what may interfere with effective treatment among healthcare providers, Walker and Lloyd (2011) analyzed providers' reactions to their patients on a number of domains, which included the attitude of the healthcare professional, countertransference, and barriers to providing treatment. They found, with respect to the attitudes of healthcare professionals, many professionals struggled to understand patients who are afraid of food. They further indicated that they would rather not work with patients with an eating disorder in part because they felt like they could not be effective with someone they perceived as vain or as knowing more than they do about eating disorders. With respect to countertransference, providers often reported feeling angry and frustrated with their patients who had an eating disorder and whom they perceived as being resistant to receiving treatment. Providers also noted that they were more aware of their own issues with **body image**; however, this was more likely to be experienced by female compared to male providers. Finally, with respect to barriers to providing treatment, the researchers found that providers were concerned about being overloaded with cases and therefore unable to devote the time necessary to adequately care for individuals with such complex concerns, and that they felt underprepared in terms of skills and training to provide adequate care.

Male therapists were more likely to experience feelings of warmth than female therapists when working with patients with eating disorders; however, males were also more likely to acknowledge feelings of anger and frustration than their female counterparts, both of which may reflect cultural role expectations more than anything else (Satir, Thompson-Brenner, Boisseau, & Crisafulli, 2009). An additional complication that may give rise to strong emotional reactions is whether or not a patient is also diagnosed with a personality disorder. Personality disorders themselves usually evoke strong reactions, and researchers have noted that countertransference reactions to patients diagnosed with a personality disorder are a "problem" in the treatment relationship (Glita, 2007). Personality disorders are organized by category or "clusters" based on the shared traits among them. There are three clusters: *Cluster A* includes personality disorders with odd or eccentric traits; *Cluster B* includes personality disorders characterized by dramatic, emotional and erratic behavioral traits; and *Cluster C* disorders are characterized by anxious and fearful traits (American Psychiatric Association [APA], 2013).

Many individuals with eating disorders have a personality disorder diagnosis, which likely falls under Cluster B or Cluster C (Satir et al., 2009), and healthcare providers' reactions to such clients are often strong and generally negative in nature (Betan et al., 2005). In particular, Betan et al. (2005) found that psychologists and psychiatrists were likely to experience the countertransferential reaction of feeling parental or protective when working with individuals diagnosed with a Cluster C disorder, and criticized or mistreated when working with someone with a Cluster A disorder. The majority of reactions were found among clinicians working with individuals diagnosed with a Cluster B disorder. These reactions included feeling overwhelmed or disorganized, helpless or inadequate, positive, sexualized, disengaged, and criticized or mistreated. Colli et al. (2015) supported these findings in that they reported treatment providers' emotional reactions to patients with eating disorders may be more likely in response to the patient's personality characteristics rather than the eating disorders symptom themselves.

Coercion is a common response among treatment providers (McEneaney, 2007) and is often experienced by the patient as the therapist's (or family member's) effort to control the patient (Zerbe, 2008). As such, countertransference can be considered in terms of ethics and ethical behavior when working with patients with eating disorders, particularly when coerciveness is used to either compel patients to seek treatment or to force patients to seek treatment involuntarily (Matusek & Wright, 2010). Eating disorder patients are often described as stubborn and resistant to the help provided by healthcare professionals and friends and family members. Therefore, when interacting with someone, regardless of the diagnosis or context, who is perceived as stubborn and willful, it is not unlikely for others to respond by psychologically pushing back and trying to "make" the patient do what he or she is told to do. This can be problematic and is likely to result in something called **psychological reactance**.

Psychological reactance refers to a reaction that people have when they feel like some form of freedom is threatened. For example, if a child is told he or she cannot have a cookie before dinner, the child may very well experience psychological reactance and either have a tantrum or sneak a cookie when no one is looking. Likewise, if a patient is told he or she will have to eat or receive treatment no matter what, the patient is likely to rebel in one way or another, which is a form of psychological reactance and which is likely to be experienced unfavorably by others. An unfavorable reaction such as frustration or anger may seem reasonable given the life or death nature of eating disorders and the patient's seeming desire for self-destructiveness (Melamed, Mester, Margolin, & Kalian, 2003); however, when considered from the perspective of countertransference, such a reaction ought to be examined in terms of what it says about the person experiencing the anger or frustration rather than in terms of the patient "making" others feel that way.

Complex Emotional Reactions Among Caretakers and Family Members

As noted previously, therapists are not the only ones who may have strong reactions to individuals with an eating disorder. Essentially, anyone who interacts with someone with an eating disorder on a regular basis (and who knows the person has an eating disorder) is likely to experience strong emotional reactions. In one study, examining the effect of a change in a patient's eating behaviors that occurred after a stroke or injury (not the typical onset for eating disorders) on the patient's caregivers, researchers found that the caregivers experienced a dramatic shift in responsibilities as well as feelings about the patient's behaviors and the patient himself or herself (Johansson & Johansson, 2009). Specifically, they found that the caregivers experienced feelings of discomfort, concern, anxiety and fear, grief, and guilt. One potential reason for the strong emotional reactions seen among family members, particularly those who are providing a caretaking role of some kind, is that the form of support most likely provided to patients with eating disorders is emotional support, which can be psychologically draining (Raenker et al., 2013). How caretaking is experienced may differ between male caretakers and female caretakers, and therefore indicates that they may require different types and amounts of psychosocial support (Martín et al., 2013).

Another important finding among caregivers of those with eating disorders, particularly anorexia nervosa, is the degree to which there was high *expressed emotion* among family members. Expressed emotion (EE) is understood in the context of interpersonal relationships, typically families, and refers to the reactions a family member has toward someone in the family who is struggling with mental illness. EE is measured by assessing family members' attitudes and behaviors about the family member who has a mental health diagnosis. These attitudes and behaviors include criticism, hostility, warmth, positive comments, and emotional over-involvement. High EE has been found among treatment providers working with individuals with anorexia nervosa (Treasure, Crane, McKnight, Buchanan, & Wolfe, 2011) and research examining this experience in families has indicated high levels of EE may have a negative effect on the outcome of treatment (Butzlaff & Hooley, 1998). Multiple studies have found that the typical experience of high levels of EE were feelings of protection and criticism (Zabala, Macdonald, & Treasure, 2009).

Countertransference as an Aid in the Relationship and Recovery Process

Countertransference reactions, whether they occur in a healthcare provider or in someone with a more casual relationship, can provide a wealth of information about each person in the relationship and the nature of the relationship itself. And when the person interacting with someone with an eating disorder has the courage to examine his or her own reactions and reflect on what those reactions might mean, there is a very good chance that what is learned can improve the nature of the relationship itself. In the context of psychotherapy, therapists willing to acknowledge and examine their thoughts and reactions to their patient can allow them to change their way of interacting and may even change their interventions, the result of which can be an unexpected improvement (Erlichman, 1998).

Becoming aware of the nature of countertransference reactions can potentially provide useful information regarding important psychodynamics of some patients with eating disorders (Bunnell, 2009; Huges, 1997; Thompson-Brenner, 2014). For example, when a therapist is feeling bored, it is possible that the patient has an avoidant attachment style, whereas a therapist feeling overwhelmed might indicate an ambivalent attachment style in the patient (Thompson-Brenner, 2014; see Chapter 7). By learning from countertransference reactions, treatment providers and others can interact with the patient in ways that are not typical of what they are used to experiencing. This is often referred to as a *corrective emotional experience* (Glita, 2007). When patients engage in behaviors that would typically incite anger or rejection (e.g., repeated refusal to eat sufficient calories, thereby continuing to lose weight) and someone responds instead with empathy and patience, the patient is likely to have a new experience that is atypical from what he or she is used to experiencing with other important people in his or her life. This has the potential to be corrective and healing. Of course, this cannot happen if the therapist (or family member) is not aware of the fact that his or her own feelings of anger, resentment, and the like are evidence of countertransference.

When therapists are aware of their countertransference reactions, these reactions can be used to benefit the psychotherapy process and by extension the outcome of psychotherapy. Recognizing the feelings that a therapist has about a particular patient can allow him or her to strengthen the therapeutic relationship, change the patient's commitment to making changes in his or her life, assist the therapist and patient when no action or movement seems to be occurring in psychotherapy, and may allow the therapist to recognize and empathize with the patient's ambivalence for making change (Ehrenberg, 1992). One analyst recounted his long-term work with a patient with a history of a severe eating disorder, which illustrated the importance of his identification and resolution of his countertransference reactions. Although initially the countertransference reactions inhibited treatment, his realization of what they were, how they were affecting him, and consequently his work with his patient allowed him to work more effectively with the patient, resulting in a favorable outcome to the therapy (Chessick, 2007).

The Body as a Source of Emotional Reactions

Given the nature of eating disorders and their accompanying symptoms, it is not surprising that not only are patients excruciatingly aware of their own bodies (e.g., what they look like and how they feel), but they are also aware of the therapist's body and may have a multitude of reactions to the therapist's body based on its size and what the patient may think that particular body size means (e.g., is it a body to be envied, to be repulsed; Lowell & Meader, 2005).

One target of countertransference (and, of course, the patient's transference), therefore, is the physical body (Daly, 2016; Lowell & Meader, 2005; McEneaney, 2007; Miller, 2000). Eating disorders by their very nature focus one's attention on the body of one's self and others. Individuals dealing with an eating disorder are typically in some state of dissatisfaction with their own body, trying to manipulate its size, and consistently comparing their body to others'. Body dissatisfaction has become an increasingly normal experience for most women in Western societies; therefore, it may be especially important for female therapists to have a well-developed awareness of one's own issues with body dissatisfaction and how those issues may intersect with the experiences of one's patients (Daly, 2016).

Lowell and Meader (2005) indicated that the therapist's perception of his or her own body can vary throughout a single session based on the patient's body size and comments about his or her body size. For example, they noted that a thin therapist working with a larger bodied patient may wish for a larger body that is reflective of a "rounder, 'earth mother' body, [that may] convey a sense of safety and security" (p. 243). This desire may last until the patient says negative things about his or her own body. Complications in the relationship can also arise when the therapist has or has not had a history of an eating disorder and the patient holds an assumption about that history that is contrary to reality (e.g., the patient believes the therapist has a history of eating disorders but in fact has not).

Miller (2000) discusses the body in terms of the fear contemporary professionals seem to have of their own and their patients' bodies. He recommends a number of things in order to become more comfortable with one's own body, including becoming more aware of how one uses his or her own body and how it operates/works during physical activity. Additionally, becoming more aware of the connection between one's own mind and body can help to illuminate the ways in which one's body is affected by movement or touch. Although certainly rife for positive or negative reactions on the part of one's patients, getting familiar with one's patients' bodies can help therapists notice changes that may occur from one session to the next including changes in movement, changes in weight, facial expressions, and the like. Finally, Miller recommends being attuned to one's **somatic countertransference** (e.g., "sudden in-take of breath," "slight sense of arousal"; p. 448), of which a therapist will become more aware after becoming more aware of his or her own body based on the previous three recommendations. These changes in one's body during a therapy session can signal emotional reactions within the therapist that may require attention outside the context of the therapy session, and they may prove informative in terms of selecting interventions with a particular patient.

McEneaney (2007) suggests that when working with patients with eating disorders, becoming more aware of one's own body is inevitable. This awareness not only includes awareness of body shape and size but also aches and pains, and appetite. McEneaney echoes others' admonishment that it is important for therapists to be aware of their own views on the expectations of body shape, size, and appearance. To borrow from Bunnell (2016), it will be especially important to be aware of these expectations as they apply to females and males (i.e., the **thin ideal** is the expectation for females while the **muscular ideal** is expected of males). Along with these expectations comes assumptions about how a body size is maintained and what body types are considered "good" and which are considered "bad." McEneaney notes that not only should therapists be aware of their own reactions to these culturally based assumptions about body weight, shape, and size, but also their willingness to hear what their patient has to say about these assumptions regardless of what they are. She also acknowledges an earlier identified and common countertransference reaction that involves the strong desire on the part of the therapist to change the patient's behaviors by whatever means necessary, including coercion. She also notes therapists should remain vigilant for reactions such as revulsion, disgust, and envy, which may, respectively, reflect one's reaction to a large body or the smaller body of a patient who engages in restricting, overexercising, and behaviors that fuel their perfectionism. Essentially, a therapist must be aware of his or her own comfort with various manifestations of body-related issues (e.g., dieting, sexual functioning, eating behaviors, and so on) so he or she is able to make space in the therapy relationship for the patient to address these and other body-related concerns that may be important to him or her.

When the Patient Is a Man

Although the symptoms and behaviors associated with eating disorders are roughly the same regardless of whether or not the patient is male or female, the fact that male and female bodies as well as the concepts of masculinity and femininity tend to have particular expectations that are culturally bound means that therapists may have reactions to their patients that differ *because* the patient is male or female (Bunnell, 2016).

Although there may be patterns of countertransference reactions that allow therapists to more accurately understand themselves and their clients, Bunnell (2016) cautions that therapists without much experience working with male patients, particularly male patients with an eating disorder, may find identifying their countertransference reactions to be elusive. For example, he notes that it may be difficult for some therapists to truly believe that their male patient has an eating disorder, which is likely influenced by the notion that males are not to be concerned with relationship issues in the same way that females are; moreover, they are therefore not likely to express those concerns in terms of an eating disorder. He further notes that female therapists working with male clients may need to be especially aware of their own perceptions and comfort around a male patient's expression of anger, whereas male therapists working with male clients ought to pay attention to the tendency for both men in the relationship to avoid emotionally charged interactions. The thoughts, reactions, and behaviors of both male and female therapists working with male patients with eating disorders and awareness thereof can be extraordinarily useful in identifying the therapist's own countertransference reactions as well as illuminating issues that the patient himself may be dealing with.

The Importance of Having Others to Talk to

Staying alone with one's strong reactions to anything is difficult. Staying alone with one's reactions to someone who is, in one way or another, important to you is an entirely different type of difficulty. For healthcare providers, the importance of supervision or consultation, whether formal or informal, cannot be overstated. Likewise, for the friend, family member, or romantic partner, having one's own therapist, a support group for friends and family of someone with an eating disorder, or some other unbiased source of support is equally valuable.

For healthcare providers, and perhaps therapists in particular, having a professional source of support can not only help to ensure treatment does not suffer based on their countertransference but in some cases the countertransference reactions to a patient can result in the therapist's suffering (Erlichman, 1998). Erlichman likens this kind of support to self-care and in the absence of attending to our strong emotional and cognitive reactions to patients we not only risk doing damage to the therapeutic relationship or the patient but also to ourselves as well.

Family members providing care to those with an eating disorder are benefitted from formal supports but likely benefit from informal supports as well (Coomber & King, 2011). Those treating individuals with eating disorders are in need of "constant support and supervision" (Golan, Yaroslavski, & Stein, 2011) if they are to be effective in their work with individuals with eating disorders. The initial step in being able to manage countertransference reactions and thereby receive support or formal supervision is for the treating professional to be able to recognize that he or she is having a reaction in the first place. Thus, self-awareness or self-insight is a critical initial step (Golan, Yaroslavski, & Stein, 2011; Hayes, Gelso, Van Wagoner, & Diemer, 1991; Van Wagoner, Gelso, Hayes, & Diemer, 1991).

Conclusion

Strong emotional reactions, often referred to as countertransference reactions, to patients with an eating disorder are common and can range from care and concern to frustration and rage. Acknowledging and identifying one's own countertransference reactions can help both the person feeling them and the patient as well. This is particularly true for treatment providers who can risk harm to themselves and/or the patient if countertransference reactions remain unidentified. By contrast, when countertransference reactions are identified and appropriately understood the treatment provider may learn more about himself or herself as well as the patient, which ultimately can benefit treatment.

References

Abbate-Daga, G., Amianto, F., Delsedime, N., De-Bacco, C., & Fassino, S. (2013). Resistance to treatment and change in anorexia nervosa: A clinical overview. *BMC Psychiatry, 13*, 1–18. doi:10.1186/1471-244X-13-294

American Psychiatric Association. (2013). *Diagnostic and statistical manual of mental disorders* (5th ed.). Washington, DC: Author.

Angermeyer, M. C., Mnich, E., Daubmann, A., Herich, L., Wegscheider, K., Kofahl, C., & von dem Knesebeck, O. (2013). Biogenetic explanations and public acceptance of people with eating disorders. *Social Psychiatry and Psychiatric Epidemiology, 48*, 1667–1673. doi:10.1007/s00127-012-0648-9

Beale, B., Cole, R., Hillege, S., McMaster, R., & Nagy, S. (2004). Impact of in-depth interviews on the interviewer: Roller coaster ride. *Nursing and Health Sciences, 6*, 141–147. doi:10.1111/j.1442-2018.2004.00185.x

Betan, E., Heim, K., Conklin, C. A., & Westen, D. (2005). Countertransference phenomena and personality pathology in clinical practice: An empirical investigation. *American Journal of Psychiatry, 162*, 890–898. doi:10.1176/appi.ajp.162.5.890

Bunnell, D. W. (2009). Countertransference in the psychotherapy of patients with eating disorders. In M. Maine, W. N. Davis, & J. Shure (Eds.), *Effective clinical practice in the treatment of eating disorders: The heart of the matter* (pp. 79–94). New York, NY: Routledge.

Bunnell, D. W. (2016). Gender socialization, countertransference and the treatment of men with eating disorders. *Clinical Social Work Journal, 44*, 99–104. doi:10.1007/s10615-015-0564-z

Butzlaff, R. L., & Hooley, J. M. (1998). Expressed emotion and psychiatric relapse: A meta-analysis. *Archives of General Psychiatry, 55*, 547–552. doi:10.1001/archpsyc.55.6.547

Chessick, R. D. (2007). Long-term psychoanalytic therapy as a life-saving procedure. *The American Journal of Psychoanalysis, 67*, 334–358. doi:10.1057/palqrave.ajp.3350037

Colli, A., Speranza, A. M., Lingiardi, V., Gentile, D., Nassisi, V., & Hilsenroth, M. J. (2015). Eating disorders and therapist emotional responses. *The Journal of Nervous and Mental Disease, 203*, 843–849. doi:10.1097/NMD.0000000000000379

Coomber, K., & King, R. M. (2011). Coping strategies and social support as predictors and mediators of eating disorder carer burden and psychological distress. *Social Psychiatry and Psychiatric Epidemiology, 47*, 789–796. doi:10.1007/s00127-011-0384-6

Daly, S. B. (2016). The intersubjective experience of the physical body in the clinical setting of eating disorders. *Clinical Social Work Journal, 44*, 47–56. doi:10.1007/s10615-014-0475-4

Ehrenberg, D. (1992). *The intimate edge.* New York, NY: W. W. Norton.

Erlichman, S. R. (1998). The last word: Countertransference: A neglected natural resource. *Eating Disorders, 6*, 289–294. doi:10.1080/10640269808249264

Freud, S. (1910). *The future prospects of psycho-analytic therapy: An address delivered before the Second International Psycho-Analytical Congress at Nuremberg in 1910.* Retrieved from https://readingsinpsych.files.wordpress.com/2009/08/freud-future-prospects-of-psychoan-alytic-therapy4.pdf

Glita, P. (2007). Problems occurring in the psychotherapy of adolescent patients with symptoms of pathological personality development. *Archives of Psychiatry and Psychotherapy, 4*, 65–73.

Golan, M., Yaroslavski, A., & Stein, D. (2011). Managing eating disorders: Countertransference processes in the therapeutic milieu. In J. Merrick (Ed.), *Child and adolescent health yearbook 2009* (pp. 253–270). New York, NY: Nova Biomedical.

Grotstein, J. S. (1981). *Splitting and projective identification.* New York, NY: Jason Aronson.

Hayes, J. A., Gelso, C. J., Van Wagoner, S. L. & Diemer, R. A. (1991). Managing countertransference: What the experts think. *Psychological Reports, 69*, 139–148. doi:10.2466/pr0.1991.69.1.139

Huges, P. (1997). The use of countertransference in the therapy of patients with anorexia nervosa. *European Eating Disorders Review, 5,* 258–269. doi:10.1002/(SICI)1099 -0968(199712)5:4<258::AID-ERV183>3.0.CO;2-B

Johansson, A. E. M., & Johansson, U. (2009). Relatives' experiences of family members' eating difficulties. *Scandinavian Journal of Occupational Therapy, 16,* 25–32. doi:10.1080/11038120802257195

Land, P. (2004). Thinking about feelings: Working with the staff of an eating disorders unit. *Psychoanalytic Psychotherapy, 18,* 280–295. doi:10.1080/14749730042000297344

Lowell, M. A., & Meader, L. L. (2005). My body, your body: Speaking the unspoken between the thin therapist and the eating-disordered patient. *Clinical Social Work Journal, 33,* 241–257. doi:10.1007/s10615-005-4941-x

Martín, J., Padierna, A., Aguirre, U., González, N., Muñoz, P., & Quintana, J. M. (2013). Predictors of quality of life and caregiver burden among maternal and paternal caregivers of patients with eating disorders. *Psychiatry Research, 210,* 1107–1115. doi:10.1016/j.psychres.2013.07.039

Matusek, J. A., & Wright, M. O. (2010). Ethical dilemmas in treating clients with eating disorders: A review and application of an integrative ethical decision-making model. *European Eating Disorders Review, 18,* 434–452. doi:10.1002/erv.1036

McEneaney, A. (2007). Envy in body transference and counter-transference: Female treatment dyads, patients with eating disorders. In L. Navaro & S. L. Schwartzberg (Eds.), *Envy, competition, and gender: Theory, clinical applications and group work* (pp. 155–182). New York, NY: Routledge.

Melamed, Y., Mester, R., Margolin, J., & Kalian, M. (2003). Involuntary treatment of anorexia nervosa. *International Journal of Law and Psychiatry, 26,* 617–626. doi:10.1016/j.ijlp.2003.09.006

Miller, J. A. (2000). The fear of the body in psychotherapy. *Psychodynamic Counselling, 6,* 437–450. doi:10.1080/1353333005019070

Raenker, S., Hibbs, R., Goddard, E., Naumann, U., Arcelus, J., Ayton, A., . . . Treasure, J. (2013). Caregiving and coping in carers of people with anorexia nervosa admitted for intensive hospital care. *International Journal of Eating Disorders, 46,* 346–354. doi:10.1002/eat.22068

Satir, D. A., Thompson-Brenner, H., Boisseau, C. L., & Crisafulli, M. A. (2009). Countertransference reactions to adolescents with eating disorders: Relationship to clinician and patient factors. *International Journal of Eating Disorders, 42,* 511–521. doi:10.1002/eat.20650

Thompson-Brenner, H. (2014). Discussion of "eating disorders and attachment: A contemporary psychodynamic perspective:" Does the attachment model of eating disorders indicate the need for psychodynamic treatment? *Psychodynamic Psychiatry, 42,* 277–284. doi:10.1521/pdps.2014.42.2.277

Thompson-Brenner, H., Satir, D. A., Franko, D. L., & Herzog, D. B. (2012). Clinician reactions to patients with eating disorders: A review of the literature. *Psychiatric Services, 63,* 73–78. doi:10.1176/appi.ps.201100050

Tobin, D. (2012). Psychodynamic treatment for eating disorders patients. In D. Stein & Y. Latzer (Eds.), *Treatment and recovery of eating disorders* (pp. 97–108). New York, NY: Nova Science.

Treasure, J., Crane, A., McKnight, R., Buchanan, E., & Wolfe, M. (2011). First do no harm: Iatrogenic maintaining factors in anorexia nervosa. *European Eating Disorders Review, 19,* 269–302. doi:10.1002/erv.1056

Van Wagoner, S. L. Gelso, C. J., Hayes, J. A., & Diemer, R. A. (1991). Countertransference and the reputedly excellent therapist. *Psychotherapy, 28,* 411–421. doi:10.1037/0033-3204.28.3.411

Walker, S., & Lloyd, C. (2011). Barriers and attitudes health professionals working in eating disorders experience. *International Journal of Therapy and Rehabilitation, 18,* 383–390. doi:10.12968/ijtr.2011.18.7.383

Zabala, M. J., Macdonald, P., & Treasure, J. (2009). Appraisal of caregiving burden, expressed emotion and psychological distress in families of people with eating disorders: A systematic review. *European Eating Disorders Review, 17*, 338–349. doi:10.1002/erv.925

Zerbe, K. J. (2008). *Integrated treatment of eating disorders: Beyond the body betrayed.* New York, NY: W. W. Norton.

IV

PREVENTION AND TREATMENT

PREVENTION

Introduction

The sections that follow describe prevention efforts in general and prevention programs designed specifically for eating disorders. The final two subsections address eating disorder prevention in middle school as most programs have been studied with high school students and young adults, and prevention efforts implemented via technology. Effectiveness for the various programs discussed varies; however, there are some programs that have been shown to be quite effective and others that show promise.

Types of Prevention

The three types of prevention target different stages of the development of any disease or disorder. **Primary prevention** refers to any effort designed to prevent a disease or disorder from developing in an otherwise healthy individual. In the context of eating disorders, that might look like efforts to discourage individuals from going on a diet for the purpose of losing weight since dieting is a common factor in the development of eating disorders. **Secondary prevention** involves efforts to identify the disease or disorder as early as possible before the problem gets worse. For eating disorder prevention, this might involve using eating disorder screening tools in healthcare settings, schools, and the workplace to identify those who are showing signs that an eating disorder is developing or has already developed. Finally, **tertiary prevention** includes efforts to ameliorate the effects of a disease or disorder once it has already been established. The idea is to reduce symptoms that interfere with functioning and to restore one's quality of life. In the context of eating disorders, this type of prevention is most likely going to involve formal treatment of the eating disorder from a multidisciplinary perspective (see Chapter 12).

The National Research Council and Institute of Medicine of the National Academies (2009) convened a committee to examine the most effective ways to prevent mental, emotional, and behavioral disorders in children, adolescents, and young adults. Their work culminated in an extensive manuscript that reviewed the various forms and effectiveness of prevention, systems in which prevention efforts can be implemented, and directions for future prevention programs. The committee identified three types of prevention efforts that reflect the specific goals of the prevention program, the method used to implement the prevention program, and the individuals or groups that are the focus of the prevention program. The three types of prevention are **universal prevention, selective prevention**, and **indicated prevention**. Universal prevention efforts are designed to assist the entire population with the idea that all are likely to benefit from this type of prevention. Selective prevention focuses on a subgroup of the entire population who are believed to be at greater risk for the particular disease or disorder, and indicated prevention involves efforts focused on those who have been identified (i.e., screened) or who are at specific risk for developing a particular disease or disorder.

In their report on how to prevent disorders involving problems with mental, emotional, and behavioral functioning, the National Research Council and Institute of Medicine of the National Academies (2009) identified several *core concepts* that should be part of any prevention effort and that should be adopted by all who participate in the prevention of any mental disorder. The committee suggests that the disease model approach to prevention is ultimately not effective. This approach suggests that one waits for a disease to emerge, then provides the best known treatment to cure or ameliorate the disease/disorder. A *paradigm shift* is recommended that involves considering what efforts can be enacted that will benefit a child or adolescent many years removed from when the prevention effort was implemented. Ultimately, this shift in perspective involves a focus on supporting the health and well-being of individuals while they are still healthy and well.

The second core concept identified by the committee is the acknowledgement that the mind and body are inextricably linked. Thus, when the body is ailing the mind will suffer as well and vice versa. Thus, children and adolescents who are in good physical health are also more likely to have good mental health, and those who are mentally well are also more likely to be physically well. Therefore, prevention efforts must focus on supporting mental and physical well-being simultaneously. The third core concept reflects the spirit of the second core concept in that the committee suggests that prevention is multidisciplinary. This means that knowledgeable individuals from a variety of professions need to be involved in developing and implementing any prevention effort. The fourth core concept states that mental disorders are developmental in nature and that intervention points such as early childhood or early adolescence are opportune times to implement prevention programs in the context of the child's family or primary caretakers, school, and community. Finally, the fifth core concept builds on the fourth and focuses on the importance of the community and the establishment of an integrated set of efforts implemented in multiple systems. This would include public healthcare systems, the school system, families/institutions, and the community. Coordinating and pooling resourses provides the best chance for effective prevention.

Eating Disorders Prevention

In 2005, Levine and Maine produced an informational pamphlet for the National Eating Disorders Association that outlined what prevention is and the basic principles that should underlie any prevention efforts aimed at eating disorders. They identified four principles that in many ways reflect the core concepts put forth by the National Research Council and Institute of Medicine of the National Academies (2009). The first principle specific to eating disorders prevention is the awareness that eating disorders are highly complex; they are caused and sustained by a multitude of factors including biological (e.g., genetics), psychological (e.g., self-esteem, perfectionism), and environmental (e.g., family, school, peers) factors. The second principle involves an acknowledgement that women and girls are not the only ones who can be afflicted with an eating disorder. Moreover, education for all, including males, about the tendency for females to be objectified and mistreated can help prevent some of the psychological factors that arise from being objectified or mistreated (e.g., **body image** dissatisfaction). The third principle is that prevention efforts that focus solely on psychoeducation (e.g., information on warning signs and dangers of eating disorders) will be ineffective at best and in some cases may accidentally bolster eating disorder symptoms. The final principle is that when prevention efforts are implemented, regardless of the setting or the target audience, it is important that a professional is available for individuals to talk to, in confidence, who is also well trained in the area of eating disorders and who can provide referral and other support services if needed.

A review of research on eating disorder prevention programs found that many of the existing prevention programs are able to reduce known risk factors for eating disorders and current eating disorder symptoms, and a smaller subset are able to reduce the number of people who might develop an eating disorder in the future (Stice, Shaw, & Marti, 2007; Stice, South, & Shaw, 2012). A more recent review identified nine specific prevention programs that were found to either prevent the future onset of eating disorders or reduced existing eating disorder symptoms (Ciao, Loth, & Neumark-Sztainer, 2014). Successful prevention programs have been identified as including a number of features that may account for their success. These factors include having programs that were developed based on established psychological theory (e.g., cognitive dissonance), focused on individuals who are at high risk for developing an eating disorder (i.e., indicated prevention), provided an interactive rather than didactic- or lecture-based format, targeted specific risk factors empirically identified as strong predictors of eating disorders (e.g., dietary restriction, body dissatisfaction), engaged with individuals over multiple-sessions rather than in a one-time meeting, included information related to healthy eating, media literacy, and body acceptance, and were provided by professionals rather than by those who may already be part of a particular system (e.g., teachers, untrained healthcare providers; Ciao, Loth, & Neumark-Sztainer, 2014; Stice, Shaw, & Marti, 2007).

A recent examination of the eating disorder prevention literature found promising results and identified important areas for improvement not only in terms of what effective prevention programs should look like but also how they should be disseminated (Stice, Becker, & Yokum, 2013). This review identified six eating disorder prevention programs that effectively reduced symptoms of eating disorders for several months following completion of the program. Two programs were found to effectively prevent the onset of future eating disorder incidences. Although many of the prevention programs have been delivered under conditions that are not sufficiently reflective of real life experiences, this review identified two prevention programs that were shown to be effective under circumstances that more effectively reflect a real-world environment.

The two programs found to meaningfully show a reduction in the future rate of onset of eating disorders are the Body Project and Healthy Weight (Stice, Marti, Spoor, Presnell, & Shaw, 2008; Stice, Rohde, Shaw, & Marti, 2012; Stice, Shaw, Burton, & Wade, 2006). The Body Project is a dissonance-based prevention program. Dissonance or cognitive dissonance, first identified by Festinger in 1957, refers to the psychological discomfort experienced when a person holds two contradictory beliefs. This type of discomfort can occur when someone does something that directly contradicts a belief (e.g., spending a lot of money on a luxury item when the person believes he or she is thrifty and a conservative spender), or when someone is presented with new information or evidence that directly contradicts his or her currently held belief (e.g., someone is presented with irrefutable evidence that Sasquatch is real when the person believes no such thing exists). According to Festinger, human beings are most psychologically comfortable when we are consistent or when our experiences (i.e., our actions, exposure to new evidence) fall in line with our beliefs. Thus, when we experience dissonance-based discomfort we tend to take action by changing our behavior, changing our belief, providing a justification for either the behavior or the belief so that it "makes sense" to us, or ignore new evidence that conflicts with our currently held beliefs. Any of these approaches are intended to reduce psychological discomfort, or dissonance, and thereby reestablish a comfortable state of being.

In the context of dissonance-based eating disorder prevention programs, specifically the Body Project, the belief that is usually held by participants of the program is that the **thin ideal** is worth pursuing. Since this is the belief that is already held by participants, anything that contradicts that belief will result in dissonance and cause participants to take one of the actions previously noted in order to reduce dissonance. The Body Project takes participants through a series of discussions and written exercises designed to challenge the thin-ideal. For example, participants are asked to discuss who benefits from the thin-ideal (e.g., fitness centers, diet companies) and what costs are associated with that ideal, they are asked to write a letter to an adolescent encouraging him or her to not pursue the thin ideal, and to role-play various scenarios in which someone is pursing the thin ideal and the participants' task is to say things that would encourage the individual not to pursue that ideal. By engaging in these activities designed to bolster the idea that pursuing the thin ideal is *not* a good idea, participants are likely to experience dissonance and must do something to reduce their discomfort. In this case, the research found that the majority of participants reduced their dissonance by rejecting the thin ideal as evidenced by a reduction in eating disorder–related symptoms and the future onset of diagnosable eating disorders.

In their assessment of the effectiveness of the Body Project prevention program on multiple college campuses, Stice, Butryn, Rohde, Shaw, and Marti (2013) enhanced the program by providing additional training to college clinicians and made changes to the original Body Project program by increasing participant accountability and participation for their homework assignments and in discussions/activities. They compared the effectiveness of this program to a control group that was provided educational brochures developed by the National Eating Disorders Association and the American Psychological Association, both of which focused on eating disorders and related issues. The results of the comparison between the Body Project participants and the brochure group was that the Body Project participants showed greater improvement on a number of factors compared to the brochure group. These factors included a decrease in the eating disorder risk factors of thin-ideal internalization, body dissatisfaction, dieting and negative affect, and a decrease in eating disorder symptoms. These results held after a 1-year follow-up. An additional study of this new version of the Body Project was studied again at 3 years follow-up, showing a long-term reduction in risk factors for eating disorders, eating disorder-related symptoms, and overall impairment (Stice, Rohde, Butryn, Shaw, & Marti, 2015). This study did not, however, show a reduction in the onset of eating disorders after 3 years, leading this group to conclude that other factors apart from those addressed by this program may account for the onset of eating disorders.

In a study examining the degree of dissonance experienced in prevention programs, results revealed that those who participated in a program with a high level of dissonance showed a reduction in eating disorder symptoms that was greater than that experienced by those who participated in a program with a low level of dissonance (McMillan, Stice, & Rohde, 2011). Additionally, those with stronger thin-ideal internalization and those who had an eating disorder diagnosis showed greater improvements in a dissonance-based prevention program compared to those with lower thin-ideal internalization who did not have an eating disorder diagnosis (Müller & Stice, 2013).

Van Diest and Perez (2013) examined the extent to which targeting both thin-ideal internalization and self-objectification in prevention programs would be effective. They found that when this is done, the result is a reduction in the symptoms diagnostic of an eating disorder. An interesting finding revealed by Stice, Rohde, Gau, and Shaw (2012) indicated that what may be stronger than thin-ideal internalization in predicting eating disorder-related pathology is an active denial that there are any costs associated with pursing the thin-ideal (e.g., it is not possible to exercise too much, any risks associated with severe dieting are exaggerated). Thus, while thin-ideal internalization has been shown to be a significant factor in whether or not someone develops an eating disorder, what may supersede this tendency in the first place is not acknowledging that there might be anything wrong with trying to be thin. Stice, Rohde, Durant, & Shaw (2012) found that confronting one's desire to pursue the thin-ideal, negative affect, and symptom externalization (i.e., blaming something/someone outside of one's self for any problems) can counteract the risk associated with denying that anything bad will occur physically, psychologically, or interpersonally by pursing the thin-ideal.

An interesting twist on prevention programs involves who implements the programs: professionals or peers. In a study examining the effectiveness of a peer- or clinician-led prevention program, the study found that both groups show greater reductions in important factors such as dropout, eating disorder risk factors, and eating disorder symptoms compared to those whose only prevention intervention was a brief informational brochure developed by the National Eating Disorders Association (Stice, Rohde, Durant, Shaw, & Wade, 2013). This finding has potentially broad implications as peer-led groups would be able to facilitate prevention programs reaching greater numbers of participants compared to what clinicians can do. In fact, Shaw and Stice (2016) examined peer-led and Internet-based programs as well as programs implemented by groups such as the

Girl Scouts. They found that professionals do not have to be involved to deliver effective efforts at the universal, selective, and indicated levels of prevention.

Wilksch (2015) notes that while eating disorder prevention efforts have greatly improved in their effectiveness over the years, he also notes concern that empirical focus on targeted prevention efforts has left universal prevention programs underevaluated. He indicates that research on universal prevention programs showing smaller effect sizes (i.e., the effectiveness of the prevention program of study while present is small compared to the effectiveness of targeted prevention programs) shows not that these programs are less effective or ineffective but that the small effect size is an artifact of the baseline level of pathology.

Universal programs implemented with age groups that are likely to show less eating pathology at their point in development will mean that any effect cannot be as large as that shown with programs implemented with populations in which eating pathology is already evident. Wilksch (2015) follows this by saying that risk factors such as body dissatisfaction, dieting, negative affect, and the like can result in clinically significant functioning even if those dealing with these issues do not have a diagnosable eating disorder. Thus, prevention programs targeting a reduction in these experiences absent a specific focus on the prevention of eating disorders can help slow the development of risk factors that are ultimately associated with diagnosable eating disorders. This position is bolstered by the finding that implementing prevention efforts with girls in early adolescence is essential as girls as early as age 13 have been found to display eating disorder risk factors such as body dissatisfaction and the perceived pressure to be thin, the presence of which is predictive of later onset of eating disorders (Rohde, Stice, & Marti, 2015). The age that produced the greatest predictability of later onset of eating disorders was age 14 (Rohde, Stice, & Marti, 2015).

Combined Eating Disorder and Obesity Prevention

Some researchers have suggested that given the overlap between concerns related to eating disorders and obesity screening and prevention efforts should target both those who are at risk for eating disorders or obesity (Austin, 2011; Kass et al., 2015; Shaw, 2008; Wilksch et al., 2015) while others have expressed concern that a focus on weight loss (i.e., dietary restraint, which is typically associated with eating disorders, particularly anorexia nervosa) for the purposes of addressing obesity may lead to an increase in the incidence of eating disorders (e.g., Neumark-Sztainer, 2009). Kass et al. (2015) developed a prevention program designed to address both eating disorders and obesity that focuses on healthy eating practices while discouraging unhealthy weight management strategies often associated with eating disorders (and that are often enacted by those trying to lose weight for any reason). Another group of researchers examined three prevention programs to determine which, if any, might show a reduction in risk factors associated with both eating disorder and obesity. They found that only one, *Media Smart,* was effective in this regard. Another program designed to address both obesity and eating disorders in high school students is called StayingFit and was developed as an Internet-based program (Jones et al., 2014). This program was shown to be easily implemented by teachers, was well received by both teachers and students, and found that concerns about body weight and shape decreased, healthier eating behaviors increased as did physical activity, and there was a reduction in soda consumption and time spent watching television.

There is a growing body of literature suggesting that obesity itself is not the factor of importance when considering health problems associated with this weight range, but whether or not one has **metabolic syndrome**, which can occur in normal weight as well as obese individuals; moreover, weight loss efforts designed to address the obesity issue are more likely to result in weight gain over the long term and assumed health benefits of weight loss attempts have not been reliably established (Selby, 2017). Thus, focusing on factors that contribute to the issues implicated in metabolic syndrome is warranted. Neumark-Sztainer (2009) indicated that the way to address both eating disorders and obesity is to address the things that would benefit most people regardless of their body shape and size. She recommends that an emphasis should be placed on healthy eating behaviors and physical activity that can be sustained, promote positive body image, encourage frequent and enjoyable meals with family members, focus less on weight and more on healthy eating and physical activity, and operate from the assumption that a child or adolescent who is overweight has been the target of weight-based stigma and discrimination and that this issue should be addressed directly.

Prevention in Middle School

The Body Project is among the most effective prevention programs but has primarily shown effectiveness in high school and college age females. Additionally, not all who complete the Body Project in these age groups remain eating disorder free. Examination of the differences between those who do not develop an eating disorder and those who do indicate that the latter reported higher levels of thin-ideal internalization, body dissatisfaction, negative affect, and eating disorder-related symptoms prior to going through the program (Horney, Stice, & Rohde, 2015). Some researchers have noted that many known risk factors are their most potent at age 14 (Rohde, Stice, & Marti, 2015) and others have found risk factors for eating disorders to be present for those in late childhood and early adolescence, making this time period the most ideal for implementing prevention programs (Westerberg-Jacobson, Ghaderi, & Edlund, 2012).

Most prevention programs that are effective target high school or college students and only a few were developed specifically for middle schoolers (Rohde et al., 2014). Rohde et al. (2014) modified the Body Project, which was originally developed for high school and college students, to reflect the needs of middle schoolers. This involved shortening the length of sessions (but including more sessions to cover all material), and revising the material to match the cognitive abilities of middle school age children (e.g., deficits in abstract reasoning). Their results indicated that those who participated in what they called the MS Body Project had some benefits but that these benefits were not maintained in the months following the program. They concluded that the program has promise as it produced results at least on par with other prevention programs targeting this age group. Moreover, they cited the known immediate and longer-term benefits of the original Body Project as evidence that the MS Body Project requires additional revision in order to reach the known effectiveness of the original intervention program.

Another program called Media Smart was developed for implementation with middle school students and involves eight sessions focusing on stereotypes, how media images are manipulated, societal pressures, and activism-based activities (Wilksch, Tiggemann, & Wade, 2006). It has previously shown effectiveness in its implementation by professionals, which can limit reaching the greatest number of children and adolescents possible. The effectiveness of this program as implemented by school teachers was examined and it was determined that delivering this program was a reasonable task for teachers to undertake and that their delivery of the program showed promising results, suggesting that further implementation and study is warranted (Wilksch, 2015).

Internet-Based Prevention Programs

With the increased availability and use of social media and other electronically based platforms, the healthcare field has experimented with providing services via synchronous and asynchronous programs. Many states and professional organizations have developed guidelines, and in the case of state oversight, laws, around **telehealth** services. Telehealth refers to providing healthcare services via electronic technology. The implication is that the provider and the patient are not meeting in person and may in fact be physically located many hundreds or thousands of miles away from one another.

Internet-based prevention programs are believed to be promising in that they are able to engage individuals and larger groups in ways that face-to-face programs cannot (Bauer & Moessner, 2013). Internet-based programs can reach larger numbers of people across larger geographical areas. Such programs require fewer trained facilitators, and the modality is easier to implement and to maintain standardization compared to face-to-face interventions. Using technology to implement prevention programs also allows for greater flexibility in terms of how material is presented and can be tailored to an individual's needs. The empirical literature examining the effectiveness of Internet-based prevention (and treatment) efforts is small and has shown limited success (Loucas et al., 2014). In fact, Internet-based prevention efforts are not expected to have better outcomes in comparison to face-to-face prevention programs due to the advantage that the face-to-face programs have been around for a longer period of time and have been refined to provide the best possible intervention (Bauer & Moessner, 2013).

One Internet-based program shown to have some effectiveness is Student Bodies, which is described as "an eight-session online psychoeducation intervention based on cognitive behavioral and social learning theories and designed for individuals at risk of Eating Disorders" (National Eating Disorders Collaboration, n.d.). Among several different programs examined, some produced limited benefits, but the Student Bodies program was found to have shown a modest reduction in eating disorder-related symptoms, degree of weight concern, and drive for thinness (Jacobi, Völker, Trockel, & Taylor, 2012; Loucas et al., 2014).

Stice, Rohde, Durant, and Shaw (2012) developed an Internet-based version of the Body Project called eBody Project and compared its effectiveness to the original face-to-face version of the program, a group of people who received an informational brochure about body image, and a group who watched a documentary video on eating disorders and related factors. Their results indicated that eBody Project outperformed the brochure and video groups, but did not quite show the strength of results produced by the face-to-face version of the intervention. The eBody Project specifically showed effectiveness in reducing body dissatisfaction, dieting behaviors, and negative affect, and showed promise in reducing thin-ideal internalization and eating disorder symptoms. This group studied the eBody Project at 2-year follow-up, which showed a reduction in risk factors for and symptoms of eating disorders, which were not quite as strong nor lasted as long as those found in the face-to-face version of the program (Stice, Durant, Rohde, & Shaw, 2014).

Conclusion

There is still a lot to learn in terms of how to implement the most effective forms of eating disorders prevention to the greatest number of people. Several prevention programs developed for preventing eating disorders have shown significant and clinically relevant results. Additional research has indicated that implementing prevention programs via technology may, one day, be as effective as those implemented face-to-face.

References

Austin, S. B. (2011). The blind spot in the drive for childhood obesity prevention: Bringing eating disorders prevention into focus as a public health priority. *American Journal of Public Health, 101,* e1–e4. doi:10.2105/AJPH.2011.300182

Bauer, A., & Moessner, M. (2013). Harnessing the power of technology for the treatment and prevention of eating disorders. *International Journal of Eating Disorders, 46,* 508–515. doi:10.1002/eat.22109

Ciao, A. C., Loth, K., & Neumark-Sztainer, D. (2014). Preventing eating disorder pathology: Common and unique features of successful eating disorders prevention programs. *Current Psychiatry Reports, 16,* 453–478. doi:10.1007/s11920-014-0453-0

Festinger, L. (1957). *A theory of cognitive dissonance.* Stanford, CA: Stanford University Press.

Horney, A. C., Stice, E., & Rohde, P. (2015). An examination of participants who develop an eating disorder despite completing an eating disorder prevention program: Implications for improving the yield of prevention efforts. Prevention Science, *16,* 518–526. doi:10.1007/s11121-014-0520-0

Jacobi, C., Völker, U., Trockel, M. T., & Taylor, C. B. (2012). Effects of an Internet-based intervention for subthreshold eating disorders: A randomized controlled trial. *Behaviour Research and Therapy, 50,* 93–99. doi:10.1016/j.brat.2011.09.013

Jones, M., Lynch, K. T., Kass, A. E., Burrows, A., Williams, J., Wilfley, D. E., & Taylor, C. B. (2014). Healthy weight regulation and eating disorder prevention in high school students: A universal and targeted web-based intervention. *Journal of Medical Internet Research, 16,* 28–39. doi:10.2196/jmir.2995

Kass, A. E., Jones, M., Kolko, R. P., Altman, M., Fitzsimmons-Craft, E. E., Eichen, D. M., . . . Wilfley, D. E. (2015). Universal prevention efforts should address eating disorder pathology across the weight spectrum: Implications for screening and intervention on college campuses. *Eating Behaviors, 25,* 74–80. doi:10.1016/j.eatbeh.2016.03.019

Levine, M., & Maine, M. (2005). *Eating disorders can be prevented!* New York, NY: National Eating Disorders Association.

Loucas, C. E., Fairburn, C. G., Whittington, C., Pennant, M. E., Stockton, S., & Kendall, T. (2014). E-therapy in the treatment and prevention of eating disorders: A systematic review and meta-analysis. *Behaviour Research and Therapy, 63,* 122–131. doi:10.1016/j.brat. 2014.09.011

McMillan, W., Stice, E., & Rohde, P. (2011). High- and low-level dissonance-based eating disorder prevention programs with young women with body image concerns: An experimental trial. *Journal of Consulting and Clinical Psychology, 79,* 129–134. doi:10.1037/a0022143

Müller, S., & Stice, E. (2013). Moderators of the intervention effects for a dissonance-based eating disorder prevention program; results from an amalgam of three randomized trials. *Behaviour Research and Therapy, 51,* 128–133. doi:10.1016/j.brat.2012.12.001

National Eating Disorders Collaboration. (n.d.). *Student bodies.* Retrieved from https://www.nedc.com.au/research-and-resources/show/student-bodies

National Research Council and Institute of Medicine of the National Academies. (2009). *Preventing mental, emotional, and behavioral disorders among young people: Progress and possibilities.* Washington, DC: National Academies Press.

Neumark-Sztainer, D. (2009). Preventing obesity and eating disorder in adolescents: What can health care providers do? *Journal of Adolescent Health, 44,* 206–213. doi:10.1016/j.jadohealth.2008.11.005

Rohde, P., Auslander, B. A., Shaw, H., Raineri, K. M., Gau, J. M., & Stice, E. (2014). Dissonance-based prevention of eating disorder risk factors in middle school girls: Results from two pilot trials. *International Journal of Eating Disorders, 47,* 483–494. doi:10.1002/eat.22253

Rohde, P., Stice, E., & Marti, C. N. (2015). Development and predictive effects of eating disorder risk factors during adolescence: Implications for prevention efforts. *International Journal of Eating Disorders, 48,* 187–198. doi:10.1002/eat.22270

Selby, C. L. B. (2017). *The body size and health debate.* Santa Barbara, CA: Greenwood.

Shaw, H. (2008). A dissonance-based intervention for the prevention of eating disorders and obesity. In C. W. LeCroy & J. E. Mann (Eds.), *Handbook of prevention and intervention programs for adolescent girls* (pp. 83–122). Hoboken, NJ: John Wiley & Sons.

Shaw, H., & Stice, E. (2016). The implementation of evidence-based eating disorder prevention programs. *Eating Disorders, 24,* 71–78. doi:10.1080/10640266.2015.1113832

Stice, E., Becker, C. B., & Yokum, S. (2013). Eating disorder prevention: Current evidence-base and future directions. *International Journal of Eating Disorders, 46,* 478–485. doi:10.1002/eat.22105

Stice, E., Butryn, M. L., Rohde, P., Shaw, H., & Marti, C. N. (2013). An effectiveness trial of a new enhanced dissonance eating disorder prevention program among female college students. *Behaviour Research and Therapy, 51,* 862–871. doi:10.1016/j.brat.2013.10.003

Stice, E., Durant, S., Rohde, P., & Shaw, H. (2014). Effects of a prototype Internet dissonance-based eating disorder prevention program at 1- and 2-year follow-up. *Health Psychology, 33,* 1558–1567. doi:10.1037/hea0000090

Stice, E., Marti, C. N., Spoor, S., Presnell, K., & Shaw, H. (2008). Dissonance and healthy weight eating disorder prevention programs: Long-term effects of a randomized efficacy trial. *Journal of Consulting and Clinical Psychology, 76,* 329–340. doi:10.1037/0022-006X.76.2.329

Stice, E., & Presnell, K. (2007). *The Body Project: Promoting body acceptance and preventing eating disorders: Facilitator guide.* New York, NY: Oxford University Press.

Stice, E., Rohde, R., Butryn, M. L., Shaw, H., & Marti, C. N. (2015). Effectiveness trial of a selective dissonance-based eating disorder prevention program with female college students: Effects at 2- and 3-year follow-up. *Behaviour Research and Therapy, 71,* 20–26. doi:10.1016/j.brat.2015.05.012

Stice, E., Rohde, R., Durant, S., & Shaw, H. (2012). A preliminary trial of a prototype Internet dissonance-based eating disorder prevention program for young women with body image concerns. *Journal of Consulting and Clinical Psychology, 80,* 907–916. doi:10.1037/a0028016

Stice, E., Rohde, P., Durant, S., Shaw, H., & Wade, E. (2013). Effectiveness of peer-led dissonance-based eating disorder prevention groups: Results from two randomized pilot trials. *Behaviour Research and Therapy, 51,* 197–206. doi:10.1016/j.brat.2013.01.004

Stice, E., Rohde, P., Gau, J., & Shaw, H. (2012). Effect of a dissonance-based prevention program on risk for eating disorder onset in the context of eating disorder risk factors. *Prevention Science, 13,* 129–139. doi:10.1007/s11121-011-0251-4

Stice, E., Rohde, P., Shaw, H., & Marti, C. N. (2012). Efficacy trial of a selective prevention program targeting both eating disorder symptoms and unhealthy weight gain among female college students. *Journal of Consulting and Clinical Psychology, 80*, 164–170. doi:10.1037/a0026484

Stice, E., Shaw, H., Burton, E., & Wade, E. (2006). Dissonance and healthy weight eating disorder prevention programs: A randomized efficacy trial. *Journal of Consulting and Clinical Psychology, 74*, 263–275. doi:10.1037/0022-006X.74.2.263

Stice, E., Shaw, H., & Marti, C. N. (2007). A meta-analytic review of eating disorder prevention programs: Encouraging findings. *Annual Review of Clinical Psychology, 3*, 207–231. doi:10.1146/annurev.clinpsy.3.022806.091447

Stice, E., South, K., & Shaw, H. (2012). Future directions in etiologic, prevention, and treatment research for eating disorders. *Journal of Clinical Child & Adolescent Psychology, 41*, 845–855. doi:10.1080/15374416.2012.728156

Van Diest, A. M. K., & Perez, M. (2013). Exploring the integration of thin-ideal internalization and self-objectification in the prevention of eating disorders. *Body Image, 10*, 16–25. doi:10.1016/j.bodyim.2012.10.004

Westerberg-Jacobson, J., Ghaderi, A., & Edlund, B. (2012). A longitudinal study of motives for wishing to be thinner and weight-control practices in 7- to 18-year-old Swedish girls. *European Eating Disorders Review, 20*, 294–302. doi:10.1002/erv.1145

Wilksch, S. M. (2014). Where did universal eating disorder prevention go? *Eating Disorders, 22*, 184–192. doi:10.1080/10640266.2013.864889

Wilksch, S. M. (2015). School-based eating disorder prevention: A pilot effectiveness trial of teacher-delivered Media Smart. *Early Intervention in Psychiatry, 9*, 21–28. doi:10.1111/eip.12070

Wilksch, S. M., Paxton, S. J., Byrne, S. M., Austin, S. B., McLean, S. A., Thompson, K. M., . . . Wade, T. D. (2015). Prevention across the spectrum: A randomized controlled trial of three programs to reduce risk factors for both eating disorders and obesity. *Psychological Medicine, 45*, 1811–1823. doi:10.1017/S003329171400289X

Wilksch, S. M., Tiggemann, M., & Wade, T. D. (2006). Impact of interactive school-based media literacy lessons for reducing internalization of media ideals in young adolescent girls and boys. *International Journal of Eating Disorders, 39*, 382–393. doi:10.1002/eat.20237

TREATMENT

Introduction

This chapter focuses on who is involved in the treatment of eating disorders, the various levels of care, modes of treatment, and treatment approaches available to individuals dealing with an eating disorder and their families. This is not an exhaustive look at all forms of treatment but provides an introduction to what forms and approaches of treatment are commonly used.

Treatment Team

The American Psychiatric Association (APA, 2006) recommends that a team of professionals be actively involved in the treatment of someone with an eating disorder. This reflects the highly complex nature of eating disorders and the need to be sure that not only the individual's psychological health is being attended to but also his or her nutritional needs and medical well-being. This team is referred to as a multidisciplinary treatment team and at minimum should include a licensed mental health professional, a licensed medical professional, and a registered dietitian.

Licensed Mental Health Professional

The licensed mental health professional may be a psychologist, counselor, or social worker. It is also possible that this professional may have a medical degree with a specialty in psychiatric concerns. Such professionals may include a psychiatrist or a psychiatric nurse practitioner. Regardless of the specific credentials of the professional, this individual's role on the treatment team is to provide regular psychotherapy services to the individual dealing with the eating disorder. Typically, regular psychotherapy refers to sessions that occur once each week. Depending on the severity of the person's symptoms or the degree to which he or she is in crisis, the regular meetings may occur two times per week. The licensed mental health professional is typically the person on the treatment team with which the individual diagnosed with the eating disorder has the most frequent contact.

Licensed Medical Professional

A licensed medical professional may be a physician, physician's assistant, or nurse and is often the individual's primary care provider. The primary role of the medical professional is to monitor the individual's vital signs, which will include the patient's weight, heart rate, blood pressure, and blood chemistry. Depending on the eating disorder diagnosis and the severity of the symptoms, the individual may see his or her medical professional one to two times per week or once a month. Those who have weekly or twice weekly appointments likely require that frequency to have their weight closely monitored as a higher level of care (see Levels of Care section) may be in consideration. Additionally, an abnormality in the individual's blood chemistry, heart rate, or blood pressure may necessitate frequent checkups to monitor changes in a positive or negative direction. Those who meet with their medical provider once per month (or less frequently than that) are likely in a normal to healthy weight range, are in recovery, and/or show no abnormalities in their vital signs.

Registered Dietitian

A registered dietitian has education and training in nutrition that is regulated and approved by a governing body, usually the state in which the dietitian practices. This is in comparison to a nutritionist who may or may not have the appropriate type of education and experience that would allow him or her to ethically provide nutrition advice to anyone, let alone someone with an eating disorder. The role of the registered dietitian is to develop a meal plan with the individual and his or her family when appropriate. The meal plan can help those who have forgotten what a "normal" meal looks like in terms of appropriate amounts and types of foods. The meal plan is typically developed with the patient to meet his or her nutritional needs, which can be affected by the patient's current weight and height, level of activity, medically indicated dietary restrictions (e.g., restrictions due to diabetes), and food preferences. The last element can be complicated as it is common for people with an eating disorder to eliminate specific foods or food categories (e.g., foods with fat in them) and to state that they do not like those types of foods, when it may be necessary for them to reincorporate some of these "forbidden" foods in order to be physically healthy.

Licensed Medical Professional for Medication Management

Sometimes the professional managing the patient's medications is the primary care provider; however, it is not uncommon for patients to be on more than one medication, or to have their medications changed (e.g., change in dose or type of medication) based on their diagnosis or current weight, or due to a change in symptoms. The more complex the mental health concerns with the need for medication intervention, the more likely it is that the patient will be referred to a medical professional who specializes in psychiatry and is licensed to prescribe medication. Sometimes this professional may also have training in psychotherapy, therefore he or she may provide both medication and psychotherapy services.

Other Professionals

The other types of professionals described as follows may or may not be part of the outpatient treatment team; however, it is common in higher levels of care (e.g., residential treatment facility) to have multiple other professionals beyond those of the standard treatment teams as described in the preceding paragraphs (see Section "Levels of Care").

Marriage and Family Therapist

The marriage and family therapist, as the name suggests, is focused on providing psychotherapy services for either a couple (who may or may not be married) or the family. This professional can and likely should be part of any treatment team when the patient is a minor child or if the patient is married and the eating disorder is causing difficulty in the marriage. The focus of marriage/couples or family therapy may still be on the eating disorder and how it affects everyone involved; however, the patient in this context is the couple or the family as a whole. The individual with the eating disorder may be the *identified patient* but the focus is on how the couple or family interacts with one another and what role the eating disorder may play in affecting the quality and quantity of those interactions. Family-based therapy is considered to be part of the standard of care, particularly for those with anorexia nervosa, when the individual who has the eating disorder is either a minor child or a young adult still living at home (Couturier, Kimber, & Szatmari, 2013; Stiles-Shields, Hoste, Doyle, & Le Grange, 2012).

Art Therapist

An art therapist uses various mediums to encourage individuals to express themselves. Art therapy may involve drawing or creating anything that comes to mind, or the patient may be asked to create something that represents something specific. For example, the patient may be asked to create an artistic representation of the eating disorder itself, or how he or she feels about the eating disorder. Depending on the training of the art therapist and the purpose of the art itself, these creative endeavors may serve the purpose of allowing patients another way to emotionally express themselves, or it is possible that their creations may be interpreted and viewed in terms of what their art communicates about themselves that they have not expressly articulated. For example, some drawing techniques are designed for the express purpose of getting a better understanding of how the patient views himself or herself or the family.

Movement Therapist

Some forms of movement therapy may be incorporated into the ongoing treatment. Many individuals with eating disorders are very uncomfortable with their bodies and have become detached from them in terms of how their body feels, what their body needs, and what their body is capable of. As such, movement therapy is one way to reconnect the patient with the body as he or she has to be somewhat in tune with the body to get it to move a particular way. This type of therapy can be difficult, but can be effective in alleviating a variety of psychological symptoms (Koch, Kunz, Lykou, & Cruz, 2014).

Equine Therapy

Equine therapy is a bourgeoning form of therapy that involves horses. This type of therapy involves communicating with a horse, riding a horse, and taking care of a horse. This type of intervention tends not to be as common as some of the others in large part due to the expense involved with housing and caring for horses in addition to having someone trained in this form of therapy. Through this form of therapy, patients can learn to communicate more effectively with their words, tone of voice, and body language as the horse will respond to all of those signals either as expected or not. In order for the patient to get the horse to do what he or she needs it to do (e.g., stay still so it can be washed, moved forward if riding the horse) the patient needs to fully understand all of the ways in which he or she communicates. This ultimately benefits the individual as he or she can learn via this mode of therapy how to more effectively communicate with other people in his or her life. This form of therapy can be effective for individuals with a variety of concerns, including those with a sexual abuse history (Kemp, Signal, Botros, Taylor, & Prentice, 2014).

Treatment Team Meetings

An important element of the treatment team is communication among the team members (APA, 2006). This is important for several reasons, not the least of which is to share with the other team members what they have learned about a particular patient and how the eating disorder is affecting them. For example, the patient may show signs of dehydration or malnutrition based on blood pressure readings in the medical professional's office. This information can be beneficial to all other members of the treatment team. The registered dietitian can talk with the patient about increasing fluid and/or food intake so that his or her vital signs stabilize again, and the mental health professional can benefit from this information by talking with the patient about his or her thoughts and feelings related to the medical concern and the recommendation for an increase in caloric intake. By the same token, the mental health professional can share with the other members of the treatment team how the patient has received this and other information from the other treatment team members and provide recommendations for how best to encourage and support this particular patient as he or she struggles with this aspect of recovery.

Levels of Care

The APA (2006, 2012) provides detailed descriptions of what forms of treatment are most effective for each type of eating disorder (i.e., anorexia nervosa, bulimia nervosa, and binge eating disorder) including a description of the different levels of care that may be necessary depending on the health status of the patient. The different levels of care refer to how much therapeutic intervention and oversight is necessary for the patient in order to function, in a healthy way, in his or her daily life. The APA identifies five levels of care (i.e., **outpatient treatment**, **intensive outpatient treatment**, **partial**

hospitalization, **residential treatment center**, and **inpatient hospitalization**) along with recommendations for how to determine which level of care is most appropriate. Outpatient treatment is considered the "lowest" level of care, and inpatient hospitalization is the "highest" level of care. Low and high refer here to the amount of therapeutic intervention required for the patient. When a patient receives a lower level of care (e.g., outpatient, partial hospitalization) and is not able to follow treatment recommendations, the patient's treatment team will then consider whether or not a higher level of care is warranted (e.g., intensive outpatient, residential treatment center).

The Academy for Eating Disorders (AED, 2012) in collaboration with multiple other eating disorder-related organizations developed the *Clinical Practice Recommendations for Residential and Inpatient Eating Disorder Programs*. Residential and Inpatient programs represent the highest levels of care, indicating that patients who require treatment at either of these levels have significant and severe symptoms, and in the case of requiring inpatient care, the patient would be considered medially compromised and require medical stabilization before being able to receive treatment at a lower level of care. The guidelines were developed to help safeguard patients and their families who need care at these levels, improve the quality of care provided at these levels, and provide "benchmarks" for insurance companies who are likely involved in reimbursing for at least part of the cost of treatment at these levels.

Outpatient

The outpatient level of care involves the patient receiving regular treatment from all members of the treatment team; however, the patient is not admitted to a hospital or other treatment facility. Rather, he or she is at home and attends the sessions as scheduled. Ideally, the patient's outpatient treatment will have fairly regular treatment team meetings to coordinate care. At minimum, the individual with an eating disorder diagnosis should meet with a licensed mental health provider, a licensed medical provider, and a registered dietitian. Often the patient will also see a psychiatrist who would manage any psychiatric medications the patient was taking.

In outpatient treatment, it is likely that the licensed mental health provider sees the patient the most frequently. Sessions may be scheduled once or twice per week, depending on the patient's needs, insurance coverage, and ability to schedule more than once per week. It is possible that the patient may also meet with his or her registered dietitian once per week and the medical provider once per week in the beginning of his or her treatment or upon discharge from a higher level of care. After some period of time, meetings with the latter two providers will likely be spread out (e.g., meet every 2 weeks or once per month) as needed to check in on progress. The exception to that may be if the patient's weight needs to be closely monitored for physical safety. In that case, the patient may have a standing weight check and vital signs check each week to ensure that he or she is medically stable.

If the patient shows signs that he or she is not able to adhere to the treatment plan and follow the recommendations of the providers, the frequency of meetings with all providers will likely increase as a determination is made in terms of whether or not outpatient therapy can continue to be effective or if a higher level of care is necessary. Higher levels of care from outpatient treatment would include intensive outpatient, partial hospitalization, residential treatment center, or inpatient hospitalization.

Intensive Outpatient

Intensive outpatient treatment is the next step-up from outpatient treatment. When outpatient treatment is not effective, intensive outpatient treatment may be considered. Intensive outpatient treatment involves the same interventions found in outpatient treatment; however, what is added are regular meetings at a local treatment facility (e.g., hospital, community mental health center) several days per week (e.g., 5 days excluding weekends) for a few to several hours each day. These meetings are typically group meetings and are focused on skill building. Depending on the focus of the skill (i.e., what skill is taught), the needs of the patients, and the needs of those who attend the meetings, intensive outpatient group meetings may include only those with eating disorders or may include individuals with a range of psychiatric diagnoses. For example, if a group is focused on issues related to self-esteem and self-worth, and how to improve them, it is likely that it will be a mixed group in terms of psychiatric diagnosis. If, however, the focus of the group is on body image and body-disturbance, then it is likely that only those who have or are at risk for an eating disorder will attend the meetings.

While involved in intensive outpatient treatment, the patient may continue his or her regular meetings with the members of the treatment team or he or she may focus only on the treatment provided at the intensive outpatient level until the patient is ready to discharge from that program. If the patient does continue to meet with the outpatient team, those services may be reduced given the frequency of intensive outpatient services.

Partial Hospitalization

Partial hospitalization follows intensive outpatient treatment in the hierarchy of level of care. This level of care involves all forms of treatment that one would receive if receiving treatment via inpatient hospitalization; however, partial hospitalization is not residential, meaning that the patient does not stay overnight in the hospital. The patient is, however, there all day, usually every day of the week excluding weekends. The services that an individual would receive when admitted to a partial hospitalization program include nursing care, psychiatric evaluation, medication management, nutritional counseling, and various forms of therapy including individual, group, and family. These services are typically provided in the context of a therapeutic milieu. A therapeutic milieu refers to a type of treatment involving a therapeutic community, meaning that there is a group of patients who are part of the community and all of whom are receiving care. The care is comprehensive and consistent among treatment providers and patients themselves are encouraged to hold themselves and each other accountable with respect to the rules, responsibilities, and expectations of the milieu.

Attending a partial hospitalization program is a full-time endeavor. Although patients do not stay overnight at the hospital, a partial hospitalization program is usually a full day for most days of the week. The most effective partial hospitalization programs for those with eating disorders have patients attend the program 5 days each week for 8 hours a day (Olmsted, Kaplan, & Rockert, 2003). Since all forms of treatment (e.g., psychotherapy, medication management, nutritional counseling) are provided as part of the program, the patient would not work with members of the outpatient team while admitted in the partial hospitalization program. Patients are usually expected to participate for a number of weeks or months, depending on the program itself, the needs of the patient, and the patient's insurance coverage. Successful completion of a partial hospitalization program often means the patient will "step down" to a lower level of care, which usually means the patient will attend an intensive outpatient program for a number of weeks prior to resuming exclusively outpatient treatment.

If the patient is not able to comply with the expectations of the partial hospitalization program and follow treatment recommendations, the patient will likely be recommended for a higher level of care. A higher level of care from here would involve either going to a residential treatment center or receiving treatment as part of an inpatient hospitalization program. The decision for either level of care usually has to do with how medically compromised the patient is.

Residential Treatment Facility

Residential treatment facilities are exactly what they sound like. A patient will receive treatment at a facility where the patient will live until he or she is discharged from the program. Residential treatment centers are usually highly specialized facilities and only take individuals with a specific diagnosis. For example, there are residential treatment centers designed specifically for those dealing with substance abuse issues, and other facilities are designed to treat only those with an eating disorder. Some residential treatment facilities may admit patients who have more than one diagnosis or patients who have different diagnoses from one another but for which there is overlap. For example, some residential treatment facilities admit patients who have concurrent eating disorders and substance abuse issues. Regardless of the focus of the facility, the nature of a residential treatment facility is that the patient receives all care and basic needs while admitted in the program.

The patient will have a room to sleep in (usually with a roommate or roommates), meals will be prepared and eaten at the facility, laundry will be done on-site, and so on. Depending on the center itself and the nature and severity of the issues of those admitted to the center, each individual may be responsible for taking care of chores such as laundry, cooking, clean up after meals, clean up of bedrooms and common rooms, and so on. Residential treatment centers focused on helping those with eating disorders often involve the patients in tasks such as meal planning and cooking when they are far enough along in their recovery to be able to psychologically tolerate planning healthy meals, preparing them, then eating them. Many newly admitted patients will not likely be ready to take on this type of responsibility and their food-related task initially will be to consume their meals in their entirety and in a specified amount of time, not purge their food and/or not eat more than is nutritionally necessary.

Throughout each day, those admitted to a residential treatment center will receive various forms of therapy (i.e., individual, group, family), as well as monitoring of vitals including weight, medication management, skill building (e.g., self-esteem, relaxation), and nutritional counseling. It is also common for there to be other services such as art therapy, equine therapy, physical therapy, and so on. There is also free time during which patients can rest, relax, and engage in leisure activities.

Overall, patients are admitted to a residential treatment center if they are unable to benefit from any lower level of care and they are medically stable. Although medical staff are on-site or available 24 hours a day if needed, those who require close monitoring due to serious medical symptoms (e.g., cardiac issues, electrolyte issues) and possibly the need for refeeding will be admitted to an inpatient hospitalization program. When patients benefit from the residential treatment center and are ready to be discharged, there is usually an extensive **discharge plan** in place that may include a gradual step-down process to outpatient treatment.

Inpatient Hospitalization

The highest level of care is inpatient hospitalization. Those who receive this form of treatment are admitted to a hospital where they receive 24/7 medical care. This type of treatment occurs when the patient is medically compromised and is seriously ill. For those with an eating disorder, this may mean they are at an extremely low weight, are unable to keep any food down due to purging behaviors, have abnormal heart rhythms, have abnormal blood work, and so on. Those receiving treatment on an inpatient basis are not well enough to receive treatment at any other level. One of the major concerns of those with anorexia nervosa is the complications associated with malnutrition and emaciation. Thus, a primary goal of inpatient treatment for those with this diagnosis is weight restoration. Initially, the patient is encouraged to eat food on his or her own; however, patients who are unable or unwilling to eat and keep their food down are likely to have a feeding tube inserted to get the nutrients they need and to get their weight restored. Tube feeding is categorized as **enteral feeding**.

There are a variety of feeding tubes and the type used depends on the nutritional needs of the patient as well as his or her willingness to leave a nasal tube inserted (APA, 2006). A nasogastric (NG) tube is a tube that is inserted through the nose, down the throat, and into the stomach. A nasoduodenal (ND) tube is inserted through the nose, down the throat, and into the stomach but extends further and ends at the start of the small intestine. A nasojejunal (NJ) tube is similar to the ND tube; however, this tube extends even further into the small intestine. Other feeding tubes, such as the gastrostomy, gastrojejunal, or jejunal tubes, require surgery as they enter the body through the skin in the abdominal area and nutrients are introduced directly to the stomach or intestine.

Depending on the nature of the hospital and the plan for treatment while the patient is admitted, the patient may receive mental health treatment along with nutritional counseling. Since inpatient treatment is designed to be short term, these forms of treatment may not occur on a regular basis and may not involve full therapy sessions. The goal of most inpatient hospitalization stays for those with an eating disorder is to restore normal vital sign functioning (including weight restoration) so the patient is well enough to be discharged into a lower level of care—which may be directly into a residential treatment facility.

Which Level of Care Should Be Recommended?

The decision for which level of care is best for a particular patient is not necessarily an easy one to make. Those involved in the decision-making process may not always agree on the best or necessary course of action. Moreover, a patient's insurance company may or may not approve a particular level of care and therefore will not pay for it. This means that the financial burden of treatment may be a factor in deciding which level of care is ultimately pursued. The APA (2006, 2012) has, however, provided guidelines for determining which level of care is most appropriate for someone with an eating disorder. They note that a variety of factors must be taken into account, which include how well the individual is functioning psychologically, social, and medically.

The initial criterion for consideration noted by the APA (2006, 2012) are the patient's medical status. The nature of the patient's medical status typically means the initial decision about level of care involves whether or not the patient will be admitted to a hospital on an inpatient basis. The APA lists recommended criteria for hospitalization depending on whether the patient is an adult or a child and further notes that if intravenous (IV) fluids, tube feeding, or daily lab tests are required then inpatient hospitalization is the necessary level of care. A patient may be eligible for a residential treatment facility with some signs of a poor medical status but should not need consistent monitoring, tube feeding, or IV fluids. Another factor that often results in the decision for inpatient hospitalization from any other level of care is the degree of suicidality the patient is experiencing. Generally speaking, if the patient has thoughts about suicide, knows what method he or she would use to attempt to die by suicide, and expresses a desire to die, then inpatient hospitalization is likely the necessary course of action regardless of the patient's current level of care and health status.

Many patients, though not all, who receive treatment via inpatient hospitalization are of a very low weight. Other levels of care may be acceptable even at a weight that is not determined to be healthy for the patient. Typically, however, the recommendation is that the lower a patient's weight gets, the higher the level of care that should be considered. Moreover, the patient's ability to independenttly eat and gain weight (if needed) without consistent monitoring may mean he or she can succeed in outpatient or intensive outpatient levels of care. The greater the need for structured meal times and monitoring, the higher the level of care required. Other eating disorder symptoms, the presence or severity of which may indicate a particular level of care, include compulsive exercising and purging behaviors, which may include self-induced vomiting and/or use of laxatives or diuretics. Those who are able to use self-control effectively to manage their impulse to one or more of these compensatory behaviors are likely suitable for outpatient treatment. Patients who struggle with this skill may require a higher level of care depending on what other symptoms they may be experiencing. Similarly, those who are able to control and significantly reduce how often they use purging behaviors, in cases where there are no measureable medical issues as a result of their purging behaviors (e.g., electrolyte imbalances, cardiac problems), may be eligible for a level of care from outpatient through partial hospitalization.

Additional factors for considering which level of care is most appropriate for a patient with an eating disorder include the presence of other psychiatric disorders, the patient's degree of motivation for treatment, and the degree of stressors in his or her life. Although the APA (2006, 2012) does not explicitly state which other psychiatric disorders, when present, would indicate a particular level of care, they do state that the presence of another disorder can influence what level of care is most appropriate, including inpatient hospitalization. The patient's motivation is a significant factor in determining what level of care is most appropriate for them. The higher the degree of motivation for patients to follow through on treatment recommendations, ability to develop awareness about themselves and their concerns, and their ability to control problematic thoughts and behaviors, the lower the level of care that can be recommended. Patients who are highly unmotivated, are unwilling to comply with treatment recommendations, and are unable to control problematic thoughts or behaviors may require inpatient hospitalization or treatment in a residential treatment facility. Finally, the amount of stress the person is experiencing in his or her life is also a factor in determining the appropriate level of care. Those who have good social support and are able to rely on family and friends to assist them when needed are likely eligible for a lower level of care. Those who are dealing with significantly difficult family relationships, including not having any relationship with family members or living alone without sufficient support, may require a higher level of care.

When a level of care higher than outpatient treatment is recommended, the final factors in determining what is possible for a patient is whether or not any other level of care is available in the area and/or if the patient can afford to go. Some states, for example, do not have residential treatment centers for those with eating disorders; thus, if the recommended level of care requires that the patient would have to travel out of state, this may preclude that particular level of care from being pursued. Additionally, if insurance does not cover enough of the financial burden associated with higher levels of care this, too, may mean that particular level of care is not possible even if strongly recommended. Overall, elements from each of these areas factor into which level of care is most appropriate for a patient at a particular time in his or her recovery process. The APA (2006, 2012) does note, however, that if a patient meets one or more of the recommended criteria under a particular level of care, that level of care should be considered.

Involuntary Treatment

Eating disorders are believed to have the highest mortality rate of any psychiatric disorder (Weiselberg, Gonzalez, & Fisher, 2011). The mortality rate is believed to be particularly high among those diagnosed with anorexia nervosa (Arcelus, Mitchell, Wales, & Nielsen, 2011; Papadopoulos, Ekbom, Brandt, & Ekselius, 2009). As such, the seriousness of these disorders cannot be understated. The diagnostic criteria for anorexia nervosa includes the fact that the individual is significantly below his or her healthy weight, may be unable or unwilling to eat sufficient quantities of food for proper nourishment, and often views his or her body in such a way that the patient does not see it as it really looks (APA, 2013). This calls into question at what point is it necessary to intervene even if the patient does not want someone to? At what point should involuntary treatment be considered? The answers to these questions are not straightforward. Issues of ethics and the law are at play and may be at odds with the desperate state of the patient's medical welfare.

Involuntary treatment for someone with anorexia nervosa usually occurs when the individual has symptoms severe enough that he or she is at serious risk of death (Kendall, 2014). The issue of forcing treatment on a patient who does not want it or to force feed someone who does not want to eat can be considered in terms of ethics, in that viewing involuntary treatment as an ethical dilemma is appropriate for all healthcare providers in a position to force this kind of involuntary treatment on a patient (Matusek & Wright, 2010). When the patient is an adult, in most states, there is little anyone can do to force treatment on someone with an eating disorder unless a professional (usually a physician) can document that without treatment the patient is a risk to himself or herself from starvation or death by suicide.

Mode of Treatment

The mode of treatment refers to the way in which treatment is provided, such as one-on-one, with a group of people with similar concerns, or with a family. Although treatment in any discipline can be provided in various modes, typically in the context of eating disorders and other mental health issues the mode of treatment usually refers to the way in which psychotherapy or counseling services are provided. Thus, the brief descriptions that follow focus on the mode of treatment as it applies to counseling or psychotherapy. Whereas all modes of treatment or therapy are focused on helping the individual(s) reduce symptoms and the impact those symptoms have on their lives, each mode provides something unique that the other modes cannot.

Individual Therapy

Individual therapy refers to mental health counseling or psychotherapy provided on a one-on-one basis. This is the mode of therapy that most people think of when they think about getting help for psychological concerns or specific diagnoses. Individual therapy involves the patient and a licensed mental health professional meeting on a regular basis to address the concerns that are interfering with the patient's ability to function as he or she would like to. Individual therapy allows both the mental health professional and patient to delve as deeply into the patient's concerns as desired and to address the specific needs of the patient as they arise. Additionally, should the treatment not progress as expected or desired, the patient and mental health professional have the opportunity to change course and tailor the treatment to what the patient needs at that particular time. This is beneficial as it allows for a personalized approach that is not possible in the same way when other people are involved in the treatment (e.g., other group members or family members). Another benefit of individual therapy is that what the patient shares is only accessible by the patient and the therapist, which means that the patient has to provide explicit permission to the therapist for anyone else to know about the nature of the treatment and the fact that treatment is occurring. There are, as many readers likely know, exceptions to this type of privacy or **confidentiality**. They include when the patient is determined to be a threat to himself or herself (e.g., suicidal) or others (e.g., homicidal) and when the patient is a minor child. In the latter case, parents have access to the patient's therapy progress, though in some states there are restrictions, based on the age of the child (e.g., 16 years old), that can legally prevent a therapist from revealing to the parents things related to sexual activity, drugs, or alcohol use. Outside of these legal and ethical expectations to confidentiality, therapists have the legal and ethical obligation to not reveal anything about treatment to anyone else without the patient's permission.

Group Therapy

The group therapy mode of treatment usually involves a group of eight to 10 people who have a shared set of concerns. For example, a group may be formed to address relationship problems, grief and loss, depression or anxiety, or eating disorders. Group therapy is different from a psychoeducational group that is focused on providing information and answering questions or concerns about a specific topic (e.g., effective ways to communicate, effective ways to parent).

In group therapy, the group will meet regularly, usually once per week, for 1 to 2 hours at a time depending on the nature and purpose of the group. There may be one or two therapists who cofacilitate the group sessions. The benefit of having two therapists is that one may observe reactions in group members that the other does not, and thus can interject and check in on a group member who may have had an emotional reaction to something another group member said. A significant part of group therapy (in comparison to psychoeducational groups) is that they are likely to focus not only on the concern that brought the group members together (e.g., eating disorders) but also on the nature of the interpersonal interactions group members may have during sessions. Addressing and processing interpersonal interactions within the group not only helps individual group members understand how they impact one another but also how to handle more difficult interactions, such as if a group member says something or reacts in such a way that another group member is hurt or gets angry. Group members can learn how to effectively communicate their thoughts and feelings in a safe and structured environment, which means they can take these skills and use them in their relationships outside of the group setting.

An often noted benefit that is unique to group therapy is that the group is comprised of people who are dealing with the same or similar issues. This gives individual group members the sense that they are not alone in their struggle as well as the opportunity to learn from and/or teach other group members effective ways of coping in and outside of the group therapy setting.

Family Therapy

Family therapy is precisely what it sounds like—therapy that takes place with most or all members of a family. Family members can include parents, siblings, grandparents, or other individuals (e.g., family friend, roommate, extended family member) who live in the same household and who may be impacted by the issues and concerns that brought them to therapy. Typically, there is an **identified patient** who is the member of the family that the rest of the family has identified as having emotional or behavioral difficulties. In many cases, the identified patient is a child in the family. Although the impetus behind the family seeking family therapy is to get help for the identified patient, the reality is that in family therapy the patient is the family unit as a whole. Thus, treatment is focused on helping the family cope with maladaptive interactions with the identified patient and to improve communication among all family members. Family members may also receive feedback on ways in which they interact with the identified patient that are helpful and those that may be making things worse.

Family therapy is particularly important for patients with eating disorders who still live at home (whether they are minors or emerging adults; see Family-Based Treatment section). For those with eating disorders, meal times are particularly challenging and parents are usually the ones making and serving meals which, of course, means that the parents are pivotal when it comes to knowing how to effectively encourage a child with anorexia to eat, to monitor children who may engage in purging behaviors, and to monitor children dealing with bingeing behaviors in terms of amount of food eaten and potentially food missing that may have been consumed in secret. Regardless of the type of eating disorder diagnosed, family therapy can be useful in helping all members of the family cope with the stress associated with an eating disorder.

Which Mode(s) of Treatment Should Be Recommended

The mode of treatment that should be recommended depends on a variety of things, not the least of which is the preference of the patient, particularly when it comes to individual or group counseling. Some individuals may prefer the privacy and focused attention afforded by individual therapy, whereas others may prefer the opportunity to interact with other people dealing with similar issues. There is nothing, however, that would necessarily preclude a patient from being part of individual therapy and group therapy. There are potential issues that can arise that are beyond the scope of this book, which may make taking part in both modes simultaneously disadvantageous (e.g., meeting once per week for individual therapy and once per week for group therapy may be emotionally overwhelming to some individuals).

Another factor determining what modes of treatment are utilized is the level of care (see Levels of Care section). In higher levels of care, such as residential treatment facilities, there are multiple modes of treatment throughout a day or week. It is not uncommon for residential treatment facilities, for example, to have ongoing individual therapy and group counseling, and family therapy when the family is able to travel to the treatment facility. Of course in the current day and age, it may be possible that family therapy takes place virtually in that the therapist and patient may be in a room at the treatment center and the family participates via a remote connection that allows them to take part despite being hundreds or thousands of miles away.

Ultimately, the modes of treatment that are recommended take into account the severity of the patient's symptoms, his or her current state of emotional stability, the patient's living situation outside of residential or inpatient treatment (e.g., living with other family members), and the preferences of the patient. Although the focus tends to be on the patient with the eating disorder diagnosis, there is support for the inclusion of the family, particularly the families of children, adolescents, and young adults, to not only be highly involved in treatment but to also be considered part of the treatment team (Hoste, Doyle, & Le Grange, 2012).

Treatment Approaches

Generally speaking, any treatment approach will have the goals of intervening with respect to any eating behaviors that are maladaptive at best and dangerous at worst. This can include treatment via medication or treatment via counseling or psychotherapy. Counseling or psychotherapy will also focus on identifying and addressing any factors that may have allowed the eating disorder to develop in the first place and those factors that may allow the eating disorder to continue. There are various ways to address these goals and the method(s) used will depend on the treatment approach of the licensed mental health professional, preferences of the patient and/or the patient's family, and which approach is known to be effective for that particular eating disorder. Although there are more treatment approaches than are covered in this section, what follows are brief descriptions of approaches commonly used in the treatment of eating disorders. When indicated, each description will include a comment on what is known about how effective the particular approach is for treating the different eating disorders. A brief discussion of which medications may be effective in the treatment of eating disorders is also included.

Cognitive-Behavioral Therapy

Cognitive-behavioral therapy (CBT) involves addressing maladaptive thoughts and accompanying behaviors of the patient. In the context of eating disorders, this means that inaccurate or unrealistic thoughts about food and eating or concerns such as body image dissatisfaction will be discussed and either replaced with more adaptive thinking, or a competing thought will be identified for the purpose of challenging any inaccurate or unrealistic thought. If, for example, someone with **anorexia nervosa** has the thought that eating too much food will make him or her fat, the therapist using CBT will likely talk with the individual about how realistic that is given his or her view of "too much food," and with the patient will develop a competing thought designed to undermine the maladaptive thought. For example, the new thought might be "food is necessary for me to live" or "just like a car needs gas to run my body needs fuel too in the form of food."

The intent behind CBT work is that as one's thinking changes one's behavior will change, too. So, if someone changes how he or she thinks about food, for example, from thinking food is dangerous to thinking food is necessary and beneficial, then the person may begin eating in a more healthy way. Sometimes the thoughts are identified first and connected to behaviors, and other times problematic behaviors are identified and subsequently associated with thoughts that correspond to the behaviors.

CBT has been found to be an effective form of treatment for those diagnosed with binge eating disorder, with up to 50% showing significant improvement in reduction of symptoms; it is believed to be the treatment of choice for this disorder (Williams, Goodie, & Motsinger, 2008; Wilson, 2011). CBT has also been extensively studied in the treatment of bulimia nervosa and is believed to be an effective form of treatment for this disorder as well (Spotts-De Lazzer & Muhlheim, 2016).

Interpersonal Psychotherapy

Interpersonal psychotherapy (IPT) is a short-term treatment approach designed to focus on the nature and quality of interpersonal interactions and was originally developed as an intervention for depression (Markowitz & Weissman, 2012). It presumes that interpersonal difficulties, particularly with respect to interpersonal communications and emotional attachment, are believed to play significant roles in mental illness. Thus, addressing these dynamics are thought to help the individual develop more effective and satisfying relationships, which in turn improves overall mental health.

IPT has been applied to a variety of mental health disorders and has been found to be an effective form of treatment for bulimia nervosa (Williams, Goodie, & Motsinger, 2008; Wilson, 2011) and binge eating disorder (Tanosky-Kraft & Wilfley, 2010; Wilson, 2011).

Family-Based Treatment

Family-based treatment (FBT) refers to treatment that heavily involves the family, typically the parents or primary caretakers, in the treatment process itself rather than the family/parents simply being informed about what is happening in treatment. FBT is indicated for children and adolescents, and in some cases young adults, particularly for the treatment of anorexia nervosa. The most well-known and researched of FBT models is the Maudsley method, which was developed to determine if family-based intervention was more effective compared to individual treatment. The developers noted that their study was the first "controlled trial" of FBT specifically for anorexia nervosa and revealed that FBT was more effective than individual therapy, particularly for patients whose illness had not yet become chronic and for whom their disorder began prior to the late teens (Russell, Szmukler, Dare, & Eisler, 1987).

Since this treatment was developed it has been studied extensively, modified for other eating disorders, modified to be implemented with multiple families, and has been found to be effective for adolescents and in some cases young adults (Rienecke, 2017). It is considered by many to be the treatment of choice for adolescents with anorexia nervosa. A meta-analytic study examining the literature comparing FBT to individual treatment found that at the end of treatment the two modes were equivalent; however, at follow-up 1 year later, those who experienced FBT showed greater benefits (Couturier, Kimber, & Szatmari, 2013). Another review of the literature also reported the effectiveness of FBT in the treatment of adolescents with anorexia nervosa, and growing support for the use of FBT in the treatment of adolescents with bulimia nervosa (Stiles-Shields et al., 2012). These authors indicated that additional research is needed to draw more definitive conclusions about the effectiveness of FBT in treating bulimia nervosa, binge eating disorder, or other eating disorder populations.

Use of Psychotropic Medication in the Treatment of Eating Disorders

Psychotherapy is believed to be the treatment of choice for individuals with eating disorders; however, medications may enhance treatment for some individuals (Hay & Claudino, 2012). There are very few psychotropic medications that are effective in the treatment of eating disorders. The most commonly used classes of medications are antipsychotics, antidepressants, mood stabilizers, and anxiolytics (i.e., antianxiety). The medications that have produced the clearest effectiveness are fluoxetine for bulimia nervosa and anticonvulsants or anti-obesity medications for binge eating disorder (Hay & Claudino, 2012; Mitchell, Roerig, & Steffen, 2013). Additional medications prescribed for those with anorexia nervosa have included tricyclic antidepressants, selective serotonin reuptake inhibitors (SSRIs), and antipsychotics, which have shown mixed results or no effectiveness (Mitchell et al., 2013). Moreover, there is not much known in terms of the long-term efficacy of prescribing psychotropic medications as a treatment method for eating disorders (Flament, Bissada, & Spettigue, 2012).

Difficulty Treating Eating Disorders

Eating disorders are notoriously difficult to treat and patients often exhibit low motivation to change. Treating professionals are not always effective at identifying true motivation to change and helping patients enact meaningful change. Moving from a cognitive understanding of motivation toward a behavioral view of motivation may help clinicians more effectively help their patients (Waller, 2012).

One of the purported reasons that anorexia nervosa is more difficult to treat compared to the other eating disorders is due to the ego-syntonic nature of the disorder

(Rienecke, 2017). *Ego-syntonic* refers to something that is desired and that fits with an individual's sense of who he or she is or wants to be. By contrast, *ego-dystonic* refers to something that the individual does not want nor does it fit with who he or she is or wants to be. As such, anything that is ego-dystonic is relatively easier to divest one's self of whereas something that is ego-syntonic is something that the individual will psychologically hold on to tightly and strongly resist letting go of.

Which Treatment Approach Should Be Used?

As noted in the description of each of the major approaches to treating eating disorders, **bulimia nervosa** and **binge eating disorder** can be effectively treated with more than one approach (e.g., CBT, IPT) and there are some medications that have been shown to be helpful with these disorders. Generally speaking, most individuals with eating disorders can expect to experience treatment effectiveness and overall improvement (Keel & Brown, 2010). However, with respect to anorexia nervosa specifically, effective treatment approaches are difficult to come by, either through counseling, psychotherapy, or medication.

With the exception of FBT for adolescents, research results examining the effectiveness of other forms of treatment for anorexia nervosa are unclear at best (Keel & Brown, 2010; Watson & Bulik, 2013; Williams et al., 2008). In a recent examination of what may be needed to effectively treat anorexia nervosa, Munro, Randell, and Lawrie (2017) suggested that a **biopsychosocial** approach is warranted. Additionally, addressing difficulty with trust, emotional security, and self-acceptance may help to improve treatment effectiveness. Other recently developed forms of treatment specifically for anorexia nervosa are classified as neurobiological interventions and include deep brain simulation (DBS) and transcranial magnetic stimulation (TMS). They both have shown preliminary promise but require additional research to render firm conclusions about their effectiveness in treating this disorder (Lipsman et al., 2013; McClelland, Kekic, Campbell, & Schmidt, 2016).

Conclusion

The treatment of eating disorders is complex and involves a multidisciplinary team of professionals to provide the most effective treatment. Given the nature of eating disorders and how serious the symptoms can be, it is necessary for someone with an eating disorder to require a level of care that attends to his or her psychological and physical needs 24 hours a day, 7 days per week. In extreme cases, it may be necessary to consider involuntary treatment for someone with anorexia nervosa, though this can be fraught with legal and ethical issues.

References

Academy for Eating Disorders. (2012). *Clinical practice recommendations for residential and inpatient eating disorder programs.* Reston, VA: Author.

American Psychiatric Association. (2006). *Practice guideline for the treatment of patients with eating disorders* (3rd ed.). Washington, DC: Author.

American Psychiatric Association. (2012). *Guideline watch (August 2012): Practice guideline for the treatment of patients with eating disorders* (3rd ed.). Washington, DC: Author.

American Psychiatric Association. (2013). *Diagnostic and statistical manual of mental disorders* (5th ed.). Arlington, VA: American Psychiatric Publishing.

Arcelus, J., Mitchell, A. J., Wales, J., & Nielsen, S. (2011). Mortality rates in patients with anorexia nervosa and other eating disorders. *Archives of General Psychiatry, 68*, 724–731. doi:10.1001/archgenpsychiatry.2011.74

Couturier, J., Kimber, M., & Szatmari, P. (2013). Efficacy of family-based treatment for adolescents with eating disorders: A systematic review and meta-analysis. *International Journal of Eating Disorders, 46*, 3–11. doi:10.1002/eat.22042

Flament, M. F., Bissada, H., & Spettigue, W. (2012). Evidence-based pharmacotherapy of eating disorders. *International Journal of Neuropsychopharmacology, 15*, 189–207. doi: 10.1017/S1461145711000381

Hay, P. J., & Claudino, A. M. (2012). Clinical psychopharmacology of eating disorders: A research update. *International Journal of Neuropsychopharmacology, 15*, 209–222. doi:10.1176/appi.focus.120415

Hoste, R. R., Doyle, A. C., & Le Grange, D. (2012). Families as an integral part of the treatment team: Treatment culture and stand of care challenges. In J. Alexander, J. Treasure, & R. R. Hoste (Eds.), *A collaborative approach to eating disorders* (pp. 136–143). New York, NY: Taylor & Francis.

Keel, P. K., & Brown, T. A. (2010). Update on course and outcome in eating disorders. *International Journal of Eating Disorders, 43*, 195–204. doi.10.1002/eat.20810.

Kemp, K., Signal, T., Botros, H., Taylor, N., & Prentice, K. (2014). Equine facilitated therapy with children and adolescents who have been sexually abused: A program evaluation study. *Journal of Child and Family Studies, 23*, 558–566. doi:10.1007/s10826-013-9718-1

Kendall, S. (2014). Anorexia nervosa: The diagnosis: A postmodern ethics contribution to the bioethics debate on involuntary treatment for anorexia nervosa. *Bioethical Inquiry, 11*, 31–40. doi:10.1007/s11673-013-9496-x

Koch, S., Kunz, T., Lykou, S., & Cruz, R. (2014). Effects of dance movement therapy and dance on health-related psychological outcomes: A meta-analysis. *The Arts in Psychotherapy, 41*, 46–64. doi:10.1002/14651858.CD003148.pub3

Lipsman, N., Woodside, D. B., Giacobbe, P., Hamani, C., Carter, J. C. Norwood, S. J., . . . Lozano, A. M. (2013). Subcallosal cingulate deep brain stimulation for treatment-refractory anorexia nervosa: A phase 1 pilot trial. *Lancet, 381*, 1361–1370. doi:10.1016/S0140-6736(12)62188-6

Markowitz, J. C., & Weissman, M. M. (2012). Interpersonal psychotherapy: Past, present and future. *Clinical Psychology and Psychotherapy, 19*, 99–105. doi:10.1002/cpp.1774

Matusek, J. A., & Wright, M. O. (2010). Ethical dilemmas in treating clients with eating disorders: A review and application of an integrative ethical decision-making model. *European Eating Disorders Review, 18*, 434–452. doi:10.1002/erv.1036

McClelland, J., Kekic, M., Campbell, I. C., & Schmidt, U. (2016). Repetitive transcranial magnetic stimulation (rTMS) treatment in enduring anorexia nervosa: A case study. *European Eating Disorders Review, 24*, 157–163. doi:10.12659/MSM.908250

Mitchell, J. E., Roerig, J., & Steffen, K. (2013). Biological therapies for eating disorders. *International Journal of Eating Disorders, 46*, 470–477. doi:10.1037/e500812014-012

Munro, C., Randell, L., & Lawrie, S. M. (2017). An integrative bio-psycho-social theory of anorexia nervosa. *Clinical Psychology and Psychotherapy, 24*, 1–21. doi:10.1002/cpp.2047

Olmsted, M. P., Kaplan, A. S., & Rockert, W. (2003). Relative efficacy of a 4-day versus a 5-day day hospital program. *International Journal of Eating Disorders, 34*, 441–449. doi:10.1002/eat.10216

Papadopoulos, F. C., Ekbom, A., Brandt, L., & Ekselius, L. (2009). Excess mortality, causes of death and prognostic factors in anorexia nervosa. *The British Journal of Psychiatry, 194*, 10–17. doi:10.1192/bjp.bp.108.054742

Rienecke, R. D. (2017). Family-based treatment of eating disorders in adolescents: Current insights. *Adolescent Health, Medicine and Therapeutics, 8*, 69–79. doi:10.2147/ahmt.s115775

Russell, G. F., Szmukler, G. I., Dare, C., & Eisler, I. (1987). An evaluation of family therapy in anorexia nervosa and bulimia nervosa. *Archives of General Psychiatry, 44*, 1047–1056. doi:10.1001/archpsyc.1987.01800240021004

Spotts-De Lazzer, A., & Muhlheim, L. (2016). Eating disorders and scope of competence for outpatient psychotherapists. *Practice Innovations, 2*, 89–104. doi:10.1037/pri0000021

Stiles-Shields, C., Hoste, R. R., Doyle, P. M., & Le Grange, D. (2012). A review of family-based treatment for adolescents with eating disorders. *Reviews on Recent Clinical Trials, 7*, 133–140. doi:10.2174/157488712800100242

Tanosky-Kraft, M., & Wilfley, D. E. (2010). Interpersonal psychotherapy for bulimia nervosa and binge-eating disorder. In C. Grilo & J. Mitchell (Eds.), *The treatment of eating disorders: A clinical handbook* (pp. 271–293). New York, NY: Guilford Press.

Waller, G. (2012). The myths of motivation: Time for a fresh look at some received wisdom in the eating disorders. *International Journal of Eating Disorders, 45*, 1–16. doi:10.1002/eat.20900

Watson, H. J., & Bulik, C. M. (2013). Update on the treatment of anorexia nervosa: Review of clinical trials, practice guidelines and emerging interventions. *Psychological Medicine, 43*, 2477–2500. doi:10.1017/s0033291712002620

Weiselberg, E. C., Gonzalez, M., & Fisher, M. (2011). Eating disorders in the twenty-first century. *Minerva Ginecologica, 63*, 531–545.

Williams, P. M., Goodie, J., & Motsinger, C. D. (2008). Treating eating disorders in primary care. *American Family Physician, 77*, 187–195.

Wilson, G. T. (2011). Treatment of binge eating disorder. *Psychiatric Clinics of North America, 34*, 773–783. doi:10.1016/j.psc.2011.08.011

SCENARIOS

Scenario 1: Suzanne, a 10-Year-Old, Throws Food Away at Lunch

Suzanne is a 10-year-old elementary school student in the fifth grade. She lives at home with her mother, father, and brother, who is 2 years older than she is. Suzanne has not reached puberty but, like her other female, heterosexual classmates, she has begun to develop an interest in boys and what it takes to be attractive to them. She has asked her mother to subscribe her to teen-oriented fashion magazines and often reads her mother's magazines when there is an article related to dieting, looking good, or how to attract the opposite sex.

At lunch time Suzanne, along with a few of the girls, often throw away the "fatty" or "high calorie" food that is packed in their lunches. Suzanne has recently asked her mother to stop packing cookies and chips and instead pack more vegetables and fruits, to which her mother happily agreed, assuming that her daughter was focused on eating healthy. Suzanne routinely had enough to eat and would feel full after lunch but found that she was feeling increasingly guilty for having eaten everything in her lunch. This feeling was exacerbated by observing her friends throw away parts or all of their lunches (including healthy items) because they did not want to get fat. They would comment on Suzanne eating the fruit in her lunch, saying, "Are you sure you want to eat that? You know it has sugar in it." Suzanne also began to notice that when her friends threw away food they talked about being "good" that day and when they ate all of their lunch or had a piece of fruit they talked about being "bad" that day. Suzanne requested that her mother only pack vegetables without any dipping sauce or a salad without meat, cheese, or dressing. Despite her mother's willingness to pack what her daughter requested, Suzanne did not eat all of her lunch and eventually got to the point where she would only eat five pieces of lettuce or one to two baby carrot sticks.

Suzanne's weight began to drop. Early in her weight loss her parents commented on the fact that she seemed to have lost weight and expressed mild concern. Suzanne assured them that she was eating enough and that she was not hungry; rather, she was eating healthier so "of course" she had lost some weight. Suzanne began to skip meals at home, stating that she had not only eaten her lunch but she had also had some of her friend's food, or ate snacks at a friend's house before coming home from school. Suzanne started to wear layers of baggy clothes to not only hide her weight loss but also to keep herself warm as she found even on warm days she felt cold.

It was not until Suzanne's mom accidentally walked in on her coming out of the shower one morning that she noticed how much weight Suzanne had lost. She could see each of Suzanne's ribs, the bones in her spine, and her hip bones seemed to protrude dramatically. At that point, her mother was alarmed and immediately scheduled an appointment with Suzanne's pediatrician.

Analysis

The earlier an eating disorder is identified, the greater the likelihood for recovery. It was fortuitous that Suzanne's mother happened to see how much weight her daughter had lost because it is possible that Suzanne could have successfully hidden her weight loss for weeks or months longer, making recovery that much more challenging. It is likely that Suzanne may resist going to the appointment or at minimum not think there is any reason she should go because there is "nothing wrong with eating healthy and losing a little weight."

Suzanne's pediatrician, while not a specialist in the treatment of eating disorders, recognized the signs and symptoms and listened carefully to the mother's description of her daughter's requests with respect to food and the dramatic weight loss. The pediatrician confirmed that Suzanne had lost 10 pounds since her last checkup when there would be an expectation of weight gain due to normal physical development. Despite Suzanne thinking there was nothing inherently wrong with what she was doing, she was forthcoming and answered her pediatrician's questions honestly. She shared that she had been cutting way back on how much and the types of food she ate, and that she was skipping meals more frequently. She also stated that she was worried about becoming fat and not being attractive enough to boys.

The pediatrician took Suzanne's vital signs, all of which were normal but did note that Suzanne's skin was cool to the touch—to which Suzanne acknowledged that she was feeling cold a lot of the time. Suzanne's pediatrician referred her to a licensed mental health professional, who was also an eating disorder specialist, who would further evaluate Suzanne for the presence of an eating disorder and make recommendations for treatment.

The result of the meeting with the eating disorder specialist was a diagnosis of **anorexia nervosa** along with several treatment recommendations. These included that Suzanne receive weekly therapy meetings, weekly or biweekly family meetings depending on the family's success in encouraging Suzanne to eat, weekly appointments with a registered dietitian, and weekly appointments with a medical provider to check her weight and vital signs. An additional recommendation was that Suzanne's family should be heavily involved in her treatment so they can learn how to support her in the recovery process, specifically at meal times. Suzanne's parents would be coached on how to respond to meal refusal, the refusal of specific types or amounts of food, and how to handle consequences of not following through with meal-time requirements or other treatment recommendations.

A plan for school was also made to ensure Suzanne would eat her entire lunch. Her parents and school officials identified appropriate school personnel who would monitor and check in with Suzanne at lunch time. They were instructed to be encouraging when needed but mostly to observe and record whether or not Suzanne was eating her lunch and reporting back to the treatment team about Suzanne's compliance in this regard. Lunch-time monitors would also note any difficulties Suzanne might experience such as pressure from her friends to not eat or to throw food away. Issues such as these could then be addressed in Suzanne's weekly therapy sessions.

Scenario 2: Stephen, a Freshman in High School, Was Bullied Because of His Weight

Stephen is a 14-year-old freshman in high school whose weight puts him in the **body mass index (BMI)** category of obese. He has struggled with his weight most of his life. His mother describes him as having been a "hefty baby" who "never really lost his baby fat." Stephen reports that, as far back as he can remember, adults and peers have commented on his weight. During his earlier school-age years, he describes being bullied by classmates for his weight, starting in elementary school. Typically, the bullying consisted of name calling and derogatory comments about his weight and who he is as a person. Thus, his peers not only made fun of him about his weight but proceeded to make fun of him as a person, including how he dressed, what his interests were, his sense of humor, how coordinated he was, and so on.

Stephen's parents received advice from his pediatrician to put him on a strict diet limiting not only the amount of calories he ate but also what types of food he could eat. This resulted in Stephen sneaking "junk food" into the house and hiding it. He would eat as much of the junk food as he could at one time and then hide the wrappers. His parents eventually realized what was happening and regularly checked his backpack and room for food that he was not allowed to eat. This led Stephen to use his money to buy junk food on the way to and from school and eat it all as secretly and as quickly as possible. Occasionally, some of his peers would notice him rapidly eating a bag of chips or package of cookies and make fun of him, often making animal noises. Despite the food restrictions imposed on him, his efforts to secretly buy and eat food that was "not allowed" and being ridiculed by his peers was demoralizing and made him feel depressed and worthless. He found that he was not able to stop himself from continuing to eat as much junk food as possible before anyone found out.

Stephen was acutely aware of who among his peers were well liked growing up and what people seemed to like about them. He recognized that among both males and females those who were athletic and fit were usually popular. He had no interest in sports, in large part because he was not terribly coordinated and therefore did not enjoy participating. He ultimately decided that if he could not participate in sports to garner positive attention and favor from his peers he would need to lose weight. Stephen made an effort to do more walking whenever possible but mostly decided to change how he was eating. He was able to restrict his intake dramatically and stick to his new plan for a few days at a time. Ultimately, he would "give in" to his feelings of hunger and eat as much food as possible as quickly as possible. He usually felt physically uncomfortable immediately after eating in this way and engaged in cruel self-talk that included thoughts about how "worthless and weak" or "disgusting" he was. He did not do anything to get rid of the food he ate, but vowed that he would not eat for as long as possible so that he could offset the calories he consumed.

Analysis

Stephen's motivation to lose weight in order to better fit in and be accepted by his peers seems to have contributed to a complicated relationship with food. Because his weight was a topic of conversation much of his life Stephen has presumably been focused on his body shape and size, particularly as it compares to others, especially his peers. As a result, he has engaged in eating behaviors that may meet the criteria for an eating disorder diagnosis.

Ideally, Stephen will be assessed both medically and psychologically to determine his overall health. Although his weight in and of itself may or may not contribute to health-related issues, his consuming of large quantities of high-calorie food has the potential to contribute to health-related issues such as diabetes. A physical assessment would identify any issues or developing issues that may need to be addressed. A psychological evaluation would determine whether or not Stephen has developed an eating disorder. The pattern of behavior described earlier may fit the criteria for either **bulimia nervosa** or **binge eating disorder**. He seems to be binging on a fairly regular basis although it would need to be established how frequently this occurs through the course of a month. His decision to "fast" following these binges can be considered a compensatory behavior, which fits the criteria for bulimia nervosa; however, as described it is unclear if he actually has fasted following his binges. If not, the appropriate diagnosis is likely binge eating disorder. An assessment conducted by someone who specializes in eating disorders would be able to determine the appropriate diagnosis by gathering additional information about the nature of Stephen's binges, how often they occur, how he feels afterward, and whether or not he does anything to offset the calories he consumed.

Stephen and his family would likely benefit from psychotherapy services. Depending on the types of services available in his area, he and his family would be best served by individual psychotherapy for Stephen addressing his eating disorder and the psychological contributors to the development and maintenance of the disorder (e.g., bullying, wanting to fit in). Family therapy would also be indicated to help all members of the family understand the nature of the eating disorder, how the eating disorder may impact all members of the family, and how each member of the family can assist in supporting Stephen. Stephen would also likely benefit from meeting regularly with a registered dietitian to help him learn or relearn what an appropriate meal looks like in terms of types and quantity of food. The dietitian would be able to assist Stephen and the family in weekly meal and snack plans to help him meet his caloric needs and remain healthy. Finally, regular visits to his pediatrician will be important to monitor his vitals (e.g., blood pressure, heart rate, blood chemistry, and if indicated his weight) for any indication of medical consequences of his behaviors.

A challenging element to Stephen's care will be his desire for weight loss. The dietitian can help him pursue this in a healthy manner; however, research in the area of weight loss suggests that very few people are able to sustain meaningful weight loss past 5 years. This does not mean that he should not pursue weight loss; however, it may mean that explaining his reasons for losing weight will be important in his individual psychotherapy as well as the possibility that he may not be able to lose the amount of weight he would like to in a healthy way. Thus, he may need to learn to adjust his thinking toward being healthy regardless of how much weight he may or may not lose as a result of eating well and engaging in regular exercise.

Scenario 3: Brenda, a 19-Year-Old College Student, Has a History of Eating Disorders

Brenda is a 19-year-old sophomore in college. She has a long-standing history of eating disorders, which has included both anorexia nervosa and bulimia nervosa. She has successfully hidden her eating disorder behaviors from her parents since she was 11 years old and therefore has never received treatment for an eating disorder. Although her weight has fluctuated dramatically over the years, her primary care provider has simply noted that she should *watch her weight* when her weight increased, and that she "must be doing something right" when she lost weight. She has never had a gynecological exam and has lied any time a medical provider inquired about the regularity of her menstrual cycle. She has stated that it is and has always been regular but, in fact, Brenda has never had regular periods.

Brenda would occasionally have intervals of time, often lasting 2 to 3 months, when she would be symptom free, but would always be worried about her weight, afraid of getting fat, and struggled to resist reengaging in eating disorder behaviors, which would usually start with restricting. Her restricting would result in weight loss, which for a time would reenergize her and make her feel proud of herself and highly accomplished. After weeks or months she would find that she could no longer continue to eat only a few hundred calories a day. She would *allow* herself to have a little bit of a higher calorie food such as some bread or a piece of cheese. When she allowed herself this *indulgence* she found that she would be triggered to **binge**, starting a cycle of binging and purging which for her was usually self-induced vomiting.

Over the summer, Brenda had vowed to eat *normally* like her friends and not engage in any eating disorder behaviors. She was mostly successful with this, though occasionally she realized that she would slip into severely restricting how much she ate in a day for several days at a time. She would, however, ultimately recognize this and resume eating "normally" again. Since Brenda has been back at school, she has found that the pressure of classes as well as maintaining a social life have started to overwhelm her. As a result, she has felt anxious about getting good grades and pleasing her friends by going out with them whenever they ask, even if she has a lot of homework to do or an exam to study for. Brenda began eating quick meals and snacks, which usually meant she was consuming junk food and, as a result, gained several pounds. She quickly slipped back into her long-standing pattern of restricting her food intake by trying to eat healthier, low calorie food, and a lot less food overall. She was unable to sustain this for more than a few days before she resumed binging and purging. She would buy thousands of calories worth of junk food at a nearby convenience store and sneak it into her dorm room where she would eat it until it was gone. She would feel so bad physically and emotionally that she would go to the communal bathroom and make herself throw up. She tried to do this without anyone noticing (e.g., late at night or during the times of day when most people were in class).

If she were "caught" throwing up she would say that she had food poisoning or that she had the flu. This happened enough times, however, that those in her dorm were starting to think something else was going on, and some were getting frustrated by hearing her throw up and/or seeing the "mess" if she did not clean up sufficiently.

Analysis

Although not indicated in the earlier description, one of the primary pieces of information needed to craft an accurate diagnosis is Brenda's weight. As described earlier, she seems to be alternating between anorexia nervosa and bulimia nervosa. Although this is possible, it is also possible that Brenda could be diagnosed with anorexia nervosa, bingeing and purging type. In addition to knowing Brenda's weight, it is also important to understand the nature of her binges. It is certainly possible that she engages in binges that meet the definition of binging in the context of bulimia nervosa, particularly since she has reportedly consumed several thousands of calories at a time. It will be important to discern how often that occurs since those who are suffering with symptoms more consistent with anorexia nervosa may indicate that they binge but after further explanation the binge is likely better described as having eaten more food than they would have liked to. This does not mean that Brenda should not refer to those episodes as binges as that is clearly how she experiences them; however, fully understanding what she means when she says she binges can help not only with an accurate diagnosis but also with better understanding Brenda's experience.

Regardless of Brenda's diagnosis, she is potentially dealing with a situation in which she may lose her status as an on-campus student at her university. Although she has attempted to hide her behaviors from those who live with and near her, she has not been as successful as she likely thought she was at keeping her behaviors a secret. It is possible, and should the behaviors continue it is likely, that the students and/or custodial staff responsible for keeping the bathrooms clean may complain to university officials about Brenda's behavior. It is implied from the description earlier that at least some of the students living in the dorm with her likely know that it is her in the stall making herself throw up. They may be more or less sympathetic; however, confronting someone about eating disorder-related behaviors, particularly self-induced vomiting in a shared bathroom, is not easy to do. These students may talk with her directly or they may report their concerns and frustrations to the resident assistant responsible for their dorm. Depending on the policies of the university, it is possible that Brenda's behavior can be considered a safety issue not only for her but for her fellow residents. As such, should she be identified she may be required to get counseling and may be told that she can no longer engage in her eating disorder behaviors again without being kicked out of the dorm.

Regardless of any consequences related to her living situation, ideally, Brenda will seek counseling support on campus for her eating disorder as well as have a medical checkup including a medical assessment appropriate for someone with an eating disorder engaging in self-induced vomiting. It is common for counseling centers on college campuses to not be able to provide long-term counseling. Eating disorders tend to require long-term counseling and support, so it will be important for any services she receives on campus to include appropriate referrals to off-campus professionals with experience working with eating disorders.

Scenario 4: Joyce, a 55-Year-Old Married Mother of Three Adult Children

Joyce is currently 55 years old and is married to the father of her three adult children. She dieted extensively in her teens and early adulthood. Throughout those years she was consistently concerned about her weight and how she looked. She was worried about what other people thought about her appearance in terms of her body size, but she also relentlessly scrutinized her appearance from her own perspective. She showed signs of an eating disorder early in adulthood shortly after she began dating the man who would become her husband. She began restricting how much she ate and limited the types of foods she would allow herself to eat based on how calorically dense the food was. She also increased the amount of exercise she engaged in and made sure she worked out for at least an hour every day of the week regardless of how she felt or what else was going on at the time. Things changed, however, when Joyce became pregnant with their first child.

Joyce became pregnant with her first child at age 24 and her remaining children were born within 2 years of one another. During the time she was pregnant, nursing, and caring for small children she found that her desire to attain a thin body diminished significantly. She religiously followed her OB/GYN's advice about weight gain during each pregnancy and maintaining a sufficient weight to adequately support the physical energy required to nurse each child for one and a half to 2 years. Since she had each child within 2 years of the birth of the previous child and nursed until she became pregnant again, Joyce experienced roughly 9 years of ensuring that her body had enough fuel to support not only herself but also her children. After she weaned her third child she experienced approximately 2 to 3 years of not being consumed by concern about her body shape and size. She occasionally thought about reducing her caloric intake or trying a new diet but quickly abandoned those pursuits since her mental and physical energy were predominantly consumed by her young children. After her third child began preschool, she found that she had more energy for herself and thought about starting a diet and exercise routine to get her "pre-baby body back." It did not take long for Joyce to remember the plan she had started before becoming pregnant. She limited the amount and types of food she ate and made sure she exercised at a high intensity for at least an hour each day. At times she would exercise at 9 or 10 in the evening after finally getting the children to bed and asleep. When she was unable to exercise she would become irritable and would struggle to shift her mood until she was able to exercise again. When she was unable to exercise she would be sure to eat much less food the following day.

It did not take long for Joyce to lose enough weight that her husband, family, and friends noticed the change in her appearance. They praised her for her weight loss and some of her friends expressed jealousy for her transformation, wishing they could lose weight like she did. This solidified Joyce's resolve to work even harder at weight loss because what she was doing was clearly working. Within a few months those who knew her started to express concern about how much weight she had lost. Joyce respectfully thanked them for their concern and reassured them she was fine but secretly believed they were simply jealous of her accomplishment. Over the course of her 30s, 40s, and into her 50s, Joyce pursued weight loss. When her family and friends expressed enough concern she would seek treatment to get them to "back off" but would only do the minimum of what she had to do to show she was engaged in treatment.

At the age of 55, after years of being at a low weight, Joyce was showing signs of osteoporosis consistent with that of a woman in her late 60s. One reason for this was the fact that within a year of resuming her restrictive diet and intense exercise routine her menstrual cycles became irregular and within the year following that they stopped altogether. Although she received this news from her primary care physician Joyce did not change her behaviors.

Analysis

Joyce seems to have struggled for much of her life with concerns about body weight, shape, and size. It is unclear whether or not she would have met the criteria for an eating disorder in her adolescent and young adulthood years; however, following the birth of her children and getting them to school age, her struggles seemed to resume. It is not uncommon for women who become pregnant to stop eating disorder-related behavior altogether and many may not experience eating disorder-related thoughts while pregnant. For some of these women, this respite from a focus on food and weight continues throughout nursing (if the women are able to and elect to breastfeed their children). For others, food and weight concerns resume immediately following the birth of the child. Joyce seems to have had both pregnancy and nursing follow so close to one another between her three children that she had an extended period of time during which she did not focus on food intake or weight other than to ensure that both were sufficient to support both herself and her children; however, as soon as she experienced more time and energy for herself her focus on food intake and weight shifted to a focus that resembled eating disorder thoughts and behaviors.

As is the case for many women regardless of their circumstances, Joyce was praised by friends and family for her weight loss. For many women, this confirms for them that what they are doing is working. Some may recognize that what they are doing is not necessarily a good thing, particularly if they are aware of the fact that they have an eating disorder; however, such praise for their efforts rarely deters and more likely supports and encourages eating disorder behaviors. Even after hearing from her primary care provider that her bones showed signs of accelerated deterioration, Joyce did not stop her eating disorder behaviors; thus, it is likely the case that the benefits she received from weight loss superseded any concerns about her bone health.

It is likely that the appropriate diagnosis for Joyce is anorexia nervosa. Ideally, she would seek treatment that involves weekly appointments with a licensed mental health professional, a licensed medical professional, and a registered dietitian. Moreover, it would be ideal for each of these providers to have a specialty in treating individuals with eating disorders; however, treatment may still be successful if at least one of these professionals has this specialty. Coordination of care should occur between providers to ensure all providers are communicating regularly, have a shared understanding of the nature of Joyce's eating disorder, and identify the most effective way to treat it. Additionally, Joyce and her husband would likely benefit from couples counseling to address how the eating disorder affects this relationship. Although not described in the scenario, it is not uncommon for marriages to be strained due to the presence of an eating disorder. Communication breakdowns and arguments about food and meals may be frequent, and sexual activity may decrease dramatically or stop altogether. Couples counseling can help address these issues and provide a place for Joyce's husband to express how the eating disorder affects him and his relationship with Joyce. Joyce's husband may find that individual counseling for himself may be beneficial so he has an opportunity to freely express how he feels about the eating disorder and how Joyce is dealing with it, including frustration and confusion about why she would "let" the eating disorder into her life and their life as a couple.

A focus of Joyce's treatment, particularly in her work with a licensed mental health professional, is likely to begin with her own feelings about having an eating disorder and whether or not she agrees that she is dealing with this type of concern. Assuming she agrees, Joyce may still not fully appreciate how dangerous the eating disorder can be, particularly since she flirted with one in her 20s but did not seem to fully develop one until after her children were born and in school. She may believe she can change how she eats at any time since she was able to do so previously in the context of having children and breastfeeding them. The nature of Joyce's thoughts and feelings about her eating disorder are likely to determine, in part, how long treatment may last. It is not uncommon, for example, for some individuals with anorexia nervosa in particular to want to maintain some aspects of the eating disorder, believing that partial recovery is possible long term; however, the likelihood is that partial recovery will not last and the patient will either enter into full remission of his or her symptoms or move back into a fully active eating disorder.

Scenario 5: Jacinta, a 20-Year-Old Competitive Collegiate Student-Athlete

Jacinta is a 20-year-old competitive athlete, who just completed her junior year in college. She runs cross-country in the fall and competes in distance events in track and field during the spring for a Division I university that is nationally ranked in both sports. Since her sophomore year at her university, Jacinta has consistently placed high enough in regional competition that she was able to qualify for national competition. She is expected to place in the top five nationally during the spring track and field season and is expected to continue to improve and be among the top one or two distance runners in the nation during her senior year. Although Jacinta has often maintained a strict and regimented training program, she has decided to improve on her training plan so she can meet the competitive expectations for her final collegiate year. As part of her plan she has decided to slightly reduce the number of calories she is eating and increase her training so that she can become even leaner and lighter than she is now, the thinking being that leaner and lighter will equal faster.

Jacinta has already implemented this plan and has noticed an increase in her training times during road races in which she competed throughout the summer months. She has lost some weight, which has caused her parents and local friends to express concern since she was already slim. Jacinta was able to assuage them by saying that she has simply improved upon her training regimen and that it has already paid off with improved times. Recently, however, Jacinta has noticed that she has not had as much energy as she usually does before and during her training runs, and her most recent road race resulted in a time somewhat slower than she expected, though she still won the race. She assumed that she might be getting sick, so she made sure she got enough rest and drank enough fluids but did not adjust her training schedule. Despite these efforts, she continued to feel sluggish during her training runs. As a result, she analyzed her eating and decided to cut out any "heavy" foods, which included any food with fat, sugar, or other simple carbohydrates. She did not, however, increase her overall caloric intake and found that she was eating less than she had been due to a more restrictive variety of foods.

When she returned to campus a couple of weeks prior to the start of the semester for preseason training, teammates and coaches were shocked to see how much weight she had lost. She initially met with her coach in frustration because despite her efforts to improve her training regimen her performance was suffering and she was unable to put in the training miles and times as she knew she was capable of. Her coach listened to her explain what she had been doing and recognized that she was probably not eating enough to sustain her body during her grueling training. When he suggested upping the amount of food she ate Jacinta burst into tears and began pacing the room, stating that eating more would ruin her training and her chances at becoming a national champion. Her coach, again, listened to Jacinta's concerns and recommended that since she was convinced that she was doing the right thing with her training that she should be evaluated by a sport physician to rule out a medical cause for Jacinta's low energy as well as a sport psychologist with a specialty in eating disorders to determine if she needed assistance with adjusting her approach to food.

Analysis

Jacinta is likely dealing with anorexia nervosa, though more information would need to be gathered before a definitive diagnosis can be rendered. Her restriction in calories and types of food coupled with a continuation of her intense training and strong reaction to her coach suggesting that she may need to eat more point to the possibility of an eating disorder.

Jacinta's coach handled the situation very well. Instead of criticizing Jacinta or ordering her to change her behaviors (or, alternatively, encouraging her behavior) he expressed concern for her and recommended that she be evaluated by healthcare professionals who would be able to determine what may be going on with her. Ideally, the referrals she received from her coach would be to professionals who understand both competitive sport as well as eating disorders. Having a well-developed understanding of both would allow the professionals to empathize with Jacinta's desire to get any edge she can in her training but also to recognize the seriousness of eating disorders and determine if that is what Jacinta is dealing with. Without such training or awareness even an otherwise well-trained professional may misunderstand the fine line between elite level training and when the training has become harmful, potentially indicating an eating disorder. By the same token, a professional who is well-trained in eating disorders but who does not have experience in working with competitive athletes may recommend, outright, that Jacinta cease all athletic activity and physical training (a common recommendation for those dealing with anorexia nervosa). While this is decidedly the correct call when the individual is at risk medically, prior to that determination helping Jacinta understand the caloric needs the body has to work properly as a competitive athlete and how she is now feeling the effects of being undernourished for the amount of physical activity she engages in may be sufficient for Jacinta to change her behaviors and continue with her season. However, should she refuse to make any changes it may be necessary to restrict the amount of activity she engages in (including practices/training) so that she does not further deplete her body and risk serious psychological or physical damage.

An important element of any treatment plan is the involvement of an interdisciplinary treatment team, which typically includes a licensed mental health professional, a licensed medical professional, a registered dietitian, and a psychiatrist if psychiatric medications are involved. When the individual dealing with an eating disorder is also an athlete it becomes important to involve others in the process who are not likely involved in treatment directly but in providing support. For example, keeping the coach and athletic trainer up to date with respect to how Jacinta is doing psychologically and medically will allow them to support the recommendations of the treatment team. Since coaches in particular are viewed as experts when it comes to performing one's best they are in a unique position of power that can help or hinder the recovery process. In this case, Jacinta's coach will likely be a treatment team ally in that he is likely to support and reiterate the recommendations of the treatment team including, if necessary, a hiatus from physical activity until her weight is restored and other vital signs are back to normal. The athletic trainer is also in a position to share with the treatment team what he or she observes in terms of how Jacinta is doing and can also reinforce the treatment team's recommendations. Other support team members may include Jacinta's teammates, family, and roommate; however, anyone outside the treatment team can only be directly involved with the treatment team with Jacinta's permission.

Overall, the goal would be to get Jacinta back on her team and competing in a healthy way at a healthy weight. This can occur relatively quickly (e.g., days or weeks) or may take longer (e.g., months or a year or more) depending on how strongly the eating disorder has taken hold and Jacinta's ability to follow the recommendations of the treatment team. The fact that Jacinta was identified as possibly having an eating disorder relatively quickly puts her in a better position for a full and expedient recovery than if her eating disorder was not identified until a year or more had passed.

Scenario 6: Alex, an 18-Year-Old High School Wrestler

Alex is an 18-year-old senior in high school who is a competitive wrestler. He has a scholarship to a Division I university to compete on their wrestling team and has high expectations for his ability to, even as a first-year student, compete with other collegiate wrestlers regardless of their year in college. In high school, Alex could have wrestled in one of two weight classes given that his current weight was always 5 to 10 pounds above the lower weight class. He and his coach always elected to have him compete in the higher weight class since that was where his natural weight seemed best suited. He consistently performed well in this weight class, usually winning his matches and always advancing to state level competition. During his sophomore and junior years, he advanced to national competitions and placed in the top five both years. After being recruited by and accepted into a highly competitive collegiate wrestling program, he was informed that he was recruited based on the expectation that he would be able to "drop weight" and wrestle in the lower weight class, which would make him more competitive because he would be larger than those who naturally weighed less than he did. As a result of this expectation and plan, Alex informed his coach that during his final year in high school he would learn how to drop weight and would therefore compete in the lower weight class.

Alex's coach expressed concern for this since he had never engaged in dropping weight; however, the coach had his own experience with dropping weight and other members of Alex's team regularly dropped weight. As such, his coach supported Alex's decision and talked with him about various techniques that would allow him to meet the weight class goals by the day of weigh-in. Early in the season, Alex struggled to drop weight effectively and had to therefore compete in the weight class in which he had been competing previously. This left him frustrated and performing poorly since he was more focused on his failure to drop weight than on the match itself. During the middle of the season, Alex became more adept at dropping weight and learned what techniques were best for him in terms of what he could do to drop up to 10 pounds relatively quickly.

Alex initially followed the advice of his coach and met with a nutritionist to figure out the most effective diet for weight loss. He focused on eating lean meats, larger amounts of fresh vegetables than he typically ate, and only ate whole grain bread but in limited quantities and drank only water or skim milk. Alex found that he was able to lose some weight but was not losing weight as fast as he thought he would. He became impatient and researched online rapid weight loss techniques, particularly for wrestlers. He read about restricting his caloric intake even more than he already had been and limiting the amount of liquids he consumed. He also read about sweating out the weight he needed to lose by using saunas, wearing multiple layers of clothing, or wearing garbage bags while engaged in high intensity aerobic exercise. He read that the last technique could be dangerous and could strictly speaking get him disqualified from competition at the high school and collegiate level (should he engage in dehydrating techniques while a collegiate athlete). Despite these dangers and the possibility of losing his privilege to compete, Alex tried the dehydrating techniques on the weekend to see how much weight he could lose. He found that he lost around 8 pounds in 1 day and was thrilled with his accomplishment. He devised a plan to lose weight by dehydration on weigh-in days so that he could prove to himself and his future collegiate coaches that he was capable of dropping the kind of weight they wanted him to drop.

Alex's high school coach noticed the Monday after the weekend that Alex seemed more fatigued than usual and that he had difficulty focusing not only during school but also at practice. His coach suspected that Alex may have used dehydrating techniques to lose weight but was not sure. He encouraged Alex to drink more fluids; however, Alex refused, saying that he did not want to affect his weight prior to weigh-in that day. After weighing in Alex found he had dropped enough weight to wrestle in the lower weight class. His coach pulled him aside to talk with him about rehydrating and eating enough food. He also suggested Alex not practice that day so he could give his body time to repair itself. Alex became agitated at the thought of not only not practicing but also of eating or drinking enough to result in weight gain. Alex's coach reassured him that his body needed enough fluids and calories to function properly; however, Alex seemed scared at the possibility of gaining too much weight and not being able to drop weight at the next weigh-in.

Analysis

Given the information presented, Alex may or may not have an eating disorder. His extreme weight loss techniques, while effective in the sense that he lost the weight he planned to lose, were dangerous in that severe dehydration can have debilitating effects on the body including the brain. Additionally, dropping weight to compete in a weight class below where one's natural body weight is can negatively affect performance. It is likely that if Alex continues his extreme weight loss techniques he may notice that he is not as effective as he has been and that he gets fatigued more easily.

Regardless of the impact his behaviors have on his ability to wrestle at the level he is used to, Alex's reaction to refueling and rehydrating his body suggest that he may be developing an eating disorder. Although it is far too soon to tell for sure, Alex's fear of gaining weight and not being able to lose it again when he has to weigh-in for competition may signal that he could be in the very early stages of an eating disorder. If Alex continues to refuse to adequately hydrate and fuel his body to sustain normal functioning and competitive athletics he should be referred to a sport medicine professional to determine if his health is compromised in any way and to an eating disorder specialist who has a knowledge of competitive sport to determine if Alex is in the early stages of an eating disorder.

If it is determined that Alex is in the beginning stages of an eating disorder, catching it early and getting him into treatment increases his chance for a speedy recovery and the ability to continue to compete. Depending on the conclusions made by a medical professional and an eating disorder specialist, Alex's ability to compete may be contingent on his ability to follow through with treatment recommendations, which would likely include weekly meetings with the mental health professional, regular check-ins with a medical professional, and meeting with a registered dietitian familiar with both eating disorders and the needs of a competitive athlete to work with Alex on meeting his nutritional needs and maintaining a healthy weight. Depending on how well Alex is able to respond and his ability to maintain a healthy weight, he may or may not be able to compete in the weight class desired by his collegiate coaches. It is possible that the act of dropping weight is too stressful not only on Alex's body but also his mental well-being and he may be unable to drop weight even in a healthy way without experiencing this as a triggering event that may contribute to the development or reemergence of an eating disorder.

It will be important for Alex's current coach to be regularly informed about Alex's treatment progress so his coach is able to adequately support him in his efforts to recover and/or sustain a healthy relationship with food. Keeping the coach informed will also allow the coach to support and bolster the recommendations of the treatment team, which could include cessation from practice and competition for a period of time. This is usually contingent on an athlete's health status as well as his or her ability to comply with treatment recommendations. Should Alex's symptoms get worse and he is unable to maintain a healthy weight and consume a healthy amount of food and fluids, he may require a higher level of care, which can include a residential treatment facility that specializes in working with athletes with eating disorders.

PROFESSIONAL ORGANIZATIONS AND THEIR OFFICIAL STAND ON EATING DISORDERS

Academy for Eating Disorders

The Academy for Eating Disorders (AED) is an international, multidisciplinary organization with members from the fields of mental health, medicine, and nutrition, as well as members from the public. The organization provides information for professionals, families and friends, and students (AED, 2017). In 2016, the AED published its third edition of *Eating Disorders: A Guide to Medical Care: Critical Points for Early Recognition & Medical Risk Management in the Care of Individuals With Eating Disorders*. The guide describes eating disorders and their seriousness, and lists medical signs and symptoms by physiological system (e.g., cardiorespiratory, gastrointestinal). It further outlines what a comprehensive medical assessment should include with guidelines for when a higher level of care is warranted. The guide also describes refeeding syndrome, how to prevent and treat it, as well as recommendations for effective and safe refeeding for malnourished patients.

American Academy of Pediatrics

The American Academy of Pediatrics (AAP) has a membership of over 66,000 physicians who specialize in pediatric medicine (i.e., pediatricians). The AAP was founded in 1930 to offer medical providers a place to discuss and address the needs of children. Prior to this time, physicians were not aware that children may have medical needs that are unique to them in comparison to adults (AAP, 2017). They have since published numerous *Clinical Reports* designed to inform its membership and others about the unique needs of children as they relate to myriad medical and psychosocial issues. Two of those reports are focused on eating disorders in general and one on eating disorders in athletes.

The document entitled "Clinical Report—Identification and Management of Eating Disorders in Children and Adolescents" (Rosen & The Committee on Adolescence, 2010) describes diagnostic criteria for eating disorders, guidelines for evaluating a patient who exhibits symptoms of problems related to eating, describes medical complications that can surface as a result of an eating disorder, and recommends how to interact with patients without inadvertently encouraging unhealthy eating or exercise behaviors.

Another clinical report entitled "Preventing Obesity and Eating Disorders in Adolescents" (Golden, Schneider, Wood, & AAP Committee on Nutrition, 2016) addresses not only concerns about obesity and eating disorders among adolescents but also the possibility that efforts designed to prevent obesity may be a part of the development of eating disorders among some patients. This report superficially notes that pediatricians should have a focus on helping patients develop healthy eating and healthy lifestyle habits rather than focusing on weight.

The third clinical report, "The Female Athlete Triad" (Weiss Kelly, Hecht, & AAP Council on Sports Medicine and Fitness, 2016), notes that female athletes may be at greater risk for problems associated with sport participation, including the **female athlete triad**, which involves problems related to menstruation, bone density, and disordered eating. The report describes the triad in terms of prevalence, how it is diagnosed, and what can be done when an athlete is identified as having one or more symptoms related to the triad.

American College of Sports Medicine

The American College of Sports Medicine (ACSM), founded in 1954, has an international membership of over 50,000 members from various sport-related professions. The purpose of the organization is to support research in the areas of exercise and sport and to use the findings in educational and practical settings (ACSM, 2017). The ACSM has published a variety of position stands related to eating disorders.

The report entitled "The Female Athlete Triad" (Nattiv et al., 2007) takes the position that all female athletes should be screened for the presence of an eating disorder when they undergo their preparticipation exam or annual healthcare screening, and anytime thereafter should the athlete display any facet of the triad. The report also states that it may be prudent for sport administration officials to enact regulations to ensure that unhealthy weight loss practices are not supported or encouraged among athletes or other sport personnel.

In 1996, the ACSM published a position stand entitled "Weight Loss in Wrestlers" (Oppilger, Case, Horswill, Landry, & Shelter, 1996) in their official journal. Twenty years later, they updated their information on the issue of how wrestlers cut weight despite how unhealthy and potentially dangerous the practice is (ACSM, 2016). Among other things, in the updated report, the ACSM notes that both the coaches and wrestlers need to be educated on the dangers associated with cutting weight. The report also specifically discourages common practices among wrestlers to dramatically cut weight (e.g., rubber suits, laxatives, saunas), and the report states that any weight lost as a result of such practices should be regained.

Finally, the ACSM published a report entitled "Female Athlete Issues for the Team Physician: A Consensus Statement" (Griffin et al., 2003), which includes information on a variety of medical issues unique to female athletes including information found in a subsection entitled *The Female Athlete and Disordered Eating* and *The Female Athlete and Selected Menstrual Dysfunction*. The report is designed to assist sport physicians by providing information about the rate of a particular issue, consequences associated with it, what may cause the issue, optimal treatment for the issue, and prevention measures.

In 2016, the ACSM, along with the Academy of Nutrition and Dietetics, and Dietitians of Canada, produced a joint statement entitled "Nutrition and Athletic Performance" (Thomas, Erdman, & Burke, 2016). Although not focused on eating disorders, the statement focuses on the importance of adequate nutrition for athletes, including low energy availability (EA) which, when identified, should include an assessment for an eating disorder.

Academy of Nutrition and Dietetics (formerly American Dietetic Association)

The Academy of Nutrition and Dietetics is a national organization founded in 1917 for the purpose of helping the American government better nutritionally assist the population of the United States. Currently, the Academy has a membership primarily comprised of registered dietitians with a mission of ensuring that the public sees this organization and its members as "the most valued source of food and nutrition services" (ADA, 2017). With regard to eating disorders, the organization published an article entitled "Position of the American Dietetic Association: Nutrition Intervention in the Treatment of Eating Disorders" (ADA, 2011) with a clear position on the role of registered dietitians in the treatment of those with eating disorders:

> *It is the position of the American Dietetic Association that nutrition counseling by a registered dietitian, is an essential component of the team treatment of patients with anorexia nervosa, bulimia nervosa, and other eating disorders during assessment and treatment across the continuum of care. (ADA, 2011, p. 1236)*

See the ACSM for a discussion of a joint statement entitled "Nutrition and Athletic Performance" (Thomas et al., 2016).

American Psychiatric Association

The American Psychiatric Association (APA) is an international, professional organization with over 37,000 members, most of whom are psychiatrists. Its priorities are to promote high-quality patient care, via delivery of the best standards of practice, and to promote the rights and interests of patients utilizing psychiatric services. The APA produced a substantial document entitled the *Practice Guidelines for the Treatment of Patients With Eating Disorders, Third Edition* (APA, 2006). This 128-page document describes in detail how to provide the most effective treatment for those with eating disorders, including specific recommendations by specific eating disorder.

In 2012, the APA published the *Guideline Watch (August 2012): Practice Guidelines for the Treatment of Patients With Eating Disorders, Third Edition.* This update includes information from more recent publications in the area of eating disorders, including practice guideline statements from national and international organizations.

International Olympic Committee

The International Olympic Committee (IOC), though most widely known for their hosting of the Olympic Games, is an organization that devotes time and energy to a variety of sport-related programs including promoting ethics in sport, promoting peace through sport, discouraging discrimination by promoting equality among athletes, and protecting the health of athletes (IOC, 2017). One effort to support the latter goal is through their report entitled "The IOC Consensus Statement: Beyond the Female Athlete Triad—Relative Energy Deficiency in Sport (RED-S)" (IOC, 2014). This statement is intended to update and replace their previously published statement entitled *The Female Athlete Triad* (IOC Medical Commission Working Group Women in Sport, 2005). The move away from a singular focus on the female athlete triad is intended to signal the fact that males, too, can be negatively affected by insufficient caloric intake relative to their energy expenditure. Thus, the statement explains what the **RED-S syndrome** is, what causes the syndrome, and the consequences associated with RED-S. Additionally, the statement addresses effective management of athletes affected by the syndrome.

National Athletic Trainers Association

The National Athletic Trainers Association (NATA) is a professional organization for certified athletic trainers, as well as other professionals and paraprofessionals who work with athletes and recognize the importance of athletic trainers. NATA was formed in 1950 and has an international membership of over 40,000 (NATA, 2017). The organization published a position statement entitled "National Athletic Trainers' Association Position Statement: Preventing, Detecting, and Managing Disordered Eating in Athletes" (Bonci et al., 2008) to help athletic trainers identify and work with athletes with eating disorders. In their statement, they provide information about signs and symptoms of eating disorders as well as guidelines on how to best approach an athlete who may show signs or symptoms of an eating disorder. The NATA also noted the importance of an interdisciplinary treatment as well as the importance of involving crucial athletic staff in the identification, treatment, and recovery process of athletes.

National Collegiate Athletic Association

The National Collegiate Athletic Association, more commonly known by its acronym NCAA, is the governing body for athletics in the United States college and university system. They not only ensure NCAA rules and regulations are adhered to, but they also develop and institute programs designed to promote the well-being of the nearly 500,000 student-athletes who compete for over 19,000 athletic teams nationwide. The NCAA has published a document entitled *Mind, Body and Sport: Understanding and Supporting Student-Athlete Mental Wellness* (NCAA Mental Health Task Force, 2014). The document is intended to address athletes' reported number one concern, which is their mental health (NCAA Mental Health Task Force, 2014, p. xi). The document offers firsthand accounts of what it is like for an athlete to deal with a mental illness and addresses some of the most common mental illnesses among student-athletes, which includes eating disorders. The section on eating disorders was authored by Ron Thompson (2014) and includes signs and symptoms for eating disorders as well as the reasons athletes are at risk, particularly based on risk factors associated with their sport.

Society for Adolescent Health and Medicine

The Society for Adolescent Health and Medicine (SAHM) was founded in 1968 with the focus on improving the overall well-being—physical, psychological, and social—of adolescents. The organization is multidisciplinary and attracts professionals not only interested in adolescent health but also those who recognize that the well-being of adolescents involves more than preventing, identifying, and treating illness or disease. They are also focused on ways to help adolescents maximize their satisfaction with all aspects of their life (SAHM, 2017). SAHM has a multitude of position papers, including one related to eating disorders. The paper entitled "Position Paper of the Society for Adolescent Health and Medicine: Medical Management of Restrictive Eating Disorders in Adolescents and Young Adults" (SAHM, 2015) focuses on anorexia nervosa and related disorders that involve the restriction of caloric intake. They state that medical providers are crucial members of a multidisciplinary treatment team in the identification and treatment of adolescents and young adults who may be at risk for or who already have an eating disorder.

References

Academy for Eating Disorders. (2017). *Academy for eating disorders.* Retrieved from https://www.aedweb.org/home

American Academy of Pediatrics. (2017). *AAP facts.* Retrieved from https://www.aap.org/en-us/about-the-aap/aap-facts/Pages/AAP-Facts.aspx

American College of Sports Medicine. (2016). Weight loss in wrestlers. Retrieved from https://journals.lww.com/acsm-msse/Fulltext/1996/10000/ACSM_Position_Stand__Weight_Loss_in_Wrestlers.49.aspx

American College of Sports Medicine. (2017). *About ACSM.* Retrieved from https://www.acsm.org/acsm-membership/about-us

American Dietetic Association. (2011). Position of the American Dietetic Association: Nutrition intervention in the treatment of eating disorders. *Journal of the American Dietetic Association, 111,* 1236–1241. doi:10.1016/j.jada.2006.09.007

American Psychiatric Association. (2006). *Practice guidelines for the treatment of patients with eating disorders* (3rd ed.). Washington, DC: Author.

American Psychiatric Association. (2012). *Guideline watch (August 2012): Practice guidelines for the treatment of patients with eating disorders* (3rd ed.). Washington, DC: Author.

Bonci, C. M., Bonci, L. J., Granger, L. R., Johnson, C. L., Malina R. M., Milne, L. W., . . . Vanderbunt, E. M. (2008). National Athletic Trainers' Association position statement: Preventing, detecting, and managing disordered eating in athletes. *Journal of Athletic Training, 43,* 80–108. doi:10.4085/1062-6050-43.1.80

Centers for Medicare & Medicaid Services. (n.d.). *The Mental Health Parity and Addiction Equity Act (MHPAEA).* Retrieved from https://www.cms.gov/cciio/programs-and-initiatives/other-insurance-protections/mhpaea_factsheet.html

Golden, N. H., Schneider, M., Wood, C., & AAP Committee on Nutrition. (2016). Preventing obesity and eating disorders in adolescents. *Pediatrics, 138,* e1–e10. doi:10.1542/peds.2016-1649

Griffin, L. Y., Hannafin, J. A., Indelicato, P., Joy, E. A., Kibler, W. B., Lebrun, C. A., . . . Putukian, M. (2003). Female athlete issues for the team physician: A consensus statement. *Medicine & Science in Sports & Exercise, 35,* 1785–1793. doi:10.1249/01.mss.0000089353.24886.bb

International Olympic Committee. (2014). The IOC consensus statement: Beyond the female athlete triad—relative energy deficiency in sport (RED-S). *British Journal of Sports Medicine, 48,* 491–497. doi:10.1136/bjsports-2014-093502

International Olympic Committee. (2017). *What we do.* Retrieved from https://www.olympic.org/the-ioc/what-we-do

IOC Medical Commission Working Group Women in Sport. (2005). *Position stand on the female athlete triad.* Lausanne, CH: Author.

National Athletic Trainers Association. (2017). *About.* Retrieved from https://www.nata.org/about

Nattiv, A., Loucks, A. B., Manore, M. M., Sanborn, C. F., Sundgot-Borgen, J., & Warren, M. P. (2007). The female athlete triad. *Medicine & Science in Sports & Exercise, 39*, 1867–1882. doi:10.1249/mss.0b013e318149f111

NCAA Mental Health Task Force. (2014). *Mind, body and sport: Understanding and supporting student-athlete mental wellness.* Indianapolis, IN: Author.

Oppilger, R. A., Case, H. S., Horswill, C. A., Landry, G. L. & Shelter, A. C. (1996). Weight loss in wrestlers. *Medicine & Science in Sports & Exercise, 28*, 135–138. doi:10.1097/00005768 -199610000-00049

Rosen, D. S., & The Committee on Adolescence. (2010). Clinical report—Identification and management of eating disorders in children and adolescents. *Pediatrics, 126*, 1240–1253. doi:10.1542/peds.2010-2821

Society for Adolescent Health and Medicine. (2015). Position paper of the Society for Adolescent Health and Medicine: Medical management of restrictive eating disorders in adolescents and young adults. *Journal of Adolescent Health, 56*, 121–125. doi:10.1016/ j.jadohealth.2014.10.259

Society for Adolescent Health and Medicine. (2017). *Mission.* Retrieved from https://www.adolescenthealth.org

Thomas, D. T., Erdman, K. A., & Burke, L. M. (2016). American College of Sports Medicine joint position statement: Nutrition and athletic performance. *Medicine & Science in Sports and Exercise, 48*, 543–568. doi:10.1249/MSS.0000000000000852

Thompson, R. A. (2014). Eating disorders. In G. T. Brown (Ed.), *Mind, body and sport: Understanding and supporting student-athlete mental wellness* (pp. 25–28). Indianapolis, IN: National Collegiate Athletic Association.

U.S. House. Congress, 1st Session. (2015). *H.R. 2515, Anna Westin Act of 2015.* Washington, DC: U.S. Government Printing Office.

U.S. Senate. Congress, 1st Session. (2015). *S. 1865, Anna Westin Act of 2015.* Washington, DC: U.S. Government Printing Office.

Weiss Kelly, A. K. Hecht, S., & AAP Council on Sports Medicine and Fitness. (2016). The female athlete triad. *Pediatrics, 136*, e1–e10. doi:10.1177/1941738112439685

Anorexia A lack or loss of appetite as a result of a medical (rather than mental) disorder.

Anorexia Nervosa A diagnosable mental disorder characterized by inadequate food intake resulting in significant weight loss (or lack of weight gain in children); accompanied by a fear of gaining weight and a disordered body image.

Autism Spectrum Disorder (ASD) A mental health diagnosis that appears in the first 2 years of life and includes difficulty with communication and interpersonal interactions, as well as a limited range of interests and behaviors, all of which interfere in some way in the individual's everyday life.

Avoidant/Restrictive Food Intake Disorder (ARFID) A diagnosable mental disorder characterized by an eating or feeding (in infants) problem resulting in not getting what the individual needs nutritionally and/or in terms of energy expenditure.

Binge Consuming a large quantity of food in a relatively short period of time; associated with binge eating disorder and bulimia nervosa.

Binge Eating Disorder (BED) A diagnosable mental disorder characterized by episodes of binge eating during which the individual feels out of control and often disgusted with himself or herself after a binge.

Biopsychosocial An approach to understanding human behavior that indicates one cannot fully understand or explain behavior without knowing what biological (bio), psychological (psycho), and social (social) factors may be involved.

Body Image One's perception of one's own body.

Body Mass Index (BMI) Originally developed by a mathematician to understand populations, BMI is a mathematical formula that divides a person's weight in kilograms by his or her height in meters squared.

Bradycardia Low heart rate.

Bulimia Having an excessive appetite; used medically to refer to a variety of conditions in which someone may display a ravenous hunger.

Bulimia Nervosa A diagnosable mental disorder characterized by episodes of binge eating followed by a compensatory behavior.

Comorbid Diagnosis Refers to one or more diagnoses in addition to the diagnosis of focus. Also referred to as a co-occuring diagnosis.

Compensatory Behaviors A set of behaviors designed to counteract caloric intake by getting rid of the calories consumed by self-induced vomiting, fasting, excessively exercising, or using laxatives or diuretics; associated with bulimia nervosa.

Confidentiality A legal and ethical term in the context of counseling and psychotherapy that refers to the expectation that all things communicated in the context of the client–therapist relationship will not be disclosed to anyone outside of that relationship except with their permission; there are limited exceptions to this expectation.

Corrective Emotional Experience Usually used in the context of counseling or psychotherapy, this refers to reexperiencing an emotionally charged situation, under conditions that allow the client to effectively cope with it, that is reminiscent of past circumstances with which the client was previously unable to effectively cope.

Countertransference First identified by Sigmund Freud, countertransference refers to the emotional reactions a psychotherapist has toward his or her client but that reflect conscious or unconscious feelings that can interfere with treatment.

Diagnostic and Statistical Manual of Mental Disorders (DSM) The manual used in the United States by mental health professionals to diagnose mental disorders; currently in its fifth edition, which was published in 2013 (*DSM-5*).

Discharge Plan Upon completion of treatment at a higher level of care, a discharge plan is developed to ensure the patient will continue with treatment and that there will be a continuity of care.

Distorted Body Image When one thinks about, touches, or looks at his or her body, that person sees a shape and size that does not accurately reflect his or her true body shape and size (e.g., someone with anorexia nervosa may see himself or herself as fat or significantly overweight even though in reality the person is emaciated).

Energy Availability Refers to the relationship between energy intake (i.e., caloric intake) and energy expenditure (i.e., energy used in sport or other physical activity).

Enmeshment Characterized by being defined in terms with one's relationship with another, such that one's individuality is sacrificed and the relationship is required for the individual to feel healthy; usually results in poor psychological functioning.

Enteral Feeding When caloric needs of the individual are met entirely or in part via the gastrointestinal tract; this type of feeding can include eating a food the usual way, getting one's requirements via liquid supplements, or via a feeding tube.

Exercise Dependence Uncontrolled exercise that may be accompanied by tolerance, withdrawal, anxiety, or depression.

Expressed Emotion (EE) First identified in the context of schizophrenia, it refers to being critical and hostile toward a family member that has a mental illness.

Female Athlete Triad A term used to describe symptoms found among female athletes who do not have sufficient caloric intake related to how much energy they are expending. The triad consists of an interrelationship between bone density problems, menstrual irregularity, and disordered eating. Each element is on a continuum and when one element is identified in a female athlete the other two should be assessed.

Full Remission Refers to the complete absence of any symptoms of the diagnosed mental illness.

Hypokalemia Low potassium levels in the body.

Hyponatremia Low sodium levels in the body.

Identified Patient (IP) Typically refers to the patient in a family who has been identified by the family as having a mental health issue. Usually, the family is in family therapy for the purpose of treating the issues that the IP has been diagnosed with.

Indicated Prevention A type of prevention directed at those who are known to be at risk for or are showing signs of a disorder or disease.

Inpatient Hospitalization Refers to treatment received in a hospital setting where the patient is admitted overnight. This form of treatment is usually involved when the patient's medical status is compromised.

Intensive Outpatient Treatment Refers to treatment that takes place outside of a facility at which a patient would stay overnight (e.g., inpatient hospitalization, residential treatment center). The patient receives treatment several hours per day several days per week and is often used as a "step-down" form of treatment from inpatient hospitalization or a residential treatment facility to outpatient treatment that will occur one to two times per week.

Metabolic Syndrome A set of health factors that, in combination, put one at greater risk for diseases such as heart disease, diabetes, and stroke. There are five factors, and having at least three of them indicates that an individual has the syndrome. The five factors are: large waistline, high triglycerides, low high-density lipoproteins (HDL) cholesterol, high blood pressure, and high fasting blood sugar.

Muscular Ideal The body type typically considered ideal for males in Westernized cultures. This body type is characterized by having visible lean muscle mass with low body fat.

Orthostatic Hypotension Low blood pressure evidenced by dizziness when moving from sitting to standing or from lying down to sitting up.

Osteopenia Weakened bones as evidenced by bone density that is lower than expected but not low enough to be classified as osteoporosis.

Osteoporosis Weakened bones due to excessive bone loss or the body's inability to make or replace lost bone.

Outpatient Treatment Treatment that takes place outside of a treatment facility (e.g., hospital, residential treatment facility). If treatment is occurring in a hospital setting, it may still be considered outpatient treatment if the patient is not admitted as an inpatient (i.e., staying overnight).

Partial Hospitalization Refers to treatment that takes place at a hospital; however, the patient is not admitted overnight. Partial hospitalization will involve more than 1 hour of treatment a day for several days a week and will include medical monitoring.

Partial Remission Refers to a reduction in symptoms that may mean the patient is no longer diagnosable with a mental health disorder (e.g., eating disorder) but still shows some signs and symptoms of the disorder.

Pica A feeding disorder characterized by the individual eating nonfood substances at a developmentally inappropriate level.

Primary Prevention A type of prevention focused on healthy individuals who do not yet show signs of a disease or disorder.

Psychological Reactance A reaction a person has when he or she is feeling like his or her freedoms or rights are being infringed upon; the reaction is usually contrary to the action or view the person is being pressured to take.

Purging In the context of eating disorders, this refers to a behavior designed to get rid of food/liquid intake; self-induced vomiting, use of laxatives, diuretics, or enemas.

Refeeding Syndrome A medical syndrome that can occur during the refeeding of malnourished patients. Symptoms include swelling, failure of the cardiac or respiratory systems, and muscle weakness, and the syndrome can result in death.

Relative Energy Deficiency in Sport (RED-S) Syndrome A term used in reference to a group of factors that can affect the overall health and well-being of male and female athletes. In addition to the three elements involved with the female athlete triad, the RED-S syndrome also includes physiological impairment in the areas such as metabolic rate, immunity, cardiovascular health, and so on.

Residential Treatment Center Refers to treatment that takes place at a facility where the patient stays overnight. Typically, stays at a residential treatment center last for weeks or months. The patient receives all treatment at the facility and lives there until he or she is discharged.

Rumination Disorder A feeding disorder involving repeatedly eating, then regurgitating, food that may then be rechewed, reswallowed, or spit out.

Russell's Sign The presence of calluses on the back of the hand, often on the knuckles, indicating long-term self-induced vomiting.

Secondary Prevention A type of prevention focused on those who show signs or symptoms of a disease or disorder in which efforts are made to prevent the disease or disorder from progressing.

Selective Prevention A type of prevention focused on a particular subgroup of a population known to be at risk for a particular disease or disorder.

Somatic Countertransference Also known as body-centered countertransference; in the context of counseling or psychotherapy, it refers to changes in the therapist's physical state (e.g., change in breathing or muscle tension) based on the physical state of the client.

Specifier Related to the *DSM* diagnosis, this refers to descriptors of a particular diagnosis that help to indicate shared features, severity of symptoms, and course of the disorder, all of which help to inform treatment.

Subtype Related to *DSM* diagnosis, this refers to descriptors indicating shared features a subgroup of those diagnosed with a particular disorder have that others also diagnosed with the same disorder do not have.

Telehealth Healthcare provided via technology such as telephone or video calls.

Tertiary Prevention A type of prevention that focuses on reducing the effects of a disease or disorder once it has already been established.

Thin Ideal The ideal body type for females in Westernized cultures. It is characterized by being lean with very little body fat.

Universal Prevention A type of prevention focused on an entire population with the assumption that the effort will benefit everyone regardless of his or her current health status.

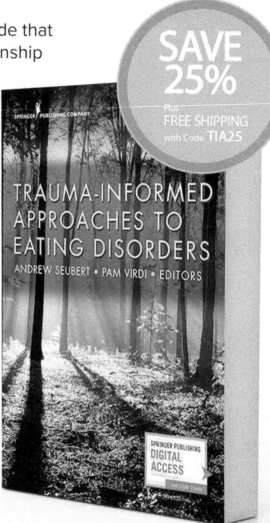

CPSIA information can be obtained
at www.ICGtesting.com
Printed in the USA
LVHW062202290123
738193LV00011B/513